How to
Get Started in
Active Trading
and Investing

David S. Nassar

McGraw-Hill

New York Chicago San Francisco Lisbon
London Madrid Mexico City Milan New Delhi
San Juan Seoul Singapore Sydney Toronto

The McGraw·Hill Companies

Copyright © 2004 by The McGraw-Hill Companies, Inc.. All rights reserved. Printed in the United States of America. Except as permitted under the United States Copyright Act of 1976, no part of this publication may be reproduced or distributed in any form or by any means, or stored in a data base or retrieval system, without the prior written permission of the publisher.

1 2 3 4 5 6 7 8 9 0   DOC/DOC   0 9 8 7 6 5 4

ISBN 0-07-144096-8

This publication is designed to provide accurate and authoritative information in regard to the subject matter covered. It is sold with the understanding that the publisher is not engaged in rendering legal, accounting, or other professional service. If legal advice or other expert assistance is required, the services of a competent professional person should be sought.
—*From a declaration of principles jointly adopted by a committee of the American Bar Association and a committee of publishers.*

McGraw-Hill books are available at special quantity discounts to use as premiums and sales promotions, or for use in corporate training programs. For more information, please write to the Director of Special Sales, McGraw-Hill Professional, Two Penn Plaza, New York, NY 10121-2298. Or contact your local bookstore.

This book is printed on recycled, acid-free paper containing a minimum of 50% recycled, de-inked fiber.

This book is dedicated to my beautiful sons, Zachary D. Nassar and Weston S. Nassar. I am very proud of you both!

CONTENTS

FOREWORD

As a long-time Commodities trader, I have attended many symposiums and events on the topic of "making money in the market." Usually within a half hour of listening to a presentation, I get bored with the speaker and just get up and leave because the information tends to be all theory without actual trading experience behind the information. David Nassar is one of the few who keeps me thoroughly intrigued.

My firm, MBF Clearing Corp, is the largest clearing firm on the New York Mercantile Exchange (NYMEX). I have been trading since I was eighteen and teaching others for almost that long. In 2002, I authored the book, *The Logical Trader, Applying a Method to the Madness*. After the book was published, I began conducting a series of trading seminars and live trading demonstrations in which I invite a select few to join me at the NYMEX. David Nassar is one of the rare and few worthy of speaking at our highly sought-after events on Wall Street. Great traders are hard to find and those who can transfer their knowledge to others are even harder—David is one of those people.

I have a large team of proprietary traders who trade my money, as well as customers who rely on me for quality information. My role is to continually help them to be successful, therefore, quality information is at a premium. The problem is, finding quality information is rare. The first time I listened to David, I was immediately impressed with his views of the market and his methods of trading them. I knew immediately he was focused on the same basic principles of the market that I have been trading and teaching about in the futures markets for the past 20 years. Working with seasoned pros and other market icons, I can tell you that timeless strategies that have worked on the floor of the exchange are also transferable to virtual screen-based markets. These are methods that few people truly understand because of the jaded views that form due to media influences but that will open the reader's mind to an unobstructed view of how to make money in all markets.

When trading on the floor of the NYMEX, learning to trade is "baptism by fire." You are taught by hanging on to the wing of active traders all around you who are moving large amounts of money in real time. There is little time for theory—only action! Today, the markets are virtual and open to all participants. This creates the opportunity for a structured learning environment that the exchanges did not readily provide. The way I and many others learned to trade on the floor was through harsh reality and experience, which created many casualties among traders. Today that has changed because of traders like David, who can teach how they trade.

Reading *How to Get Started in Active Trading and Investing* was like reading an echo of myself. His obsession with risk management and his approach of combining discrete market trading patterns with market psychology are the same views I have expressed in *The Logical Trader*. If you only read one book this year, read David Nassar's comprehensive guide to the markets. It will teach you how to become your own analyst while acquiring a tremendous fundamental, technical, and psychological background into the markets. This book will be an invaluable trading tool for the day trader, swing trader, and long-term investor regardless if you trade stocks, bonds, or futures contracts. It should be required reading for all traders and investors. It is a rare opportunity to get into the mind of a highly successful trader.

Finally I will state that trading has been the greatest living I could have ever imagined. It has given my family and me tremendous opportunities, while allowing me to follow my passion. My 15-year-old son paid me a father's greatest compliment recently when he stated that he too wants to learn how to trade the markets. I hope David Nassar will be one of his mentors.

Mark Fisher
President, MBF Clearing Corp

ACKNOWLEDGMENTS

I want to offer special appreciation to the MarketWise team of professionals I work with everyday. The material presented is the result of a team effort. In particular, I would like to acknowledge the following contributors to the book who have worked many nights and weekends to see its completion.

Brian Shannon is our Chief Market Technician and head of Research at MarketWise. Brian, who has a business degree from Merrimack College, has been published in many industry magazines and is a recognized speaker around the country and abroad.

Eric Erickson is a research analyst and instructor at MarketWise who has contributed greatly to the project. Eric has a strong background in mathematics with a degree in physics from Western Washington University. Eric conducts regular online classes, which are very well subscribed to.

John Seckinger is a research analyst and instructor at MarketWise. John holds an MBA from Regis University.

I also want to thank all the talented and supportive people at TerraNova Trading, LLC. Special appreciation to my partners MarrGwen and Stuart Townsend, founders of Townsend Analytics, Ltd. and the RealTick® trading platform; Chris Doubek, President of TerraNova Trading, LLC.; and Jerry Putnam, CEO of Archipelago® Exchange. I also want to thank my editor at McGraw-Hill, Stephen Isaacs. This is the fifth book I have done with Stephen, and he has always been outstanding. I would also like to thank Jeffrey Krames for his continued support. Appreciation to all the wonderful people at McGraw-Hill who edit, format, and publish the material. Finally, and most importantly, I would like to thank my loving and supportive wife Tracy.

INTRODUCTION

History teaches us many lessons, and it seems the lessons of the market are taught more often by the bear than the bull. During the last bull market cycle, like those that preceded it, the energy was electrifying. The bulls ran through the Streets (Wall Street and Main Street) with the blood of any short sellers dripping from their horns. When the "new economy" was fed to the public by industry spokespeople disguised as CEOs of Internet companies, it was swallowed whole by the media and the trusting public alike. Analysts dove into the fray and were a driving force behind the entire circus act, fooling themselves into believing the garbage they themselves spewed. As long as the market rallied, many analysts were willing to disregard ethics for instant gratification. Most were not motivated by sound research, but by investment banking deals and CEO influences.

Many investors believed they were invincible, racking up thousands if not millions of dollars, but it didn't take long for the self-cleansing mechanism of the market to take its course. The business of trading is Darwinist—survival of the fittest—and most didn't survive. Those who survived were able to dismount the bull and remount the bear, but as industry statistics prove, they are few. Regardless which bull market we describe, the attitudes and results have been nearly the same. Statistics prove that it takes more than a bull market to be profitable. History also proves this. I believe the eighteenth-century mathematician Daniel Bernoulli unknowingly described what it takes to survive the market best—"Human Capital!"

Human capital describes, among other attributes, one's education, talent, and ability to perform. Most people pay too little attention to human capital and too much attention to the ideas and methods of others. As we have learned from the most recent bear market, this diversion is at their own peril. The public took to Internet trading like a fish to water—or should I say a sheep to the slaughter. The analysts and brokers fed investors ideas and the bull market made these players heroes. As such, most participants didn't consider risk. Beginner's luck syndrome quickly developed and most participants did not fully appreciate the risks embedded within the analysis they consumed. New participants tended to be gullible and trusted data fed to them from analysts under the guise that big money equals smart money. But we must not be confused and turn the bear market into a scapegoat for the reasons most investors lose. Luck breaks down with the emergence of a bear market, but bear markets are not to be blamed—the lack of knowing how and when to sell is the reason. Investors who don't know why they bought won't know when to sell. Analysts didn't miss the call to sell. They had no incentive to make it in the first place as Chapter 1 will explain. As a result of this misguided trust the public placed on the analysts, luck quickly ran out and human capital suffered with little personal investment into self-development.

Back in the 1700s Bernoulli introduced another factor of paramount importance that can be applied to today's stock market—The Law of Diminishing Returns. This law states that not all risk can be defined in intrinsic or mathematical terms. Bernoulli discovered that "the utility resulting from any increase in wealth will be inversely proportionate to the quantity of |wealth| previously possessed."* Because wealth is relative to each participant, each person must make their own decisions regarding risk. What may be acceptable risk for one person may not be for another. Therefore Bernoulli's law of diminishing returns reminds us that trading and investing is a very individual endeavor. This historically valid discovery applies today, explaining why successful traders and investors tend to remain profitable. The combination of patience and fear contribute to decision making. Objectively analyzing and waiting for the right trade while relentlessly protecting downside risk are among the best skills a trader can acquire. Decision making at an institutional level where all participants of a fund are subjected to the same risk does not address such personal risk tolerances.

Even objective market analysis does not cancel out all subjective factors, such as fear or the psychological pressures of the market. Like it or not, when you commit your capital, you also commit your emo-

*See Against the Gods, 1996, pg. 105.

tions. In bull markets, greed too often takes a front seat to fear, but it is a healthy dose of fear that develops discipline—something most investors never learned. I believe that no participant, regardless where they are in their career, escapes the psychological demands of the market! Perhaps the easiest way to describe this is to say that the analysis of markets (stocks, options, bonds, futures, currencies, etc.) are determined by objective considerations (statistical analysis, probability, back testing, technicals, fundamentals, etc.), but the motivation to act on the analysis is personal and influenced by the laws of diminishing returns. Do the potential gains warrant the risk? The conundrum created for many who contemplate these very real issues (consciously or unconsciously) often lead to a form of ambiguity. The way that many people deal with dubiety is to delegate the decision making to others—hence the contradiction. This raises other important questions regarding the risk/reward relationship.

This theory of risk and utility is known as *The Petersburg Paradox*, and was only translated to English in 1954, 216 years after its creation! The only reason it was translated was because the modern-day economist John Maynard Keynes made reference to it in his great work, *Treatise on Probability*. Both published works are readily available and deserving of your study. The salient points and relevance to the market are quite enlightening. Is a millionaire proportionately happier with each additional million dollars acquired? The law says no, and his happiness is only incremental and eventually it diminishes because he is less willing to take risks. The paradox in today's terms is that as you accept the responsibility of doing your own analysis, you begin to understand the very real risks embedded within the markets. Most investors never truly understand this until too late. Investors who rely on others for research perhaps temporarily escape the paradox by not understanding the true risks, but are later punished for their apathy. Bull markets tend to provide a false sense of security and even overconfidence which only sets up the greater fall. Ignorance is not bliss and the delegation of risk management to institutional funds is not the answer that many seek. The oddity can be surmised by stating that while acquiring market knowledge also reveals its risks; equivocating the responsibility to others exposes even greater risks. This is not to say that money should never go into managed accounts, but if these accounts are used, the risks the fund is taking must be fully understood.

Regardless of age, gender, or status, all participants will find the market to be an evolutionary process and challenge every step along the way—an endeavor of relentless demand yet limitless bounty. Therefore, every participant must answer this question about risk. Those who cut corners and hunt for an easy solution to the market have the most to explore and the least to find. Those who accept the responsibility of finding their own path are in a position to achieve success. Research done by others does not account for the individual subjectivity of each person. The confluence of using objective analysis for making decisions and the ability to define individual financial risk is the role you must accept. The act of following research and analy sis for which you have had no hand in is clearly the greatest risk. The individual who trades their own capital becomes the trader, the analyst, psychologist, coach, and risk manager. This begins to define both the objective (analytical skills) and subjective (psychological demands) knowledge one must possess in order to be successful. There are no divine answers.

What is certain is that the cash (equities) markets are not a zero sum game. Yes. That is the magic of the markets (capital markets, not derivative). It is not a zero sum game. As long as others buy after you do, like in the case of long positions (buy low sell high strategy), or others sell after you do, like in the case of short positions (sell high buy low), many participants can simultaneously make money. Risk is not linear or equal to all participants. Conjointly, institutions want you to react to their analysis because they can tolerate more risk than any individual. Accordingly, the influences they imbue upon the market naturally create reactionary pressures most individuals fall victim to. The market cliché "if they don't scare you out, they will wear out" comes to mind. The first step is to avoid being the "dumb money" that is bamboozled by this classic market activity by becoming your own analyst and understanding how this activity is manifested in the market. Once this manifestation can be seen through objective data (which will be discovered throughout the text), decisions can be made with predetermined risk that meets your own individually defined parameters. The same firms that employ analysts and brokers produce news that moves and gaps the market. These firms not only help to produce the tsunami of market moving news, but they are better prepared both through prior knowledge and capital wherewithal to "batten down the hatches" to deal with it. It isn't the average investor. This book is an introduction to understanding the forces at play in the market to not only avoid foreseeable risk, but to also gain an edge to compete and win.

An entire generation of traders and investors have been conditioned to follow the analysts' ratings, research, and brokers. This diversion from the truth is at the expense of building the requisite skills of understanding one's self and developing the human capital as your own analyst. I draw on history to make an important point; history repeats itself because human nature is not prone to change. The study of the market is the study of human nature, and the past teaches us important lessons that must be applied. In other words—be Market Wise!

David S. Nassar

PART I

THE LANDSCAPE

1

TRADITIONAL WALL STREET—TRUMPERY, TYRANNY, AND TENDENCY

In a rare time of disintermediation whereby money management is flowing to the individual and public domain, there is no better time to understand the economy and the capital markets. In management theory, the *Peter Principal* is a phenomenon that describes a level in which incompetence is obtained. In other words, even after successive promotions, little can be achieved beyond one's abilities. I believe traditional brokerage firms and the analysts that work for them have reached and surpassed this level of incompetence. As stated, big money does not mean smart money, and the journey you are about to embark on will prepare you to understand and deal with the market, to make your own decisions, or at a minimum, prepare you to filter the advice of others before blindly investing.

Countless battles take place each day on Wall Street. In this arena powerful people rely on the public's order-flow to navigate a world of greed, fear, regulations, and even corruption. The markets are populated with large institutions down to small investors. To the uneducated, the markets may seem covered in a blanket of fog where movements are mysterious. Therefore, in order to participate in the financial markets, these uneducated participants pay for a guide to lead them through the fog. There is trust placed in this guide and participants believe they are being led toward their best interests. At times the guide leads participants safely through the shrouded world, but other times the guide leads participants in a way that only furthers their own interests. This analogy too often describes the relationship between the amateur market participant and their money manager or broker. The relationship between an investor and their money manager is a tricky one, taking on different tones in different market conditions.

During a strong bull market, almost every stock's price increases. This is great news for the investor, both big and small. In most cases, if a person invests any money at all in the stock market during this time, they will most likely see a profit. A strong bull market is also where true greed rears its ugly head, tempting those in positions of influence to put their own monetary gain before the masses that trust them to honestly guide them through the fog. As with most things in life, what goes up must come down. When markets decline and the bearish side shines through, people begin to lose the money they have invested. It is at this time that the exceptional greed and corruption at high levels is uncovered, breaking the trust between broker and investor. Investors begin to understand the trumpery or nonsense being fed to them. This in turn causes confidence levels to plummet. During this time of low confidence, market participation decreases and Wall Street searches for ways to gain back the trust of the investor. Typically regulators jump on this opportunity to step in and enact rules designed to bolster confidence. These rules allow the investing public to feel that the corruption has been stamped out and won't happen again. This bull and bear cycle has been repeated time and again throughout the history of the stock market. History is our teacher and lessons can be learned that apply today.

This cycle reaches as far back as the economic boom of the 1920s, and much farther if we exclude regulation. After World War I, the U.S. economy began to rebuild. In the 1920s the use of electricity expanded and consumerism rose. With this rise in consumerism the stock market rose as well. In fact, the market was driven upward in a craze. Most participants made money and little thought was given to regulation, and the theory of the day was a laissez-faire approach to just "let things be." The crash happened near the end of October 1929, when the Dow lost over 39 percent from the high it made in September of the same year. By June 1932 the Dow had lost over 90 percent.

Many investors borrowed money to participate in the stock market rally, and as prices fell, banks collected on loans made to investors who now had holdings worth very little. Many banks also invested depositors' money in the stock market, and the combined result was that banks had large, uncollectible loans and worthless stock. As word spread and panic set in, people tried to retrieve their money as banks failed by the hundreds. This is what modern day fund managers call a "run on money," and it represents a repeatable crowd reaction we still see in the market today.

In response to the great crash, the Federal Government set up the Federal Deposit Insurance Corporation (FDIC) to prevent such disasters from happening in the future. If an FDIC-backed bank failed, then the government would reimburse depositors. The FDIC still stands today.

After the crash in the 1920s and the ensuing depression, there was a consensus that in order for the economy to recover, the public's faith in the markets needed to be restored, similar to the sentiments felt after the stock market decline that began in 2000. In 1933 and 1934 Congress passed two Securities Acts that required public companies to tell the truth about their businesses and required people who trade, buy, and sell securities to put the investors' interest first. The SEC was founded in 1934 to enforce these rules. Notice the pattern—the market goes up and irrational buying takes place, then the market comes down and people lose money and consumer confidence drops, then regulation is enacted to renew the confidence of investors. See Figure 1-1 for a chart of the Dow during this period.

Direct parallels can be drawn to the Internet bubble in the late 1990s. During the 1990s the stock market grew at an unprecedented pace, led higher by high-tech companies. After the market crested and fell, people once again lost money. Regulators asked questions and uncovered information that contributed to falling confidence. The SEC quickly enacted regulations to increase confidence, and the cycle of market activity followed by regulatory intervention. The common denominator that spans the dimension of time is human nature. History helps us understand the problems that occur today by understanding the problems of the past. To link the similarities, we must have an

FIGURE 1-1   *A chart of the Dow that illustrates the crash of 1929.*

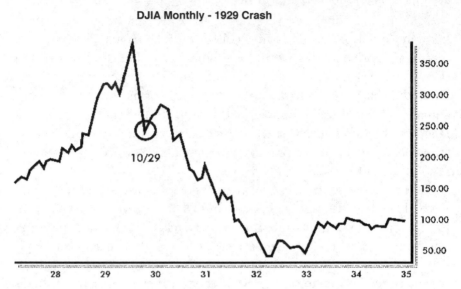

understanding of how things really work in the markets. The first piece of understanding comes from the knowledge of how information is filtered through the market participants of Wall Street.

Success on Wall Street is based on information. It is a world of tyranny, where important information is given to a select few. The majority of amateur market participants base their decisions on fundamental information given to them by brokerage firms or the public companies themselves. It is key to understand how this information is handed down and how it can be altered. To use a metaphor, a long line of participants clamor and compete for market information. We see this information as "market food." The food chain describes where various participants exist within the information hierarchy. Once this information is received, we must then ask what nutritional value remains. The digestive system of the market operates on a very fast metabolism. These participants include institutions and high producing commissionable accounts that receive the best market food with their commission dollars. As they act on this information, stock prices often discount in value before the public reaches the same information, only now depleted of its nutritional value. In most cases, the public is at the end of the intestinal system, where the "market food" is—well, you can finish the analogy for yourself! But the digestive process describes what the analyst, brokers, and media do with the market food they receive (research and ratings reports) before it reaches the public, who are the last to receive it. Pretty gross, I agree, but I want you to get the message—by the time the market food reaches you, it is not wise to consume it. This explanation illustrates why Wall Street insiders consider the public to be "dumb money." The first step in changing your place in the system is to understand the system itself, and that begins with investment banking.

INVESTMENT BANKING

The first set of relationships to understand are the ones built by a private company that decides to sell their stock publicly. These private companies are located at the beginning of the food chain, where all the relationships start. Initial Public Offerings (IPOs) can be very profitable for the company going public and the investment bank alike. There are a variety of reasons a company may decide to go public. The company may want to use the proceeds from the sale of stock to enlarge their business, pay off debt, or may want to spread risk from the current owners over a larger area. To do this, the company must find initial buyers for the stock they intend to sell. The initial buyers are found through the underwriter. Underwriters are generally institutions that specialize in taking companies public; as a group they are called *investment bankers*. Understanding this process is in your best interest and will set the foundation of knowledge you need to understand Wall Street.

The next step is to understand how financial institutions make money and the relationship of the broker, analyst, and investment banker. This is important to understand because you need to know where their interests lie and if they conflict with yours.

WHY A BROKER CAN MAKE YOU BROKE

A *broker* is an individual, who is licensed to buy and sell securities and has the legal power to act on the behalf of a customer. If someone wanted to buy 1000 shares of stock, they would have to go to a person or firm who has access to the market, and this is a broker. Brokers are in the sales business, and most get paid on a commission basis. Much like a real estate agent, who makes money when a house is bought or sold, each time a stock is bought or sold through a broker, they charge a commission. As long as a transaction is incurred, the broker and the firm they work for gets a commission, regardless of whether their client makes money or loses money. There seems to be an obvious conflict of interest between how a broker gets paid, when that broker is paid to manages an investor's money. Many argue the broker's incentive to do a good job in investment management is to retain and attract customers, and this keeps the interests of the customer and broker aligned. History proves otherwise in many ways, such as churning and poor performance to name a few, because brokers are generally not trained as analysts; they are trained to sell. Even if trained as analysts, their interest and your interest align poorly.

ANALYSTS

An *analyst* is a person who researches companies then makes buy-and-sell recommendations based on their findings. They often specialize in a certain industry sector or a group of stocks. Analysts prepare recommendations and reports that are usually disseminated through the firms they work for or to market participants and institutions to help make investment decisions. They have their own vernacular of grading stocks, and their recent performance of reading the future is quite dismal as a group. Some analysts have enjoyed a spectacular track record as have many fund managers, but as we shall soon discover, something has gone awry. To some degree the reasons are new, but to a much larger degree, it has everything to do with an age-long flaw—greed. Figure 1-2 shows the various ratings systems of the different analysts.

Many investors lack the time or interest to put a great deal of time into researching a company, so they heed the advice of the analyst. Thus, the analyst is frequently placed in a position of trust. The lessons

FIGURE 1-2 *The rating systems that analysts use to convey their outlook on securities vary, but the rationale behind the research is often the same. It is subjective and often unjustly influenced. With either good intentions or bad, the nutritional value of this market food is highly questionable and filled with unhealthy risk.*

Analyst Recommendations

Brokerage Firm	Rating System
Credit Suisse First Boston	Outperform, Neutral, Underperform
Goldman Sachs	Outperform, In-Line, Underperform
JP Morgan	Overweight, Neutral, Underweight
SG Cowen	Strong Buy, Outperform, Market Perform
UBS Piper Jaffray	Strong Buy, Outperform, Market Perform, Underperform

to be learned should forever remind all participants that risk can never be properly evaluated without having a hand directly in the analysis.

CORRUPTION IN THE FOOD CHAIN

From 1792 to 1975 brokers charged for their services on the basis of a minimum commission schedule. The commission price was set at a high amount. As a result, most financial firms and institutions made most of their money through commissions. Brokers enticed their clients to make transactions, while analysts were paid from the commissions that the firms made. The analysts were truly motivated to make good recommendations, and when clients made money they were naturally motivated to trade again based on the next recommendation the analyst made. Essentially, the analysts were rewarded for being right and objective. This was a good system, whereby the analyst and the public were reasonably well aligned.

In May of 1975 (known as "May Day"), the SEC eliminated fixed commissions after an unexpected intervention by the U.S. Justice Department [who also interceded in 1996 to lead the "order handling rules" that opened the door for Electronic Communication Networks (ECNs) and direct access trading as we know it today] who questioned the need for fixed commissions. The rationale for the repeal of fixed commissions was to eliminate price collusion among firms. While price collusion occurred, its repeal forced firms to find other ways to quench their greed. As we shall soon see, which is the lesser of two evils?

After these fixed commissions were eliminated, discount broker-ages such as Charles Schwab emerged and exploded in popularity, and commission prices fell precipitously. The financial firms and institutions, which made the majority of their profits from commissions, saw revenues fall. This caused an increase in investment banking business, and this resulted in more and more companies going public through the 1980s and 1990s. This helps explain how many companies with no fundamental value exploded into the market during the Internet boom, while contributing to a new feeding frenzy of greed for big brokerage.

During this period analysts saw their value to the commission side of the firm decrease. Meanwhile, an increasing number of analysts began to subtly work with the investment banking side of the firm, which handled IPOs and mergers. Their research became increasingly motivated by supporting the IPO process, instead of being motivated by objective research and accuracy. Being accurate regarding the company outlook meant that the research was worth the high commissions to investors, but the IPO process paid them well regardless of accuracy. Pre-IPO craze, if their research was poor, so was the commission income since investors would stop relying on research. This aligned brokerage and the public as well.

To the outside world, the large financial firms maintained that there was a "Chinese wall" that separated research and banking. A *Chinese wall* is a set of procedures that restricts access to nonpublic information within the firm reaching the brokers who would undoubt-edly pass it on to their customers. The Chinese wall is in place to avoid the illegal use of inside information gained by analysts from their close work with companies getting disseminated to the public through the seemingly unrelated divisions of the broker. On the inside, the wall began to crumble and corruption and greed flourished. The timeless human nature of Wall Street participants emerges again.

CORRUPTION BEHIND THE SCENES

Analysts began to recommend that investors invest their money in public companies that had investment banking relationships with the firm. This had nothing to do with fundamentals or objective analysis, but it did influence investors to buy stocks where both the firm and the company benefited from the higher stock price. By the late 1990s this practice was out of control. Soon analysts were using buy recommendations to get business for the investment banking side, and the analysts received bonuses if they helped secure large investment banking deals. While some companies were rewarded for investing with a certain firm, others were downgraded as a form of punishment for investment banking with the competitors' firms. The Chinese wall truly crashed down as executives of major companies leaked information to analysts. When a company leaked earning numbers to the analysts, analysts, in turn, adjusted the earning prediction so the company would beat the estimate. This in turn influenced stock prices to go higher, and the executives and the investment banks made big money. In the past, analysts had to be accurate in their market calls in order to earn additional commissions for their firms. Now, however, many analysts and the firms they represent found even greater success by supporting the stocks they took public, merged, or offered secondary offerings. In this sense, the repeal of fixed commissions hurt the market by taking away the incentive for firms and analysts to make accurate calls.

Inside information as well as valued IPO allocation and the like was then fed to institutional clients high up in the food chain. These institutional clients have very large accounts and trade often. The analysts and investment bankers, as well as the firms' institutional clients, had access to the valuable information before the rest of the market. The number of downgraded companies decreased as analysts learned that if they downgraded a company, then the executives stopped leaking information and turned to another firm for investment banking business. These relationships are a strong indication that corruption was taking place behind the scenes and the Chinese wall had fallen.

A company that was planning on going public would talk to investment bankers and analysts, who in turn found support for their stock. The company went public and the analyst recommended the stock to investors. This created an underlying demand for the stock or a base of buyers, and as the price rose higher and higher, the major

FIGURE 1-3   *The circle of profitability where both analysts and corporations prospered from their relationship.*

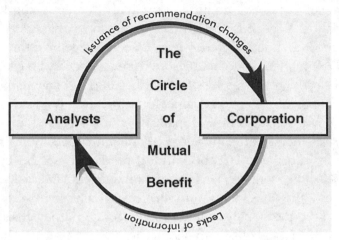

players—including the executives and the investment banks—printed money once again. In return for recommending the company's stock, the executives leaked information to the analysts. This created a circle of profitability where most everyone profited. See Figure 1-3.

As long as the stocks kept moving higher, most everyone, including the small investor, saw profits and felt good, but the house of cards had to fall. Eventually, the cyclic nature of the markets kicked in. After the large run up, there had to be a substantial pull-back. History has proven this time and time again. This is by no means a recent phenomenon. This is human nature. This is greed. This is the market.

ENTER THE REGULATORS

As investors started to lose money and companies started to go under, people began asking questions and investor confidence fell. In the summer of 2000 after the market had retracted sharply from its long-term upward movement, the SEC passed Regulation Fair Disclosure or

Reg. FD. This required companies to release important information to all market participants at the same time and not to only a select few.

This helped tremendously to level out the playing field between the institutions and small investors. Although this regulation helped eliminate the filtration problem, there were still some relationships and information that squeezed through the cracks.

Even after Reg. FD was put in place there were still leaks of information and research reports that were untruthful. As companies started to go under, investors wondered how analysts repeatedly upgraded them several months before the companies filed for Chapter 11 bankruptcy protection. The tricks that some companies were doing with their accounting were uncovered. In a period of just a couple years, trust was lost yet again, investor confidence fell yet again, and new regulation was enacted to bolster the confidence of the investor yet again. This regulation was passed in 2002 and is called the *Sarbanes-Oxley Act.*

Sarbanes-Oxley sets rules to protect investors by improving the accuracy of corporate disclosures. It now becomes obvious that it was the small investor who was lied to repeatedly by analysts and companies alike. These scandals tarnished the brand names of many financial institutions, and investors don't seem to know whom to trust. Perhaps there is no better message to the investor that responsibility must ultimately rest on their shoulders. Even if direct decisions are not to be made by individuals, each person must understand the information that impacts their capital.

So is it the role of Government to correct these scandals? Certainly the regulators need to play an important role, but as history shows, the forces of greed have always found a way to prevail. This is one last representation of how rampant the greed was during the last bear market. It only confirms what history already knew.

THE MUTUAL FUNDS ROLE

More recently there have been mutual fund scandals that have hit the marketplace. They have shown undeniable wrongdoing. Several mutual funds allowed a limited number of mutual fund customers to trade after the market was closed. While the small investor was stuck with their position, a select few industry professionals and possibly even employees of some funds were allowed to enter and exit trades. This enabled a select few to be ahead of the masses. These acts show perhaps the greatest breach of trust given the wide participation of all demographic segments. How does the individual gain trust in the market after all the deceptions? There needs to be a filter.

While the conditions stated are more recent, history has plenty of examples of the same dynamics at work—all driven by trumpery, tyranny, and the human tendency. It is with this historical reference that we can begin to predict the cyclical nature of markets, without the need to consume market food that is unhealthy for us. See Figure 1-4.

FIGURE 1-4   *The breakdown of how market information is filtered through different participants.*

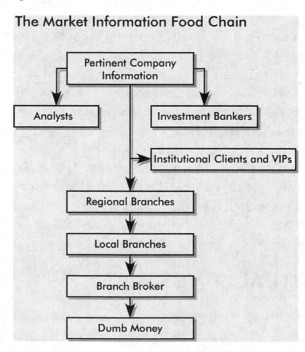

WHERE IS THE MARKET FOOD?

The small investors have some responsibility here as well. Admittedly, history shows they have been repeatedly taken advantage of by big brokerage, but instead of doing their homework in order to make smart decisions, most blindly base their investment decisions on the advice of others, and this is simply irresponsible. Market food is therefore found shortly after accepting responsibility. Market participants need a filter, or a framework with which to be able to sort through the vast amount of information being fed to them. The first step in creating a filter is taking responsibility for trading decisions. The cliché "no one will take better care of your money than you" holds much truth. In today's environment, it is more important than ever to take an active role in the management of your money. An active hand includes researching and trading your own ideas, understanding what your professional money manager is doing, and being able to filter the information given to you by your broker or investment professional if you use one. Realize that being a responsible money manager is not complicated or mysterious. The responsibility is learnable, and most people can filter out useless market information while identifying truths through objective data. While data can be altered or changed, it cannot lie. Regardless, if you make your own decisions or simply use the information about to unfold to filter the advice of others, acting blindly on the advice of others or handing over money to mutual funds without researching the funds rationale is irresponsible. With a little understanding of the market and a true interest in the behavior of markets, dumb money will quickly become smart money.

CHAPTER 2

THE BUSINESS CYCLE

In Chapter 1 we touched on information that disseminates from Wall Street and why participants cannot blindly follow the advice, direction, and research of others. The question raised, then, is where do participants find nutritious market food? Good food is available once responsibility is accepted to do one's own research and in the course of doing so also measure personal financial risk. It is found under the guise of the market behavior of its participants— or crowd psychology. This market psychology, as we will refer to it, is manifested through the business cycle, and before we can direct our attention to specific methods of market engagement, we must understand this cycle.

Before exploring and defining the business cycle, it is imperative for all participants to understand market principles and the possible influences they have on the markets. Seeing the market from the macro level is truly seeing the forest from the trees, and avoiding the often-myopic view participants develop. In fact, understanding the complexities of inter-market relationships will open up all participants' eyes to a number of important facets that take place in the market daily, uncovering many trading and investing opportunities. Conditioning the mind to only see one perspective of the market not only limits opportunity, but also expands risk. As you will discover throughout the text, the proper understanding and perspective of the economic process will define perhaps the most important questions of the market—when to have conviction and when to be disciplined. To borrow a cliché from the card playing community—you gotta know when to hold'em and when to fold'em.

In addition to understanding our domestic economic process and its effects, market engagement has certainly rooted itself globally, so the importance of world events also cannot be ignored. The process of analyzing the markets from a macro level and filtering data to a micro level is referred to as *top-down analysis*. The logical beginning of this analyzing process is an explanation of the business cycle. The term *business cycle* describes economy-wide fluctuations in output, incomes, and employment. Basically, a business cycle can be described as the upward and downward movement in an economy's aggregate output. Looking back in history, there have been many constant predictable periods of low output generally followed by periods of expansion. Therefore, a cyclical trend can be established and used as a benchmark going forward. Time and history have proven the cycle over and over based on many different drivers connected by one enduring ingredient—risk. Without the element of risk, the business cycle would be at the hands of oracles and soothsayers. Risk represents the adventures of man, and perpetuates the cyclical nature of capitalistic markets. Risk is what makes the future our friend. The anticipation of what may occur drives excitement, hope, fear, and uncertainty. These emotions are manifested in perfect harmony with the economic cycles of our nation and much of the world. Essentially, the business cycle reflects the byproduct of sentiment and emotion. This makes the cycle measurable and therefore somewhat predictable, but only if seen from the higher ground. In modern day western society, our economy can be viewed as a giant machine. This machine requires lubrication in order for it to run as efficiently as possible. This does not guarantee the machine won't occasionally run rough, but as history has proved, our machine of capitalism continues to avoid breakdown and represents the smoothest economic and political mechanism on earth. Perhaps the most important gear in our economic machine, as it applies to the business cycle, trading, and investing, is the Federal Reserve (Fed). One of the commonly accepted roles of the Fed is to control swings in the business cycle, accomplished by influencing interest rates and the money supply. The Federal Open Market Committee's (FOMC) monetary policy setting power gives it the ability to influence these aspects of the economy through the buying and selling of government securities and the governance of short-term interest rates.

Therefore, the Fed will loosen monetary policy when output seems to be slowing and tighten when economic expansion appears to be rapid. Accelerated expansions tend to fuel inflation, which can undercut long-term growth. These expansion cycles can last for years (typically three to five) before reversing, and the state of the economy will certainly be influenced by the actions of the Fed regarding interest rates. The Fed and their role in the economy will be discussed in greater detail in Chapter 3. For now, understand the components of the business cycle as explained below and the impact the Fed has on it.

THE BUSINESS CYCLE COMPONENTS

The components of the business cycle are outlined below:

- *Expansion*—Also known as *recovery*, expansion is characterized by increases in business activity throughout the economy. The expansion stage is actually the normal state of the economy.
- *Peak*—As activities expand to a peak, employment and income rise. When near full employment is reached along with rising incomes, we refer to this period as prosperity (inflation).
- *Contraction*—As business activity begins an overall period of decline, the economy is said to be going through a contraction. If there is a decline in the Gross Domestic Product (GDP) for two or more consecutive quarters, the official term is *recession*. *GDP* is defined as the annual economic output of a nation (all of the goods and services produced by the workers and capital located within it). It is important to note that recession does not take into consideration changes in other variables. Changes

in the unemployment rate or consumer confidence are ignored, and using quarterly data makes it difficult to pinpoint when a recession begins or ends. This means that a recession that lasts 10 months or less may go undetected. More severe contractions of longer duration (any economic downturn where real GDP declines by more than 10 percent) may be deemed depressions. The last depression was from May 1937 to June 1938, where real GDP declined by 18.2 percent.

- *Trough*—At the bottom of a contraction is a period in which business activity stops its decline and begins the long road back through expansion toward prosperity. This bottom of the business cycle is known as a trough.

There are some patterns found within the business cycle, and these are published by the Department of Economics at the University of Minnesota. One pattern suggests that expansions generally last longer than recessions, with the average post-World War II expansion lasting about 50 months, while the average recession lasted about 11 months. Therefore, the average post-World War II cycle was about 61 months, or five years. This said, participants could begin to understand the timing aspect of the business cycle as it applies to markets.

Economists love to talk about where we stand in this cycle, and they use many forms of measure to make their arguments. While it seems that there are as many views as there are economists, as quoted by John Kenneth Galbraith in the *Wall Street Journal* (January 22, 1993, C1): "There are two kinds of forecasters: those who don't know, and those who don't know they don't know." The one common theme to all arguments is short-term interest rates. Short-term rates are a common focus because both consumers and producers are directly impacted. They represent the best variables as they relate to the financial market, in the way of bond prices and yields via pricing in the next cycle of the economy. In other words, many economists believe that the bond markets will directly influence the stock market in a forward-looking manner. It is therefore important to understand which indicators are leading, coincident, or lagging with predicting the economy.

- *Leading indicators*—Leading indicators are those factors that appear to reliably predict trends in the economy. They give us a heads up idea of where the economy is headed. Leading indicators that economists use most often include and are directly influenced by the cost of money (interest rates):
  - Hours of production workers in manufacturing
  - New claims for unemployment insurance
  - Value of new orders for consumer goods
  - S&P 500 Index
  - New orders for plant and equipment
  - Building permits for private houses
  - Fraction of companies reporting slower deliveries
  - Index of consumer confidence
  - Change in commodity prices
  - Money growth rate (M2)

  Positive changes in any of these leading indicators (such as a bull market, expansion of the money supply, issuance of more building permits, and increases in orders for consumer goods or plant and equipment) lead economists to believe that there will be more spending, production, and employment in days to come. Negative changes in leading indicators give rise to a more pessimistic outlook among economists and politicians, as possible downturns and recessions loom. Simply stated, when the cost of money is low, increases in money supply fuel consumer and producer spending.

- *Coincident indicators*—Coincident indicators are those measurable factors that vary directly and simultaneously with the business cycle. They tell us where we now are. Coincident indicators include:
  - Nonagricultural employment
  - Personal income
  - Index of industrial production
  - Manufacturing and trade sales

  Personal income and industrial production are representations of what is already "in play." Production, for example, represents that the machines are already running, while changes in interest rates may affect output if they stay running. This is an oversimplified example, but it puts the indicators in context of the economist view.

- *Lagging indicators*—Lagging indicators are those factors that change after the economy has already started to follow a pattern or trend. They tell us where we were. Lagging indicators include:
  - Average duration of unemployment (in months between periods of employment)
  - Ratio of deflated inventories to sales, manufacturing, and trade
  - Labor cost per unit of output (manufacturing)
  - Commercial and industrial loans outstanding
  - Corporate profits
  - Ratio of consumer installment credit to personal income

The indicators speak for themselves. For example, corporate profits are directly affected by the cost of money. When short-term rates rise, earnings for most corporations are adversely affected as we will discuss in greater detail in Chapter 3.

As you can see, these indicators and clues are a cross section from the Stock, Bond, and Commodity markets. The importance of following the reports given throughout the year can help the trader and investor see the big picture and the trends that are building. While this view is far too broad to make any investment decisions, perhaps its greatest value is to help form one's conviction about the maturity of the stage of the business cycle. In fact, the stock market has predicted 12 of the last 18 recessions. Looking at Figure 2-1, there is a general tendency for bond prices to rise as the business cycle enters and deepens into the contraction cycle. During the trough phase, equity prices tend to rise and the stock market begins to price in or anticipate better times, portending a move into the expansion cycle. During this expansion cycle, commodity prices rise, and there is usually a general pick-up in inflation. The economy will continue to rise and handle the inflationary pressures within the manufacturing pipeline and at the retail level, until eventually there

FIGURE 2-1   *This illustrates the common relationship among stock, bond, and commodity prices in relation to the business cycle. This understanding alone will help participants to direct attention to various investment vehicles during the stages of the cycle.*

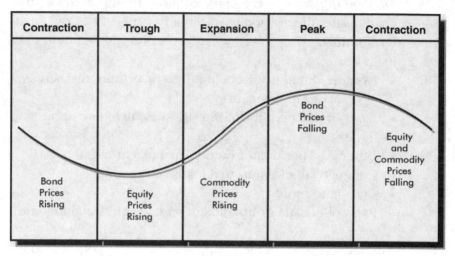

is a peak in the cycle (preceded by a move lower in bond prices). Coming full circle, stocks (as well as commodities) fall and we once again enter the contraction phase. Having this broad understanding will help keep a proper perspective of the financial marketplace.

THE ROLE OF THE GOVERNMENT (FISCAL POLICY)

The Government is the single largest spender in the economy, which means its impact on the markets is the largest. When the economy is zipping along at full employment, deficit spending by the Government is a bearish indicator because the issuance of Government debt competes with corporate bonds for the public's money. This tends to lead to higher interest rates, as competition for money requires a stronger yield (coupon). Excess Government spending can also lead to inflation and force the Fed to raise short-term interest rates. Either way, higher interest rates make interest-earning securities or money market accounts relatively more attractive, and this siphons off money from the stock market. The size of the federal debt is such a big issue in the minds of investors that just about any attempt to reduce deficits short of raising interest rates is greeted with enthusiasm by Wall Street. However, when the economy is clearly in the contraction phase of the business cycle, deficits are bullish because the additional spending by the nation's largest spender leads to a lot of economic activity in the private sector.

If the Government decides to slow down an overheated economy, it can do so in several ways, including:

- Raising taxes
- Reducing the money supply (*tight monetary* policy)
- Reducing Government spending

Each of these activities reduces consumer demand, business spending, and investment. On the other hand, if the Government decides it would be beneficial to stimulate a sluggish economy, it can do so by:

- Reducing taxes
- Increasing the money supply (*easy monetary* policy)
- Increasing Government spending

These activities stimulate the economy by encouraging consumer demand, business, and investment spending.

Once you begin to understand the complex nature of the domestic economy without further complicating it with the World economy, you can then understand the nature of the business cycle and the impact the two primary players (the Government and the Fed) have on it. Remember this always—the act of understanding and forecasting the economy is the work of economists. The ability to anticipate the reactions of the far less educated amateur participants is the work of traders. The public represents the less educated participant (dumb money). Therefore, your role here is to understand, not predict nor forecast, the economy. Through understanding, you gain an insight into the likely reactions of participants. As economic news is disseminated to the market nearly every day, these reactions tend to cause overreactions since the amateur tends to act like an economist, trying to relate the news into forecasts that have little to do with the current market. Economic news in almost all cases (the exception would be the FOMC, which will be discussed in Chapter 3) is much more forward-looking. The confusion of amateurs is perpetuated because they associate the sudden volatility in the market with the news released. The media helps this misconception as well. In fact, professionals hide behind the news as the cause for the volatility, but their true motivation is to "fade" the anticipated public reaction or go the other way. The public's emotional reactions of buying and selling are most often directly countered (faded) by professionals taking the opposite side of the transaction. The moral of the story is to understand the economic news and information well enough not to react like the public, or fade the public reaction like a professional.

FEDERAL RESERVE ECONOMIC POLICY (MONETARY POLICY)

The Federal Reserve Board's policies on the size, movement, and growth of the money supply compose its monetary policy. The Federal Government's policies on taxation and spending make up the country's fiscal policy.

MONETARY POLICY

Money and banking are directly and immediately impacted by the Fed's monetary policy.

FEDERAL OPEN-MARKET OPERATIONS

- The Fed's most important and flexible tool is open-market operations. When engaging in open-market operations, the FOMC buys or sells U.S. Treasury bonds in the open market in order to expand or contract the money supply. When the economy is sluggish and the Fed wants to expand (or loosen) the money supply, it buys U.S. Treasuries from member banks. By selling bonds, the banks receive cash that they can use to make new loans, thereby increasing the money supply. If the economy is in danger of overheating and the Fed wants to contract (or tighten) the money supply, it sells U.S. Treasury securities to banks. By selling securities, the Fed pulls money out of the banking system, forcing banks to make fewer loans and contracting the money supply. The Fed's second most important tool for affecting the money supply is raising and lowering the discount rate—the interest rate the Fed charges its members for certain very short-term loans. By lowering the discount rate, the Fed tends to stimulate the economy by making it easier for banks to make new loans. By raising the discount rate, the Fed tends to counteract inflation by making it more difficult for member banks to make new loans.

These decisions are made eight times per year. In the simplest way, traders will want to avoid having a position go into an FOMC meeting and leave the guesswork of its outcome to the gamblers. This is the one time that all positions should be closed and both traders and investors should stand aside. Traders using a technical approach will better serve their interests to trade a reactionary move than to try to predict the unpredictable. This is why gambling Web sites allow people to make bets on the outcome of an FOMC meeting—it's a gamble.

CHAPTER 3

THE BROAD MARKET AND THE WAY THE ENGINE RUNS

Now that we have gone through the different business cycles and the roles of the Government and the Fed, it is time to take a detailed look at the different gears that turn the "engine of the market." In this chapter, we will start with the broad equity markets, work through the fixed income arena (Bonds), and cover sectors and currencies. Real estate will be covered in Chapter 4. The analogy can be seen in Figure 3-1.

As Figure 3-1 shows, there are many "gears" within the powerful engine of the market, with some garnishing more "torque" than others. Nonetheless, all of the listed inner workings of the markets cannot be simply discarded as "noise." Each has an important role that, if spun hard enough, will affect the entire business cycle.

BROAD EQUITY MARKETS

THE DOW JONES INDUSTRIAL

When breaking down one of the main gears, the broad market indices, a good place to start is with the most popular benchmark, the Dow Jones Industrial Average (DJI). Despite being widely recognized by

FIGURE 3-1 *Participants should have a solid understanding of the marketplace. Some will be capable of trading in all environments, but all must understand the impact of each gear as indicators and beacons of the business cycle and the capital markets alike.*

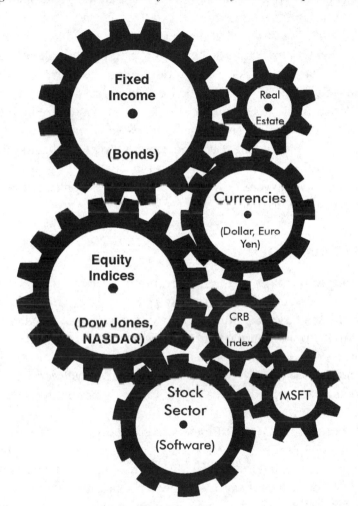

investors as the main index, one inherent problem with the Dow is that it uses only 30 stocks to gauge the sentiment of over 10,000 other stocks. If one stock in the Dow comes out with bad news and its price moves significantly, then this average of only 30 stocks is highly influenced and not necessarily reflecting all 10,000.

Evolving from 11 stocks during its inaugural year under Charles Dow in 1896, the Dow Jones is composed of actively traded high-quality stocks that are price weighted, meaning that the price of each constituent stock is added together and divided by the number of stocks to get a value. The stocks that make up this average have an excellent reputation and demonstrate sustained growth. For the sake of continuity, changes in the stocks used to determine the Dow are rare and happen only if there is a dramatic development in a particular company. For example, the Sears Roebuck Company was removed from the Dow in 1999 because it was seen as reflective of an era past, while Wal-Mart was seen as direct competition and better reflected the current and future era; so Sears was replaced by Wal-Mart. In other words, the market elected Wal-Mart as a better representative of the group than Sears Roebuck.

THE S&P 500 INDEX

The majority of the investment community regards the S&P 500 as the true benchmark of broad market performance. This index is calculated using a base weighted aggregate methodology. In other words, the level of the index reflects the total market value of all 500 component stocks relative to a particular base period. The statistical value of the S&P 500 offers a far better benchmark for the technician since they are so well regarded by the institutional community. See Figure 3-2 for data on the index.

Although the S&P 500 Index was created in 1957, it is projected from 1941–43 in order to form a basis for comparison. In practice, the daily calculation of the index is made by dividing the total market value of the 500 companies by an index divisor that is adjusted to keep the index comparable over time. The 500 constituent stocks that make up this index are selected by an independent committee. This means that companies cannot nominate themselves, nor can investment banks or other entities nominate them. This committee usually meets every month to discuss how corporate actions will affect the index. They also discuss inclusions and exclusions to the index. The companies selected for the S&P 500 index represent important industry segments and generally have the largest market value within their respective industry. Careful

FIGURE 3-2   *Notice the correlation the S&P 500 has to the Dow (91 percent) as of this printing. The value of this information is that these two indices are not directly pegged to each other, as many amateurs believe. Additionally, the Nasdaq Index also represents a broad market indicator, but primarily for technology. Therefore, a huge variance can and does occur among broad market indices. Traders and investors must recognize each index for what it measures and its market impact. This will direct trading and investing decisions on many fronts including risk, volatility, relative strength, and even arbitrage techniques. (Image provided by* www.sandp.com.)

S&P 500

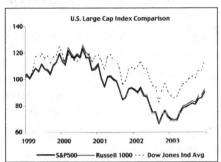

U.S. Large Cap Index Comparison

——S&P500—— Russell 1000 · · · Dow Jones Ind Avg

Portfolio Characteristics — S&P 500

No. of Companies	500
Adj Market Cap ($ bill)	10,286.25
Company Size (Adj $ bil):	
Average	20.57
Largest	311.07
Smallest	0.90
Median	9.11
% Wgt Largest Company	3.02%
Top 10 Holdings (% MktCap Share)	22.75%

Price Index Performance Statistics

	S&P 500	Russel 1000	Dow Jones Ind Avg
Returns			
1 Month	5.08%	4.62%	6.86%
3 Months	11.64%	11.73%	12.71%
YTD	26.38%	27.54%	25.32%
Returns (%pa)			
1 Year	26.38%	27.54%	25.32%
3 Years	-5.56%	-5.30%	-1.04%
5 Years	-1.99%	-1.55%	2.63%
7 Years	5.97%	6.06%	7.15%
Risk (% pa)			
3 Years Std Dev	18.29%	18.29%	18.47%
5 Years Std Dev	17.13%	17.22%	17.40%
Sharpe Ratio			
3 Years	-0.095	-0.091	-0.021
5 Years	-0.066	-0.058	0.012

Sector Weights — S&P 500

Consumer Discretionary	11.29%
Consumer Staples	10.98%
Energy	5.80%
Financials	20.65%
Health Care	13.31%
Industrials	10.90%
Information Technology	17.74%
Materials	3.04%
Telecommunication Services	3.45%
Utilities	2.84%

5 Year Tracking Statistics

	S&P 500	Russel 1000	Dow Jones Ind Avg
Correlation			
S&P 500	1.0000	0.9957	0.9168
Russell 1000		1.0000	0.9056
Dow Jones Ind Avg			1.0000
R–Squared			
S&P 500	100%	99%	84%
Russell 1000		100%	82%
Dow Jones Ind Avg			100%
Tracking Error (% pa)			
S&P 500	0.0%	1.6%	7.0%
Russell 1000		0.0%	7.5%
Dow Jones Ind Avg			0.0%

consideration must be made for additions and deletions since many large institutions have S&P 500 index tracking funds. When a stock is added to the index, one is subsequently removed in order to keep the index number at 500. This information is valuable because institutions are indexed to these specific issues and they will sell the stock that leaves the index and buy the stock that is added. This has a large impact on both companies and provides a good trading opportunity due to changes in money flow. Money flow patterns are important measures since mutual funds compete with the S&P 500. Indexing means that they own the same stocks in their portfolios as the components within the index. The funds that beat the index do so by having a heavier weight in the outperforming shares of the index.

Your role is to understand the impact these funds have on the index and trade direction of the trend they set. These funds simply have more money and leverage to set the trend than any single investor, hence the cliché, "the trend is your friend."

THE NASDAQ COMPOSITE INDEX

The Nasdaq Composite Index is another wide-based market value weighted index (like the S&P 500). It takes into account all of the common stock listed on the Nasdaq exchange and is one of the broadest indices for technology stocks. The Nasdaq mainly tracks technology stocks, so it is not the best indicator to track the overall market. Created in 1971, this index includes over 3000 securities. To be included in the Nasdaq, the security must be both listed on the Nasdaq and be either an American depository receipt (ADR), common stock, ordinary shares, real estate investment trust (REIT), shares of beneficial interest (SBIs), or a tracking stock. If at any time a component security no longer meets the eligibility criteria, the security is removed from the index.

THE NASDAQ 100 INDEX

This index is made up of 100 of the largest market capitalization stocks that are nonfinancial listed on the Nasdaq stock exchange. Still considered the standard for technology stocks, the Nasdaq 100 was launched in 1985 and focuses on several industry groups including computer hardware and software, telecommunication, retail/whole-sale trade, and biotechnology. As a pure technology index, the Nasdaq 100 (NDX) is the best broad market representative. To be listed on the Nasdaq 100, securities must be in the top 25 percent market capitalization for the prior six months, having an average trading volume of at least 200,000 shares as well as being a nonfinancial company.

FIXED INCOME MARKET: BOND BASICS

The other main sprocket that complements the broad indices is the fixed income arena, reporting an average daily cash volume of roughly $630 billion versus $70 billion for the three major stock exchanges. Moreover, at the end of 2002, there were over $20 trillion worth of outstanding fixed income securities compared to $11 trillion of total stock market capitalization.

The definition of a *fixed income security* is simply a certificate of debt issued by a government or corporation guaranteeing payment of the original investment plus interest by a specified future date. For purposes of our discussion, the term *bond* will be synonymous with the U.S. Treasury bond. This instrument is defined as a negotiable, coupon-bearing debt obligation issued by the U.S. Government and backed by its full faith and credit, as well as having a maturity of more than seven years (if less than seven years, the correct term is *Treasury note*). Interest on Government bonds is paid semi-annually and exempt from state and local taxes. Bonds are nothing more than the physical evidence of a loan made among the parties. Most bonds are fixed-rate bonds that pay a fixed annual rate of interest to the bondholder. This fixed interest rate is called the *coupon rate.* Bonds are usually issued to meet long-term obligations, to improve the working capital of the issuer, or to fund growth. Issuing bonds is the alternative to issuing stock (or selling equity).

When it comes to pricing bonds, the value of a bond is equal to its expected cash flow (coupons issued semi-annually) throughout the life of the bond discounted at a certain rate. The result equals the present value (PV) of a bond. An example of calculating the PV of a bond is shown in Figure 3-3:

Example

- Par Value = $1000
- Maturity Date is in five years
- Annual Coupon Payments of $100, which is 10 percent (100/1000)
- Market Interest Rate of 8 percent—The Key Variable

The Present Value of the Coupon Payments (an annuity) = $399.27

The Present Value of the Par Value (time value of money) = $680.58

The Present Value of a Bond = $399.27 + $680.58 = $1079.86

It is important to understand that there is an inverse relationship between interest rates and price. For example, if Company A and another company both issue bonds at 8 percent, these securities will have the same initial cost since they are equally attractive (assuming credit risk is identical). If, on the other hand, the economy deteriorates and interest rates fall to 6 percent, what will happen to the price of these bonds? They will still pay 8 percent; however, since the overall market can now only offer 6 percent, the bonds from Company A will have to demand more than what they did before (called a *premium*). These investors that pay more to get the 8 percent (or $8 per bond if par is $100) will, however, only get a 6 percent return. Why? Let's say Company A's bonds went from a par of $100 to $133. Take the $8 (coupon) and divide by 133. Then multiply by 100. This equals 6 percent. Of course, the holders of these bonds have a 33 percent capital gain they have to contend with.

FIGURE 3-3   *Present value calculation for a fixed income security.*

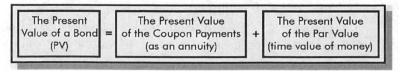

| The Present Value of a Bond (PV) | = | The Present Value of the Coupon Payments (as an annuity) | + | The Present Value of the Par Value (time value of money) |

A common misconception is that bond yields and bond interest rates are the same. They are not. A bond's yield does not have to fall with interest rates, as seen in past practice when the Fed has raised rates while yields actually fell. Therefore, yields can have a life of their own, representing investor psychology and reflecting a perception of risk used to "grade the Fed" on how its monetary policy is working. Remember, in late 1999–early 2000, it sure didn't make sense for an investor to pass up stocks that were generating 30 percent annual gains for a small 30-year yield that fell from 6.5 percent, to 6 percent, and then 5.75 percent, most likely due to the Fed raising interest rates. The market will always tell us later "why" the market was buying the higher yields. To calculate yield for bonds and notes, divide the coupon rate by the market price.

Figure 3-4 is a good illustration of how yields and rates differ.

FIGURE 3-4   *This chart illustrates the difference between current interest rates and yields, ranging from 91-day T-Bills to 30-year Treasury bonds.*

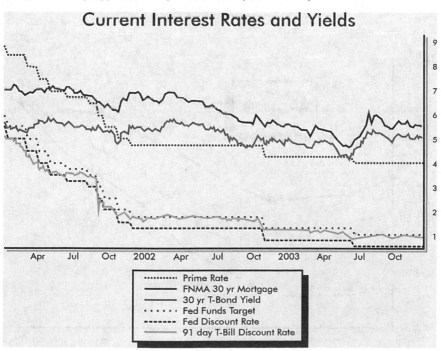

Another important understanding of the bond market is that there are different maturities issued by the U.S. Treasury. Ranging from four weeks to thirty years, the different slope of the yield curve can definitely tell a different story about the economy. It should be noted that bonds with longer maturities normally fall or rise more than bonds with shorter maturities. If, for example, interest rates fall 1 percent, the price on a 20-year bond will generally rise more than a 5-year bond. See Figure 3-5.

A situation in which long-term debt instruments have higher yields than short-term debt instruments is referred to as a *positive yield curve*. This is common. If, however, long-term interest rates have lower yields than short-term interest rates, it is called a *negative yield curve*.

FIGURE 3-5 *This chart illustrates the difference in yields between short- and long-term Treasury notes and bonds; thus forming a "yield curve" that is either positive (shown) or negative. A positive yield curve is when yields within longer-term bonds are higher than for short-term notes.*

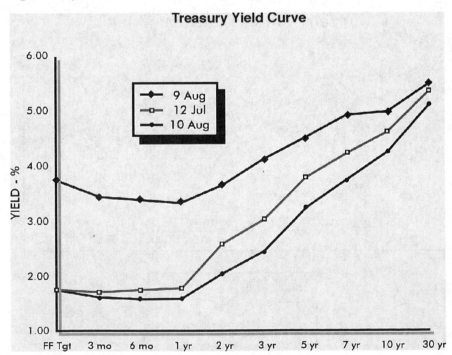

Steepening occurs when the yield curve gets more positive. This can be done a variety of ways, but usually happens via the buying of shorter-term maturities (lowering yields) and selling of longer-term maturities (raising yields). The opposite is called *flattening*. If traders ranging from speculators to foreign central banks are lowering long-term exposure to either a depreciation of the U.S. dollar or falling confidence, there could be a flight-to-quality resulting in more assets on a relative basis being put into short-term notes, thus steepening the curve.

The following rate structure will help explain the impact short-term rates have on the market.

- *Prime rate* is the base rate on corporate loans at large U.S. money center commercial banks. The prime rate is relatively stable but reacts quickly to policy changes made by the Fed.
- *Federal funds rate* is the interest rate charged on reserves traded among member banks for overnight use in amounts of $1 million or more. The federal funds rate is the most volatile of all interest rates, changing daily in response to the needs of borrowing banks, and represents a daily average of the rates charged by the lending banks. The rate fluctuates hourly.
- *Discount rate* is the rate charged on loans to depository institutions by the FRB of New York.
- *Call money rate* is the rate charged on loans to brokers on securities used as collateral. This rate forms the basis for the rate charged to customers of the broker for purchasing securities on margin.
- *Commercial paper rate* is the rate on commercial paper placed directly by GMAC or the rate on high-grade unsecured notes sold through dealers by major corporations.

As you can see, the rates within the market are also top-down and the power of short-term interest rate changes can have a dramatic impact on short-term and even long-term market direction. This does not mean that rising short-term rates mean the stock market will always fall (inflationary posture) or that falling rates will always support market rise. This is not certain; it is only certain to know that the effects of short-term interest rate adjustments can add to market volatility while contributing to a longer lasting trend. It is important to understand that rising rates cost publicly traded companies money based on the bond discussion above, and this makes these companies less valuable in the absence of other factors. Simply stated, rising interest rates means a rising cost of doing business and that means less earnings.

What is the correlation between interest rates and equity prices? Looking at the following two charts in Figures 3-6 and 3-7, the correlation may not be perfect; however, there is reason to believe that, in general, lower interest rates spell out higher equity prices.

Because earnings, as we know, are the true bottom line, and all the speculation we do in the markets is centered on factors that attempt to predict and estimate earnings, earnings are directly under

FIGURE 3-6   *The chart depicts the movement of interest rates over the long haul, illustrating the relationship of the prime rate to the federal discount rate to the long T-bond yield.*

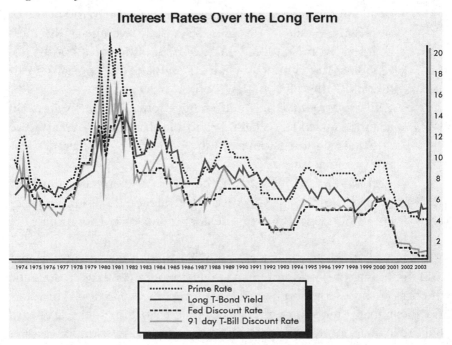

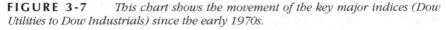

FIGURE 3-7 *This chart shows the movement of the key major indices (Dow Utilities to Dow Industrials) since the early 1970s.*

attack when rate hikes occur. This can cause quite a stir in the equity markets. Conversely, other factors that drive investment decisions are not so clearly related to earnings, and this opens the door to subjectivity. Certainly different participants come up with different conclusions, but the complexities of these factors are good reasons to stand aside and let "price" sort it out. The market discounts all factors and reflects the consensus of all opinion in its price. So why broach the subject of interest rates, you make ask—because rate changes are the "fundamental exception."

As we have made clear, interest rates matter, affecting markets dramatically as they are the universal language of all companies within the S&P 500, the market, and the world. The factors noted earlier may only apply to certain sectors or stocks, but interest rates are broad market indicators because they affect all stocks and therefore the broad market.

Here is a universal example using the objectivity of the math. Suppose a company has a present value of $5 billion and a present cost of money of 9 percent (adjustable rate) on debt funding for 10 more years. If the cost of money increases to 10 percent, the company's present value is reduced by $450 million (PV = FV/(1 + R)^t) due to the drag on earnings. This 9 percent reduction in value can have a dramatic and lasting impact on stock prices.

If a company carries little or no debt, many would surmise the impact would be minimal. We must also remember the consumer of the goods and services of the publicly traded company will also be affected through reduced buying power. Higher cost of money equals lower buying power. The Fed therefore becomes somewhat of a drug dealer. The drug is debt, and the cheaper it is, the more the money supply is eased, and the more buying power created. If debt is expensive, the cost of money is higher, which in turn means lower buying power, and less spending (tightening money supply). The drug is given, the drug is taken away—and America likes this drug.

WHAT ABOUT BOND FUTURES?

Bond futures are a standardized, leveraged instrument with specific coupon and specific maturities that trades at the Chicago Board of Trade (CBOT) as either a hedging instrument for cash traders, a market for speculators, or simply a benchmark for observers who use the moment in bonds to possibly reflect sentiment in equities. A futures account allows you to buy/sell a contract for much less than the face value of a bond (100 equals 100,000), since margin is only a few thousand dollars. Every tick ($1/_{32}$) debits or credits $31.25 into your account. There are no dividends paid and very few traders hold the bond until delivery. Futures, by definition, give traders an idea where yields might be down the road.

Futures accounts must be opened separately from equities under a commodity futures trading account regulated by the Commodity Futures Trading Commission (CFTC). Equity accounts are regulated by the SEC. Consequently, funds cannot be commingled with an equities account.

COMMODITIES

Commodities are the physical product. They represent the earliest descendents of speculation tools such as coal, oil, iron, copper, agricultural products, etc. Yet the markets today operate around the risk management of the commodity for which the producers of the actual commodity play little part. The farmers of grains, butchers of frozen pork bellies, or producers of orange juice generally have little impact on the derivative markets that trade their physical goods. Instead, the futures market leads this domain as a means of managing risk. This at least was the original purpose of said market, but today, the evolution of markets has given way more to speculation than to risk mitigation.

In theory, futures contracts act like insurance policies, whereby the risk and protections provided by the insurance company is somewhat predetermined in exchange for the insurance premiums collected. One party pays a premium for protection while the other promises to protect against a certain unknown outcome. They are called premiums because the cost of such protection generally exceeds the risk of the exposure. Both parties are obligated to the contract for as long as the agreement is in place. This is how insurance companies make money. In the case of commodities, similar contracts exist.

The producer of a good essentially buys a contract that allows them to sell the good at a predetermined future date at a predetermined fixed price. This ensures and removes risk to the producers who may develop volatile goods in terms of price based on the supply/demand environment in the future (unknown). This way, through a commodities futures contract, the producer may sell a product at a determined price that they have not even produced yet. This principal reduces the risk to the producer and can give the producer incentive to go forward with the production. They essentially give up the opportunity for selling at higher prices in the future in exchange for certainty today. Just like an insurance policy; we pay a premium today to eliminate risk tomorrow. The premium paid for the commodity is the potential upside profit available in the future. Like insurance companies, the risk from the insurance company's point of view, like that of the commodity futures issuer, is less than the premium received, hence the profitability.

On one hand this market is created to hedge risk for the producers of the commodity, while on the other hand it has become a game of chance for speculators to try and guess future pricing. This makes it a game of chance and a zero sum game as well. For every winner there is an offsetting loser with one exception. The bookie in the middle bringing the parties together called the exchanges and clearing firms. These intermediaries make the "vig" on transactional revenue with little risk. This is clearly the best business to be in!

The commodities markets were once not easily assessable to ordinary investors. They were something that your average everyday investor did not speculate in. Over the past several years, however, there has been an increased interest and increased money flow into the commodities markets. With the introduction of mini-sized commodities futures contracts that trade electronically, most investors and traders now have the ability to participate in the commodities market directly. The influx of money into commodities is mainly due to the fact that they can be a good hedge and are great trading vehicles. Throughout history, gold has been a hedge to risk. When there is mistrust about the future of the financial markets as a whole, there has typically been an influx from equities into treasuries and gold. As participants in financial markets buy a set of equities, they will typically hedge their investment in some way. More and more there has been a transition from going to treasuries and gold as a place of safety to going to energy. Two of the fastest growing commodities contracts are the light, sweet crude oil futures contract and the natural gas futures contract.

Crude oil is known as black gold for good reason. First of all oil is valuable and many fortunes have been made or lost because of it. Secondly, it trades much like gold. Crude oil is currently one of the world's most actively traded commodities, and the most liquid futures contract on crude oil is traded on the New York Mercantile Exchange (NYMEX). The movements of crude oil are direct descendants of supply and demand as well as the perception of supply and demand. Since much of the oil supply for the U.S. comes from other countries, the price is highly affected by world events. This could be terrorist acts, worker strikes, or war—any disruption of supply. These causes will typically also cause equities to decline, making it an ideal hedge. All of these types of events have an effect on the price of crude oil. Anything that adversely affects the supply of oil into the country will drive prices higher. During the 1990s the par value of oil was $18–21. Anything lower than $18 for oil was considered cheap and anything over $21 was considered rich. In the early 2000s par value was raised. The par value for crude oil moved to the $30-a-barrel area. With the U.S. oil supply so dependant on foreign nations, the market for trading crude oil is very volatile and liquid, as shown in Figure 3-8.

As a final note, Saudi Arabia is the biggest supplier of crude oil to the U.S., and the ruling family is getting older and one day a change will occur in the rule of the country. This will have a direct effect on the price of oil.

Natural gas is another commodity that is increasing in popularity. The natural gas market is purely driven by supply and demand. The factors that affect the supply and demand make this a uniquely traded instrument. There are many countries around the world that have large supplies of natural gas. The trouble with natural gas is that it is

---

FIGURE 3-8　*The bar has been raised to the $30 area for crude oil. When there is uncertainty about the disruption of the supply of oil the price spikes. (Chart courtesy of www.wtg.com.)*

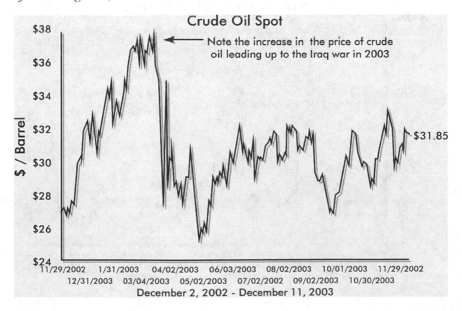

not easily transportable nor stored since it must be compressed or liquefied and is highly explosive. This makes it a natural terrorist target. Imagine a ship filled with liquid natural gas. Since natural gas is explosive, it makes it a floating bomb. There is no insurance company that would insure this type of shipment.

The U.S. is becoming increasingly dependant on natural gas each year. Being that natural gas is not easily transported, the main supply comes from within the U.S. and Canada, and this makes supply limited. The internal infrastructure within the U.S. for getting natural gas out of the ground is getting old. When the large energy trading firms went bankrupt, the scheduled repairs to the infrastructure didn't happen. As a consequence the equipment breaks down often, which disrupts supply and affects the price of natural gas. Weather may also impact the price of natural gas. In cold weather, people may use more natural gas. Energy is taking the place of gold and treasuries in the portfolios of many people as a hedge to long side exposure in the equities markets. See Figure 3-9.

FIGURE 3-9   *Notice the volatile nature of natural gas. (Chart courtesy of* www.wtrg.com.*)*

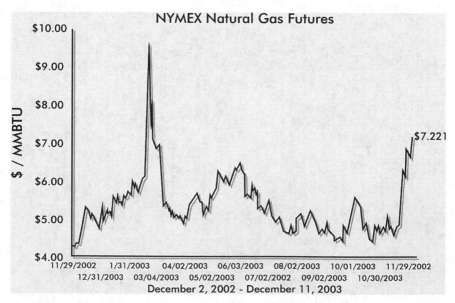

When fitting commodities into the sprocket relationship outlined earlier, there is normally an inverse relationship between Bond and Commodity prices (CRB Index). This is because a higher CRB Index usually means more inflation, which in turn generally pressures bond prices.

There are also many other commodities that are actively traded. These include coal, cocoa, coffee, sugar, and pork bellies. As with any other traded item, it is a simple matter of supply and demand. Prices are affected by rain in other parts of the world and forecasts of El Niño and La Niña seasons. These commodities may trade in unique ways but you should know that these markets exist and they are necessary to help supply meet demand. If all of a sudden the supply of sugar were cut off, the price of sugar would rise until there wasn't any more and there is a real problem. Many products couldn't be produced, people would lose jobs, and it would come to a point where it would turn into sheer madness. Though you will probably not trade any of these products, you need to know that in the overall picture they are important and necessary.

There are many ways of measuring the market. There are different ways of looking at the market depending on what you are trading. It is necessary to formulate an overall view of the market whether you are trading it actively or investing. Now that you have a taste of what is out there you can decide which indices and indicators you like personally. Though most of the focus of the book is on technical analysis, if you plan on participating in the market for any length time it is necessary to touch on a fundamental understanding of these products and indices and their market impact.

CHAPTER 4

SECTOR ANALYSIS

A s you begin to understand the gears of the economic machine, the logical progression of top-down analysis is to relate economic forces to the market and stocks you trade. Many of the influences we have studied thus far will have varying degrees of impact during the business cycle. There are times when economic news has little impact on the prevailing trend and other times when the market seems to stand still until the Fed speaks. The point here is that while the gears of the machine can seem complex and inconsistent in relation to market trend, the understanding of economic influences will contribute to market analysis.

This chapter is a strong step in that direction. Sector analysis is specific to market analysis, yet it is important to remember the foundation we have built so far. The previous chapter outlined the effects of short-term interest rates on securities and the basics of commodity contacts. This chapter helps you analyze which sectors are most influenced by such events. In the simplest context, sectors that stand the most to gain by interest rate changes tend to lead markets and sectors that are hit the hardest when rates rise tend to lag the market. Traders want to buy leading sectors in bull markets and sell (short) weak sectors in bear markets. This is a simple concept that has given traders the edge for many years.

Sector analysis involves focusing on a particular industry or sector of the economy. This can range from industry-related sectors such as software, technology, and drug manufacturing to economic influences such as banking, utilities, currencies, and real estate. The range is broad but the component issues within each are defined by the sector. The impact of broad market influences help narrow the search where participants should likely expect reaction. For example, a significant move in the bond market, as discussed in Chapter 3, allows the possibility of interest-rate sensitive issues to have reactionary moves (Freddie Mac and Fannie Mae). Therefore, it would make sense to focus on the banking sector for relatively strong (longs) or weak (shorts) issues. Moreover, there are certain sectors of the market that have historically been shown to be a leading indicator to the overall markets, such as the Dow Jones Utility Average and the Amex Oil Index.

THE DOW JONES UTILITY AVERAGE

The Dow Jones Utility Average (UTY) debuted in January 1929, making it the youngest of the three Dow Jones Averages. This capitalization-weighted index, composed of 19 geographically diverse public utility stocks listed on the New York Stock Exchange (NYSE), has traditionally provided a haven for investors who fear recession and unstable returns on other investments (these issues tend to pay high cash dividends). In theory, a rise in utility stock prices indicates investors anticipate falling interest rates, since utility companies are big borrowers and their profits are enhanced by lower interest costs. Conversely, the utility average tends to decline when investors expect rising interest rates. Due to the index's interest-rate sensitivity, the utility average is regarded by many as a leading indicator for the stock market as a whole.

With regard to the Dow Utilities as a leading indicator of equities, the correlations have become clear since 1972. In November of that year, the utilities peaked a few months before the Dow, and then formed a bottom just 10 months later, leading the Dow. Moreover, the utilities peaked in the beginning of 1981, while the blue chips formed a high only three months later. These similarities continued in 1982, with both averages bottoming and rallying together until August 1987. From an investor's point of view, the correlations since 1972 have been remarkable.

Research found in *Technical Trends* by John R. McGinley, Jr. has shown that the Dow Utilities has led the Dow Jones at every peak since 1960 with only a few exceptions (most notably the 1977 peak). When looking at lead times, on average the Utility Index peaked three months prior, with a variance of one to ten months. Relatively speaking, that is not a bad track record at all.

AMEX OIL INDEX

The other index that has historically shown itself to be a leading indicator to the overall markets is the Amex Oil Index (XOI), a price-weighted index comprised of companies involved in the exploration, production, and development of petroleum. The XOI Index was established with a benchmark value of 125.00 on August 27, 1984. The theory of the index holds that higher oil prices become inflationary, and this in turn has negative implications on the Dow. However, just like with Fed fund hikes, the Dow can trade in step with higher oil prices for quite some time before inflation is perceived by investors to be out of control. This is an important caution since cheap oil prices do not necessarily mean good news for the Dow Jones Industrial Average.

Remember, oil is considered an import product; therefore, cheap oil has the tendency to bankrupt small oil producers and oil equipment companies, especially those in the U.S. These companies usually only make a profit if oil prices are at least $16 to $18 a barrel. Cheap oil increases dependence on foreign oil imports, resulting in larger trade deficits. More importantly, cheap oil historically results in significant job loss in oil and related industries in the U.S. Several studies indicate there is a negative correlation between the fluctuations in the oil price and the gross national product of Western countries. From 1982 to 1986 when oil prices were high, the economies of the U.S., Japan, and Western Europe were expanding, whereas in the second half of 1980s, when prices collapsed, a recession took place. These are important representations of the global economy as well.

CURRENCIES

Since the U.S. dollar is the de facto global reserve currency, its trading behavior is exceedingly important for investors and speculators around the world to monitor. To monitor the U.S. dollar is to watch the U.S. Dollar Index. This U.S. Dollar Index is a futures contract that trades on the New York Board of Trade. Futures traders and futures-options speculators around the globe relentlessly trade these U.S. Dollar Index futures contracts to actively speculate on the U.S. dollar.

The U.S. Dollar Index compares the U.S. dollar to a basket of global currencies rather than just one. As of this printing, the Dollar Index consists of a trade-weighted geometric average of seven currencies, including the European euro, Japanese yen, British pound, Canadian dollar, Swedish krona, and Swiss franc. (Note: There is a chance that within a few years the Chinese yuan will be included, especially if the massive emerging economic power of China is combined with the world's first major gold-backed currency in decades. A golden yuan could rapidly dominate Pacific and Asian trade and it would be hard not to include it in the U.S. Dollar Index.) See Figure 4-1.

INTERNATIONAL TRADE

There are a number of important factors to consider when looking at the overall health of the U.S. economy and the U.S. dollar. For example, the United States' *trade balance* can have an effect on the economy and the value of the dollar in relation to foreign currencies. Since changes in a country's economy affect stock prices, it is important for us as traders and investors to understand this relationship. For example, in 1987 the "Asian Flu," as it was known, was named for the economic "bug" that began with currency (Baht) and spread from country to country, infecting otherwise healthy economies with weakened currencies, sudden credit defaults, and extreme stock market volatility.

We incur a *trade deficit* with a foreign country when we import more goods than we export. To import goods from other countries, we need to exchange our dollars into their currency in order to buy their goods. This is the process. If the foreign country doesn't want as much

FIGURE 4-1 *A weekly chart of the U.S. Dollar Index.*

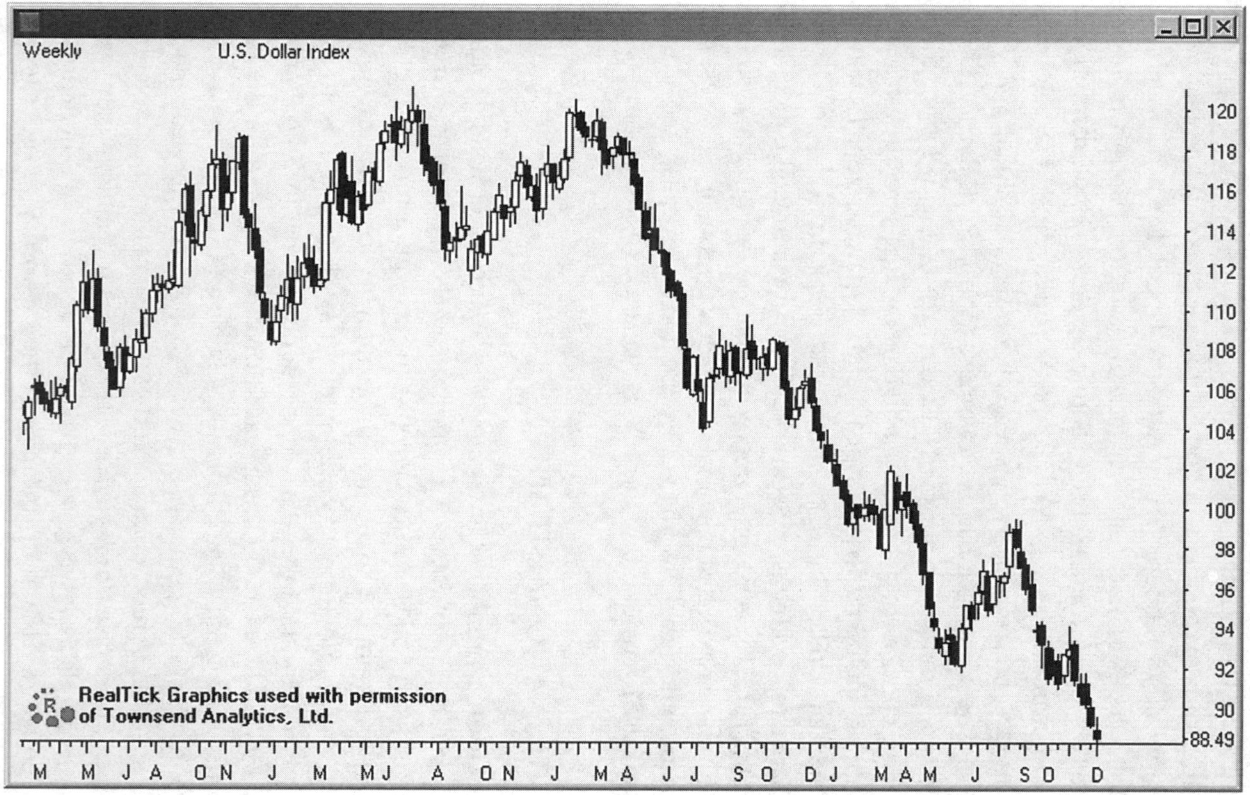

Weekly   U.S. Dollar Index

RealTick Graphics used with permission
of Townsend Analytics, Ltd.

48

of our goods, then they won't need to exchange as much of their currency for our dollars. That causes an oversupply of dollars in the exchange market and leads to a fall in the exchange rate. In relative terms, we would say the dollar is "weak." On the other hand a strong economy can make the dollar "strong" (raise the exchange rate) in spite of a trade deficit. The reason is that a strong economy attracts investment capital from abroad and foreign countries need to exchange their currencies for dollars to invest in the U.S. This is where the U.S. stock market can help absorb trade deficits. This drives up the demand for the dollar, resulting in a stronger currency. Exporting more than we import (*trade surplus*), coupled with a strong market, substantially strengthens the dollar. Many believe that as the world leader in technology development, the culmination of our trade surplus in technology, coupled with its impact on the U.S. stock market, drove exponential growth to the dollar as well as the equity markets. Many also fear that becoming uncompetitive in technology could be devastating to the U.S. economy. California, one of the world's largest economies overall (countries included), has shown signs of losing competitiveness in technology (Silicon Valley, etc.). This could be a wake-up call or a foreteller of the future.

Trade deficits or surpluses are important because they give us clues as to the direction of the dollar and the stock market. A rising dollar combined with a booming economy in the U.S. and weakening economies in Asia attracts investment and drives up our stock market. Rising trade deficits put downward pressure on the dollar and mean that American businesses are having trouble competing abroad, both of which can cause foreign and domestic investors to put their money elsewhere. The most important feature of the world economy is that money is always on the lookout for a better home. This is true domestically and abroad. Capital generally flows worldwide to where the prospects of return relative to risk are the greatest. The best tip to mastering the economics is to constantly think about all the investment alternatives available worldwide. Be aware that anytime liquid investments look relatively better, it will attract money (money flow) from all over the world and bring down the prices of the relatively less-profitable alternatives. The huge waves of Asian money that flowed into the U.S.

financial markets in 1997 and 1998 will flow back out along with American money, riding the wave as soon as the trend in the yen and Asian economies looks better than the trend in America!

The dollar's high correlation with the U.S. equity markets is very interesting, hitting highs and lows with the S&P 500 many times over the years in tandem. When foreign investors seek to put their surplus capital in the U.S. as an investment, the primary destination of this capital is most likely the U.S. stock and bond markets (main two sprockets). When stocks are going up and euphoria exists, demand for dollars increases as foreign investors sell their local currencies to buy dollars in order to buy U.S. stocks. Therefore, increased dollar demand drives up the international price of the U.S. dollar. The reverse is true as well. As foreign investors already invested in the U.S. equity markets watch the U.S. stock indices fall, foreign investors not only face equity losses but currency translation losses as well. So, as the stock markets fall, foreign investors want out so they sell their U.S. stocks for dollars and then sell these dollars to buy back into their own local currencies. Therefore, increased dollar supply drives down the international price of the U.S. dollar.

For example, American investors could be down 5 percent while foreign investors are down 10 percent when their currency losses are added to their U.S. equity losses!

These rapidly compounding losses are almost certainly going to lead to increased selling of U.S. stocks and dollars by foreign investors seeking to flee the ongoing U.S. financial carnage.

THE EFFECTS OF INTEREST RATES ON THE DOLLAR AND GOLD

There is also a solid correlation between interest rates after inflation and the dollar.

In the past, when the Fed cut interest rates and yields fell, the rates of return that both American and foreign investors could earn in short-term treasuries fell and the dollar paused. As soon as real rates of return after inflation began to plunge due to active Fed manipulation of short-term interest rates, the U.S. dollar decline accelerated dramatically.

Just as declining equity markets can accelerate the dollar's slide, so do declining real returns in the U.S. bond markets. Foreign investors are less willing to hold U.S. bonds and finance the U.S. debt if they are going to lose real purchasing power because of inflation. As some of them start to sell and repatriate their capital back into their local currencies, the dollar's decline will accelerate, leading to even larger losses for the remaining foreign holders of U.S. bonds.

Watching the dollar's trading and dominant trend is very important for American bond investors and speculators because any widespread foreign selling will hurt the prices of bonds and lead to rising longer-term interest rates, which could start a vicious cycle that affects equities negatively. What does benefit as the dollar falls? Gold.

Gold and the dollar are usually inversely related, since any weakness in the U.S. dollar should cause an increase in the U.S. dollar gold price as long as the international gold price remains relatively constant. This is true because gold is priced in U.S. dollars. Gold prices would, however, remain relatively low if there was physical selling in gold. If the dollar is strong, then one expects imports to be highly priced and exports to remain low. The dollar buys a lot in some countries, while other countries tend to resist importing much of our goods since their currency would be weak relative to ours. Therefore, their currency would buy fewer goods. With a strong dollar goes weakness in gold. Participants are buying the dollar since it has a higher value in other countries. As a result the price of gold falls.

In the reverse case where the dollar is weakening, the U.S. dollar cannot buy much foreign currency, causing exports to rise and imports to fall. As a result, the price of gold rises since it is universally priced and bought if participants fear further weakness in the dollar. Gold is safe and if something happened to the currency of this country, you could use gold in most any other country as currency. If the dollar is weak against other currencies, then gold prices will typically rise. The Dollar Index is therefore an important indicator. Refer back to Figure 4-1.

REAL ESTATE

A piece of the puzzle that also cannot be ignored is the real estate market. In fact, the aggregate market size was at $4.4 trillion by the end of 2000, with institutions owning slightly less than $2 trillion, or 45 percent, of the market. Despite weak economic times in the past, equity investments in commercial and residential property have generally bucked the trend and proved to be important safe havens. Remember, the dollar always seeks a better home, and investors literally like their homes as havens for money when the market is weak. That being said, it is important to recognize that there is a very low correlation between real estate and stock market returns. This is because in bull markets, real estate is also an attractive haven to many. Primarily the belief is because tangible assets that can bring comfort do not correlate well to investment decision making. This allows traders and investors a true method for diversification and even hedge against inflationary times. I am a strong believer and investor of real estate for these reasons. I trade for income and buy real estate for wealth (personal view).

FANNIE MAE/FREDDIE MAC

One company that specializes in the flow of low-cost mortgage capital in order to increase the availability and affordability of homeownership for low-, moderate-, and middle-income Americans is Federal National Mortgage Association (Fannie Mae). This company operates under a federal charter, and its primary regulator is the Office of Federal Housing Enterprise Oversight (OFHEO). *Fannie Mae* is a source of funds for mortgage lenders and investors, providing resources for customers to make additional mortgage loans or investments in mortgage-related securities. The company provides liquidity to the mortgage market for the benefit of borrowers, but it does not lend money directly to consumers. Fannie Mae operates exclusively in the secondary mortgage market by purchasing mortgages and mortgage-related securities from primary market institutions, such as commercial banks, savings and loan associations, mortgage companies, securities dealers, and other investors.

Another company that can shed light on the real estate market is the Federal Home Loan Mortgage Corporation (Freddie Mac), a stock-holder-owned corporation chartered by Congress in 1970 to keep money flowing to mortgage lenders in support of homeownership and rental housing. Freddie Mac purchases single-family and multi-family residential mortgages and mortgage-related securities, which it finances primarily by issuing mortgage pass-through securities and debt instruments in the capital markets.

The importance in following real estate is necessary because the average family has a mortgage and a significant amount of money spent on durable goods to decorate the house; therefore, a substantial amount of wealth is directly correlated to one's home. By watching a few economic numbers released each month, a trader can get an idea of the relative strength or weakness within the housing market.

Building permits, housing starts, and manufacturers' new orders for durable goods are all important economic numbers released every month that shine new light on the housing market. It is important to understand that all of these indicators are leading indicators, instead of lagging or being coincidences with the economy.

If the housing market falls, Fannie Mae and Freddie Mac start to witness a significant drop in lending. This drop in household wealth will get traders more nervous about the health of the economy and begin to contract spending outside of the home. The correlation with the market may not be direct; however, the housing market is still a solid barometer of consumer sentiment. Sentiment is important, and the following discussion on gauging fear helps pull sector analysis together.

THE FEAR INDEX

Created in 1993 by The Chicago Board of Options Exchange (CBOE), the Fear Index (VIX) measures and anticipates market volatility for approximately the next 30 calendar days using stock index option prices. By taking a weighted average of options with a constant maturity of 30 days, the VIX offers the best measure of near-term volatility. Unlike the indices noted above, these two indices are measuring volatility. *Volatility* is the relative rate at which a security moves higher and lower in price relative to volume. If the price of a stock moves up and down rapidly in a short period of time, the stock has a high volatility. On the other hand, if the stock's price is stable over time, it has a low volatility. If there is high volatility on one stock, many times there is company-specific news to blame and increased volatility as investors try to anticipate how the news will affect the company in the future. The value of this index is that it only measures volatility over a large number of stocks, which better defines underlying sentiment (fear and excitement) in the broad market.

The VIX was aptly nicknamed the "fear index" because it has generally peaked during times of turmoil and fear seen via weakness in equities. Therefore, as VIX rallies (measuring growing fear), investors benefit by selling shares or even shorting the market. Conversely, as volatility subsides and fear diminishes, investor confidence restores and the broad market rallies. This makes the Fear Index a contrarian's indicator. Just like an oscillator, when the Fear Index gets too low or too high, we can also expect a reversal in the capital markets. These extended levels of fear (peak VIX) and complacency (low VIX) also signal entry methods for reversals. Overextended highs signal buys and over extended lows signal sells. Refer to Figure 4-2 to see the correlation. Finally, volatility can also be used to measure an impending change in trend. As George Soros once said, "Short-term volatility is greatest at turning points and diminishes as the trend becomes established."

The VIX Index is the CBOE's near-term expected volatility index for stock index options for the S&P 500 Index. Historically, VIX measured the OEX options (options on the S&P 100 stocks) volatility, but recently the methodology has been updated to now measure the entire S&P 500 (SPX). Options will be covered in a later section but for now know that one of the factors that options derive their price from is volatility. Refer to Figure 4-3 to see how VIX marked many periods of extreme fear.

The CBOE has another volatility index that takes into account the volatility of the Nasdaq 100 options prices. This index is the VXN and is more heavily weighted to the technology side, so it is less reflective of the overall market sentiment. However, it is useful when trading with the technology sector. As with any other indicator, the volatility indices should not be the sole factor in making investment and active trading

FIGURE 4-2 *The inverse relationship indicates that traders should buy the market on declining VIX and sell the market on rising VIX. At extended levels, VIX can also act as an oscillator and forecast reversals.*

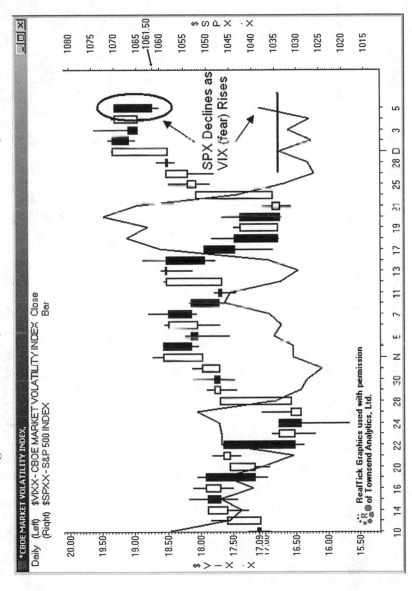

FIGURE 4-3 *Notice the large peak in volatility that occurred in the stock market crash of 1987. In October 1987 the Dow fell 508 points (22 percent) and fear was at a maximum.*

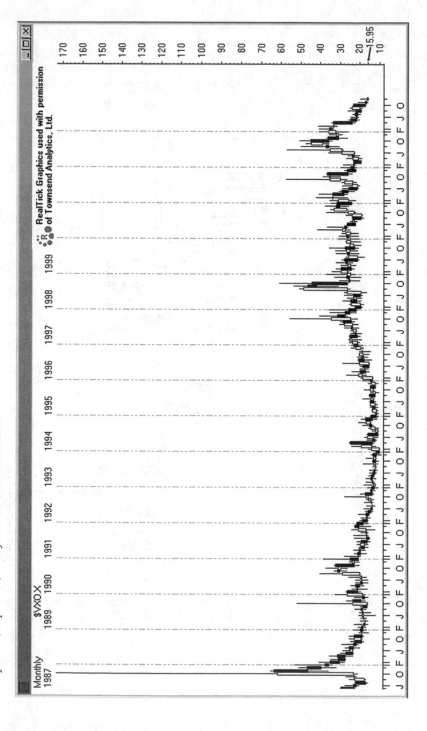

RealTick Graphics used with permission of Townsend Analytics, Ltd.

decisions. The VIX and the VXN are useful when looking at the larger picture and confirming the trading ideas that you are developing.

SUMMARY OF SECTOR ANALYSIS USING A TOP-DOWN APPROACH

When monitoring indices, groups of securities selected and tracked together give an overall impression of the movement of a particular group or sector. There are a vast number of indices that make up these capital markets, acting as points of reference or benchmarks by which other securities and sectors can be judged. By comparing individual securities to the benchmark index (S&P 500), the security can be identified as strong or weak. This comparison is called *relative strength* and is important to the top-down approach.

The importance of comparing these sectors relates directly to money flow. *Money flow* is a representation of institutional attention. When institutions are attracted to certain sectors such as semiconductors or biotechnology, money will flow into the sector and bellweather stocks (components) that make up the sector. Therefore, our objective is to measure the market's appetite for any given sector and then relate that sector's strength to the overall market indices (S&P 500, Dow Jones Industrials, Nasdaq). Once the sectors that are driving the trend can be determined, we can then analyze the stocks that lead those sectors. This is directly opposite of how most mutual funds do their research, which is *bottom up*. *Bottom-up investing* involves choosing specific securities within a particular sector under the guise that good security selection buffers any market level disturbances. As we know, good companies still get punished in bear markets just as mediocre companies can do well in bull markets. While this may not make fundamental sense, perception is reality and perception drives markets. The bottom-up analyst often misses this point.

Bottom-up investing is purely fundamental. Fund managers and research analysts study companies at the grassroots level, such as visiting the factories; testing the goods, products, and services they provide; meeting with management; etc. This approach is very prone to manipulation and subjective opinion. Obviously management of these companies wants mutual funds and other investors to buy their stock, so

they are naturally biased to be overly optimistic or perhaps hide diffi-
culties the company may be having. The bottom-up approach can be
a real poker game. It is for this reason, among others, that the technician continues to endorse and follow a *top-down approach*, allowing
the data of foundational variables to do the talking rather than biased
human interest. Price, time, volume, velocity, and the charts that represent this data cannot lie—but people can. Price accounts for all good
and bad news in the market, and the market is always right!

THE "EDGE" IS EMERGING

From a broad perspective on trading, it's helpful to have a feel for the
major forces that affect the entire market. If it is clear that economic
forces are positive, then you should have a bullish bias in your trading,
meaning you should trade more long opportunities than short situations. Use the enthusiasm of the market to improve your odds. If the
forces are negative, you should trade with bearish bias and favor
shorts to play. Economic forces will have a more pronounced effect on
longer-term trades and less impact on momentum trades. An economy
that is either entering a contraction period or coming out of one will
lend a bias to the market, but what is even more relevant to traders
and investors are the announcements of changes in policy and the
anticipation of announcements. Chapters 2, 3, and 4 presented a broad
overview of the economic forces and institutions that influence the
economy and market. To further our interest and help to see the
"statistical edge," we must now begin to put our knowledge to work
by viewing specific sectors and stocks through some of the tools provided by the market. Chapter 5 begins this process and lays the
groundwork for Part II of the book, "Pictures of Perception." These
pictures will follow the same logic as the business cycle itself, only on
a more micro level. Think of each sector and stock we study as micro-
economies unto themselves. The confluence of applying macroeco-
nomic events and their impact on the business cycle will directly apply
to the same patterns seen on individual stocks (cycles). The alignment
of patterns will lead to decisions that increase odds while reducing
risk. The collective value of this approach is undeniable.

PART II

PICTURES OF PERCEPTION

CHAPTER 5

OPINION VERSUS ANALYSIS (DATA)

Before we can dive directly into charting and measuring what the market is saying about itself objectively, we need to lay the foundation for analyzing the markets in analytical or chart form. The most important lesson I can offer at this juncture as we get ever closer to actual decision making is to remember the first rule of analysis. Remain objective! It is very easy at this point in the journey to feel excitement and overconfidence regarding trade patterns and set-ups. This is the point where a little knowledge is very dangerous. The next seven chapters are the heart of the analysis—where objectivity supersedes all opinion. Those who act too quickly and trade on opinion instead of analysis can experience catastrophic financial results.

Like it or not, when you commit your capital to the market, you also commit your emotions. What separates winners from losers is the ability to control emotions. Without this control, there is no difference between trading and gambling.

Gambling is attempting to make decisions about future outcomes based on odds or even just plain luck. Trading requires something more. The goal of this endeavor can be simply stated: minimize and control risk before seeking gain. For example, if someone is playing blackjack for the first time, the odds of consistently profiting, or winning, are low. As the player learns the intricacies of the game, the odds begin to improve. Once the player is very good and can play systematically or even count cards, the player can actually gain an epsilon of an edge or advantage. In terms of risk management, the skilled card player bets small while losing and folds quickly then presses his bets while winning. This is a systematic, unemotional approach that reduces risk and controls emotion while gaining a statistical edge.

There are many myths in the market—perceptions and fallacies that people cling to, but data is not one of them. Market data is what it is, it does not lie, yet it is still prone to subjective interpretation. To reduce the influence of emotion and opinion while trading and investing, we rely on the analysis of data along with the confluence of several indications that confirm the same bias.

RAW MARKET DATA

Data is a broad term and can mean several things including earnings estimates, economic numbers, company reports, etc. This kind of general market data can be subjected to outside influences. What you, the investor, are looking for is a set of basic building blocks of information that are true pieces of data not prone to manipulation. The most basic of market data is what we call raw data, consisting of price, volume, and time. If a person buys 1000 shares of stock at $20, the price is $20 and the volume is 1000 shares, which is hard data. There is no manipulation because a transaction occurred with a specific size at a certain price, at a certain time. A derivative piece of information, velocity is also considered a building block, but even though velocity is highly important, it is a derivative of price and time. Figure 5-1 illustrates the basic building blocks of market analysis.

In the earliest days of Wall Street, raw market data was all there was, but now, the evolution of technology has provided many complex ways for viewing this data. There is no question these advancements are improvements, but only if this information is not diluted in value through over-complication. Effective trading methods are timeless, enduring, and historical, and today in the age of technology their

The Basic Building Blocks of the Market

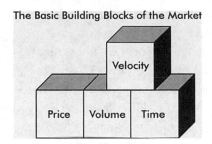

FIGURE 5-1 *The four building blocks of market analysis, whereas velocity is defined as changing price divided by time.*

simplicity is their greatest disguise. In the earlier days of Wall Street, the data for particular stocks was kept on chalkboards. Traders could track the movement of the market by watching the prices and volume on the board. In fact, one of the world's most famous traders, Jessie Livermore, got his start as a runner updating stock prices. He later said that he got his feel for the way the market moved from noticing how stock prices changed. The way of viewing the information may have been primitive, but the essential information was still there.

In the 1920s an understanding of electricity and the development of the telegraph made possible the ticker tape machine. The three key building blocks of data—the stock symbol, the price, and size of the transaction—were printed on a streaming piece of paper called *the tape*.

In today's electronic society the key elements of price, time, and volume are still available in a tape-like format on most trading systems. The same data that was relevant in the early days of Wall Street is still important today, and this study of raw market data (the three key building blocks) is called *technical analysis*.

THE BASIC PREMISE OF TECHNICAL ANALYSIS

Technical analysis is the study of charts and other objective data to predict future market movement, and a person who studies the technical aspects of the market is called a *technician*. There are several basic beliefs or foundations of technical analysis. These foundations make up the backbone of all technical analysis in the market. The first foundation is that history repeats itself. History in the market is based on the psychology of the masses. Market psychology is the collective thoughts and emotions of the millions of market participants, and one may assume that these technical charts are a physical form of measuring this psychology. The technician seeks to uncover the deeper psychology behind the movements of price, volume, and time by analyzing charts. While the actions of one person are extremely difficult to predict, the actions of millions of people fall into certain predictable patterns. When market participants are placed in certain situations, they react in a certain way, not unlike the predictable nature of mobs and crowds in emotional situations. For most, participating in the market is an emotional situation. This works to our advantage.

Another foundation of technical analysis is that price discounts everything. This means that the price at which a stock is currently trading takes everything known to all market participants, both current and anticipated, into account. The psychology and motivations of all participants is reflected in the current price of where the stock is trading. If some market participants obtain information prior to the public and act upon it before the general public, the technician will observe these actions as they happen through price, volume, time, and velocity, not by word of mouth or through the media. This raw market data accounts for all manipulations, fundamentals, and news through its consensus of value, called *price*. Hence, the discounting characteristic.

In an ideal bullish example of market pricing, both the economy and the stock market move higher in unison. As the economy shows the smallest signs of improving, professional traders anticipate good news about the economy. These economic reports are then released from the Government (unemployment rate, GDP) and by independent sources such as the Institute for Supply Management (ISM) or from companies themselves (earnings). It is important to realize that most economic data is reverse looking and indicates how the economy has done, not how it is doing at the present time (lagging indicator). Professional traders anticipate how the market is doing at the present time by reading the subtle signs that the market posts. By the time the good economic numbers are released, no one is surprised except the amateur. Upon hearing the news, the amateur tends to react, precisely what the professionals hope they will do. In most cases, the amateur misses the boat because economic news is most often anticipated by professionals, and these participants are more inclined to trade ahead of news, creating the price action prior to its release. In the case of upward price action for example, the average investor then wants to participate in the market and jumps in and buys stock upon the release of positive forecasts. For this reason more than any other, amateurs consistently lose. This phenomenon of price discounting can be summed up in an age-old market cliché, "buy rumor, sell fact."

Consider once again the food chain of market information. If certain market participants get relevant market information before other people and act upon this information, then this is reflected in the price of the security. For example, people at the top of the food chain receive positive information about a company and buy a particular stock before the news gets to the public. As the news trickles through the food chain, other participants receive this same positive information as well as having the benefit of seeing the price starting to move. They too act on this news. The technician views this market activity through data and therefore, though not privy to the information at the top of the food chain, they can view the actions of those at the top through price and avoid being caught up in the often manipulative information within the food chain.

The final premise of technical analysis is that price moves in trends. The price of a security is much like that of an object in motion. Sir Isaac Newton's first law states that every object in a state of uniform motion tends to remain in that state of motion unless an external force is applied to it. The same theory applies to stock price. A stock that is moving higher continues to do so until it moves to a level that motivates sellers, (the external force) to offer out enough stock to overwhelm the buyers and halt the advance. If a stock is moving lower, it will continue to do so until enough motivated buyers begin to overwhelm the sellers and change the direction of price. The psychology behind trend is based on the fact that as information becomes more known, amateurs will begin to react. The media reports the price action, the charts have already shown the move, and the trend gains strength as the amateurs join in. The important point here is they represent the last contributors to trend, and once the trend comes into question, professionals are the first to leave—leaving the amateur holding the bag. With these concepts in mind, we begin with the most basic form of charting. You may ask why it is that seemingly dated techniques are covered when modern tools exist. The answer once again lies within the belief that history is our greatest teacher, and the basics to follow will force you to understand the foundation of all modern-day charts, price, volume, time, and velocity.

CHARTING

A chart can be created in many ways, including a point and figure chart, a line chart, a bar chart, or a candlestick chart. Each chart has its own advantages and disadvantages, but most charting methods are just slightly different ways of viewing the same thing. As you become more educated, you automatically move up the food chain. Understanding charting is the first ingredient in this recipe. We will review each charting method as well as the pros and cons of each.

POINT AND FIGURE

A *point and figure chart* is a tool that plots price movement only and doesn't reflect the passage of time. It is a system that only displays larger moves and filters out the small movements or noise of the market. Time is automatically mitigated by only populating the chart with extensions of range (high or lows). In theory, many days could go by where a given security trades within a tight range, making no new highs or lows. In this case, the chart would not reflect any activity, hence mitigating time. The point and figure chart is typically updated daily using end-of-the-day data and consists of a series of Xs and Os, where the Xs represent demand and the Os represent supply. The easiest way to learn point and figure charting is to actually build a chart. The reversal box repre-sents a condition when a trend is being called into question by trad-ing opposite the trend by a standard three-box minimum. Using the three-box standard, this means that if the stock fails to trade lower by three price increments (user defined), in the case of a rally, it will not be reflected on the chart. By having no reflection or populated box, market noise is automatically filtered out. If the stock reverses direction from the previous trend by more than three boxes, another column of populated boxes is drawn to signify a change in trend.

This can be a bit confusing without the aid of an example. To begin with, if XYZ has been trading higher, say in a $23 to $25 range, the initial point and figure chart that represents this action is shown in Figure 5-2.

If on the second day the stock stayed within the same range as Day one, you would do nothing to the chart and it would look exactly the same as Day one's chart. If the stock didn't break Day one's three-point range to the downside, the movement would not be charted since this would be considered an "inside range," meaning prices remained inside the Day one price range. By not charting the inside price action, the chart remains clean and free of noise.

Continuing with the example, if on Day two the stock opened at $25, traded up to $26, and had a low of $24, the chart would get an X next to $26 and would look like the chart labeled Day two in Figure 5-2. The box achieves an "X" at $26 since a new high was achieved and the current trend remains intact. Note that the high and low price of the day is all that matters. Opening and closing prices are ignored. This condition is important to understand since we only seek to measure the elasticity of the market's emotion (bullish or bearish). The highs represent the extent of bullishness and the lows the extent of bearishness.

Now suppose that on the third day the stock trades in the range from $24 to $26. Again the chart would not change; since it is

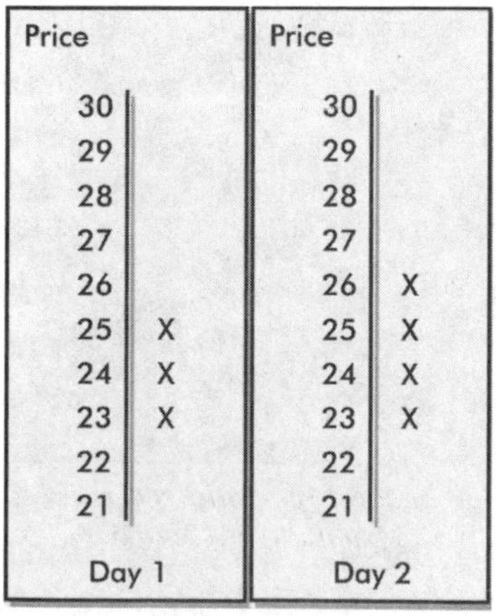

Price		Price	
30		30	
29		29	
28		28	
27		27	
26		26	X
25	X	25	X
24	X	24	X
23	X	23	X
22		22	
21		21	
Day 1		Day 2	

FIGURE 5-2   *Since on Day one the stock was initially moving higher and in a range between $23 and $25, there are three Xs between $23 and $25. On Day two the stock had a high of $26, so an X was placed next to $26.*

trading within the range (inside range) and the lack of range extension is considered market noise. On the other hand if the stock continued its trend higher and traded up to $27, you would put an X in the $27 box.

To trigger a reversal box, the stock must trade below the highest box by three boxes (points in this example). In Figure 5-2 the level to watch to the downside is $23 since this qualifies as a three-box reversal. Within the low of $23, a column of Os is drawn on the chart to indicate a three-box (point) change in trend. The Os are used to show supply or downward movement. Note, when the three-box reversal occurs, the successive two boxes above the $23 also get populated with Os to identify the trend reversal. See Figure 5-3.

This charting method may seem confusing at first, but it provides a unique view of the stock since it only shows high and low range price movements, while filtering out fluctuations (noise) less than three boxes (points). Though still a fairly popular method for charting, the point and figure chart excludes time, and without time, velocity cannot be determined—so you only have two of the four foundational variables. For more information on point and figure charting and another iteration that introduces time and puts a different twist on this type of charting called *market profile*, refer to *Steidlmayer on Markets* by Peter Steidlmayer. This book offers an excellent lesson on the intricacies of the method while also including the other foundational variables and is still widely held today.

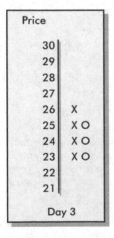

FIGURE 5-3   *The stock has a three-point reversal on day three and trades down to $23 from the last X at $26.*

THE LINE CHART

The *line chart* is one of the most basic forms of charting. In this type of chart, the closing prices of a specified period of time are connected to form a line. For example, if looking at a daily timeframe for a certain stock, the closing price for each day is connected, thereby creating a line that shows the movement of that stock price. See Figure 5-4.

Figure 5-5 is an example of an actual chart of stock XYZ tracking the closing price of the stock for the last 200 days. Note that we use the fictitious symbol of XYZ since the method is timeless and applies to all issues. Price is on the vertical axis and time is on the horizontal axis. What is missing from the line chart is "elasticity" within the day. While price may rise and fall throughout the day, the line chart only reflects the closing prices as presented and can only reflect day to day volatility, missing an impotent component of intraday volatility (elasticity).

THE BAR CHART

The *bar chart* shows the closing price as well as several other pieces of information. This additional information illustrates how the stock

FIGURE 5-4   *Notice how the closing price of each day is connected and makes a line that illustrates the movement of the stock price.*

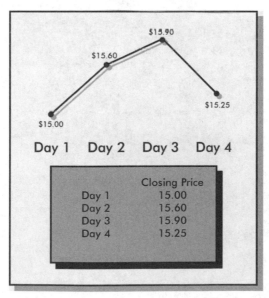

	Closing Price
Day 1	15.00
Day 2	15.60
Day 3	15.90
Day 4	15.25

FIGURE 5-5 *A line chart of XYZ on a daily interval.*

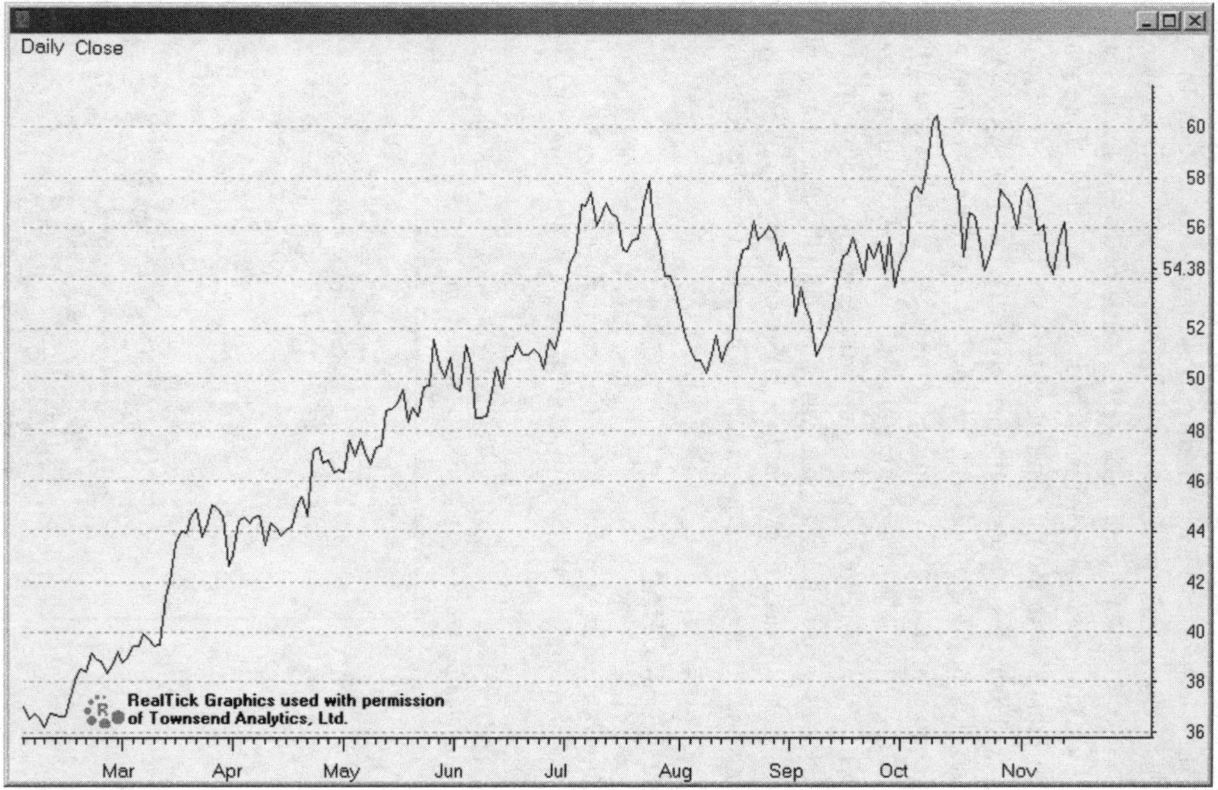
Daily Close
60
58
56
54.38
52
50
48
46
44
42
40
38
36
Mar
Apr
May
Jun
Jul
Aug
Sep
Oct
Nov
RealTick Graphics used with permission
of Townsend Analytics, Ltd.

traded during a specified period (intraday range). Included in the bar chart is the high price of the period, the low price of the period, the opening price, and the closing price. See Figure 5-6.

In Figure 5-6 there are four pieces of data for each period being measured. The highest price the stock reaches during the specified period is at the highest point of the bar. The lowest price the stock trades at is displayed at the lowest vertical extension of the bar. The bar that sticks out to the left is the opening price, and the bar that extends to the right is the closing price of the period. Figure 5-7 is a daily bar chart of the same stock over the same period as Figure 5-5.

Notice how the bar chart in Figure 5-7 is similar to the line chart in Figure 5-5. The general pattern of the charts is the same but the bar chart includes data on the range of each period. These periods can be measures in months, weeks, days, hours, or minutes. This range can be important in many situations, which will be discussed later in this chapter.

THE CANDLESTICK CHART

The *candlestick chart* is similar to a bar chart in that it gives data on the high, low, open, and close of the period being measured. The information is given in the form of a candle that is white if the close is above the open, and shaded dark if the close is below the open. See Figure 5-8.

The candlestick chart contains the same information as the bar chart, but when using a candlestick chart, it is easier to tell whether the stock finished up or down for the period being measured since it is color-coded. Figure 5-9 is an example of a candlestick chart on a daily timeframe for the same stock used in Figures 5-5 and 5-7.

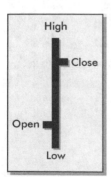

FIGURE 5-6   *A single bar that illustrates the high, low, open, and closing price.*

FIGURE 5-7 *A bar chart of XYZ stock on a daily timeframe of 100 days.*

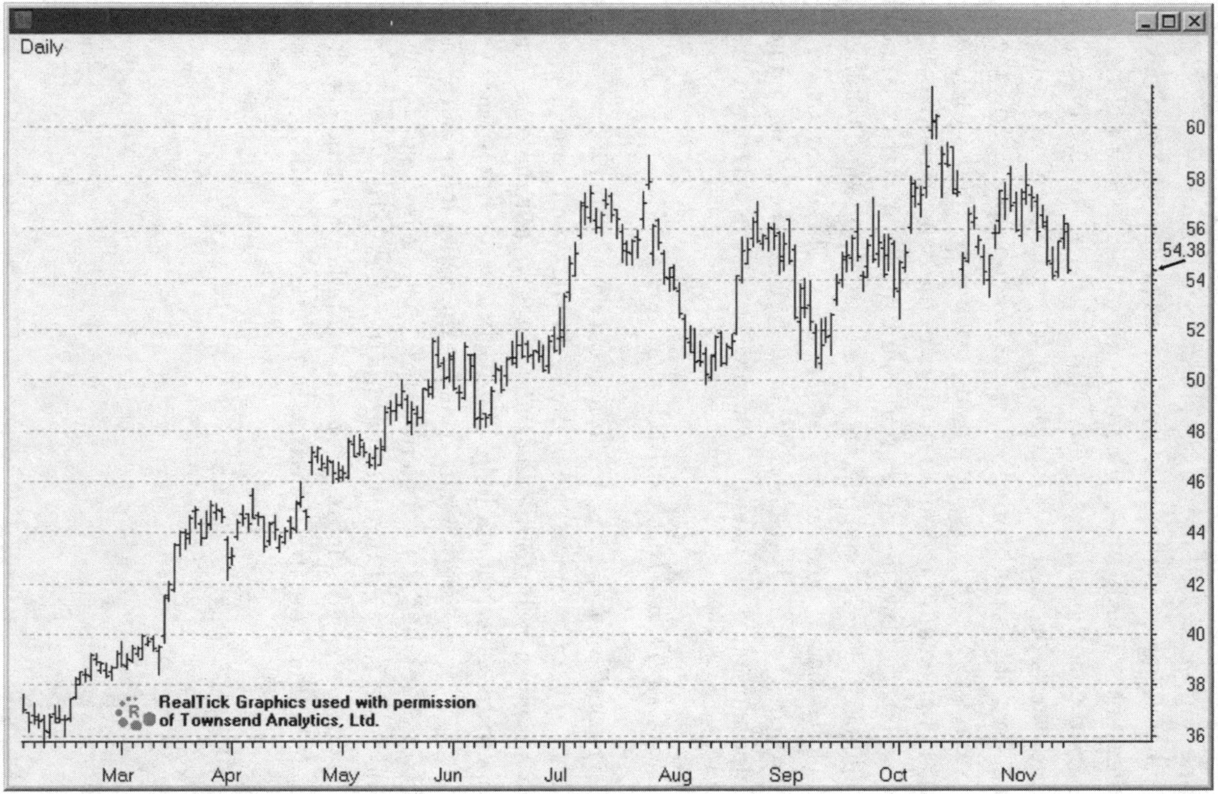

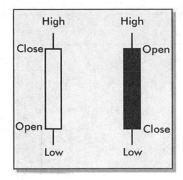

FIGURE 5-8 *A white candle occurs when the closing price is higher than the opening price. A shaded candle occurs when the closing price is lower than the opening price.*

Compare Figure 5-9 to Figures 5-5 and 5-7. The same pattern of price is revealed. The candlestick chart displays more information than the line chart but the same information as the bar chart. When examining the bar chart and the candlestick chart more closely, it is apparent on the candlestick chart whether the closing price was above or below the opening price as denoted by the color of the candle. Refer to Chapter 10 for more information on basic candlestick formations.

VOLUME

Most of the hard market data discussed earlier is included in the charts; however, the one missing variable is volume. Whether it is a line, bar, or candlestick chart, volume is typically represented by a vertical bar beneath the period that is measured. This vertical bar indicates how many transactions took place over the course of the entire period. A transaction is the amount of securities that have changed hands. For every transaction there is both a buyer and a seller so volume has no direction. Figure 5-10 illustrates a graphical depiction of how volume is viewed on a chart over a specific period of time.

The volume bar shown in Figure 5-10 displays a bar representing all the transactions that took place over a specified period. The height of the bar indicates the number of transactions that occurred in the period, thus the more transactions, the higher the bar will be. Figure 5-11 demonstrates the three different charting methods discussed earlier with the addition of volume bars. The most important thing to look at when noting volume is the relative change. It is not

FIGURE 5-9 *A daily candlestick chart of XYZ stock over 100 days.*

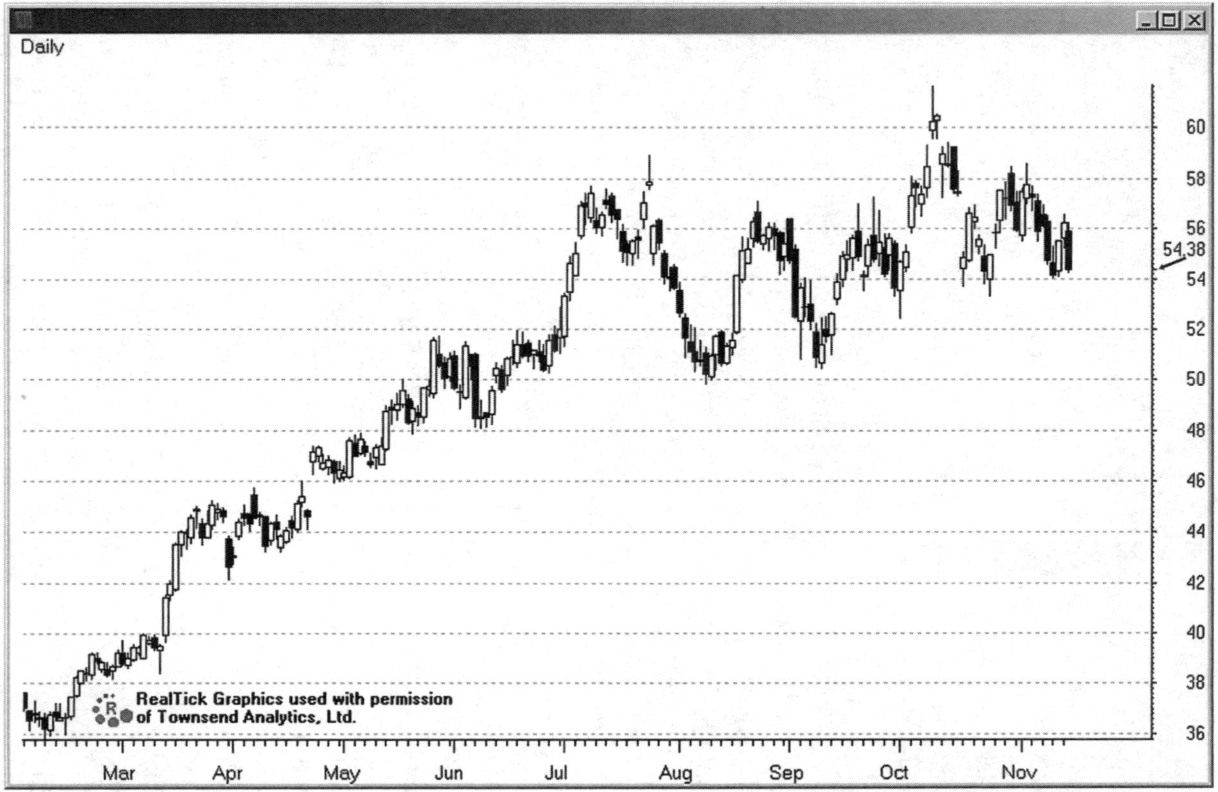
Daily
60
58
56
54.38
54
52
50
48
46
44
42
40
38
36
Mar
Apr
May
Jun
Jul
Aug
Sep
Oct
Nov
RealTick Graphics used with permission
of Townsend Analytics, Ltd.

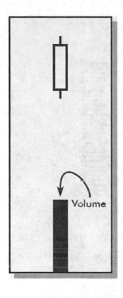

FIGURE 5-10   *Volume is the amount of transactions that have taken place over a specified period. It is represented as a vertical bar at the bottom of the chart.*

as important what the actual volume is, but note what volume is relative to what it was in the past; a moving average on volume is one way of measuring this.

Of the three charting methods, the bar chart and the candlestick charts contain the most information. Throughout the rest of the book, the candlestick chart will be used to illustrate selected concepts, however, it is important to note that the candlestick chart is not superior to other charting methods. Refer to Figure 5-11 for reassurance that each method is measuring the same data. The same information is included in both candlestick and bar charts and it is a personal preference as to which you decide to use. Those who are visual will prefer candles, while those who prefer reading each bar will be inclined to the bar chart.

TIME

Charting the time period is highly customizable. Long-term timeframes, such as monthly and weekly periods, can give you a general idea of the larger picture. Looking at a long-term timeframe is like standing on a cliff and overseeing a vast forest spread out below you. As you shorten the period on the chart, it is like zooming in on the same forest with a

FIGURE 5-11   *A daily chart of a stock using three charting methods, including volume.*

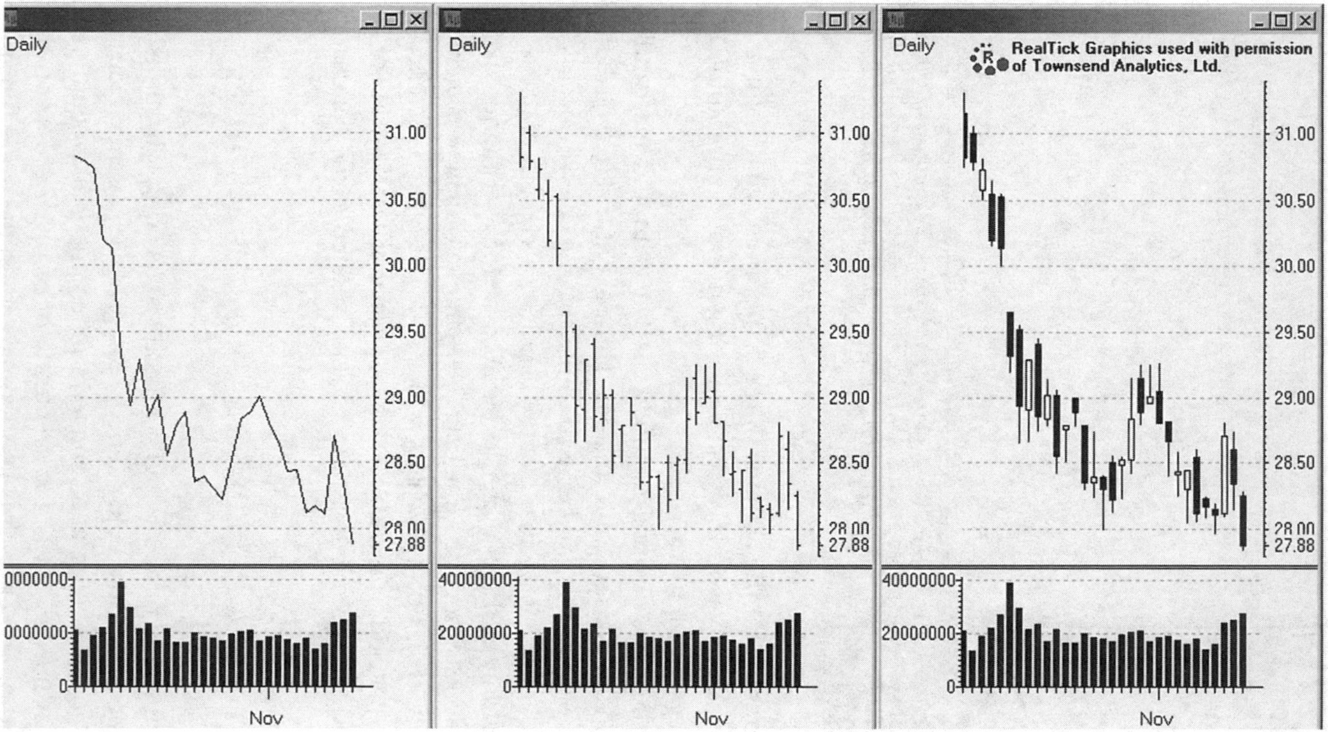

pair of binoculars. As the forest is magnified, each tree begins to distinguish itself. The individual branches appear and demonstrate unique features of their own. The vista has now changed so you see the individual trees instead of the forest. Figure 5-12 illustrates a weekly chart for a particular stock. Note the general shape of the price movement.

Now by switching to a smaller period, the magnification is increased. Figure 5-13 shows a daily chart of the same stock that appeared in Figure 5-12.

Take a close look at Figures 5-12 and 5-13. Notice that the extreme right side of Figure 5-12 has a similar shape to Figure 5-13. The effect of decreasing the period length is akin to zooming in on the right side of Figure 5-13. Taking the magnification one step further, examine Figure 5-14.

By comparing Figures 5-13 to 5-14, it is now obvious that decreasing the period is in effect looking at a magnified view of the far right side of Figure 5-13.

By now the basics of charting should be clear and the question that has most likely entered your head is "How will this information help me?" The next section will help answer that question. For now though, the most important thing to understand is that everything that we have charted is raw, hard data. The high, low, open, close, and the volume are firm pieces of data that truly happened. The data has not been manipulated and you can receive this information at the same time as everyone else, leveling the playing field. With other forms of news, this is simply not the case, and herein lies where the edge begins to emerge. Once you learn how to evaluate this raw market data effectively, the edge is obtained since most amateur participants won't put forth the effort to become marketwise.

ELASTICITY—THE RANGE OF EMOTION EQUALS THE RANGE OF PRICE

As stated earlier, when comparing the line chart to the candlestick or bar charts, there are several differences. The line chart connects the close of the period while the bar and candlestick charts display

FIGURE 5-12 *This is a 300-week chart that shows the long-term price movement of the stock. Each candle represents one week of trading activity, with price on the vertical axis and time plotted on the horizontal axis.*

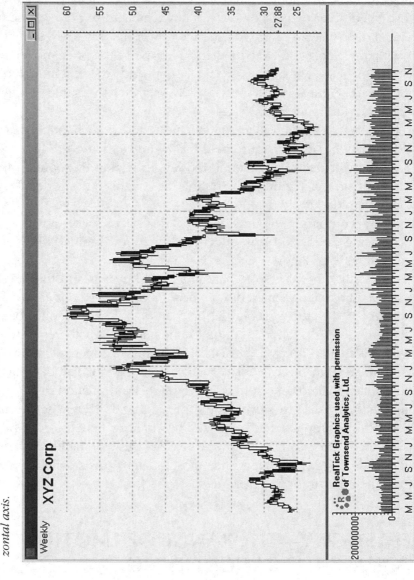

FIGURE 5-13 *This is a daily chart of the same stock used in Figure 5-9, looking at 200 days of data.*

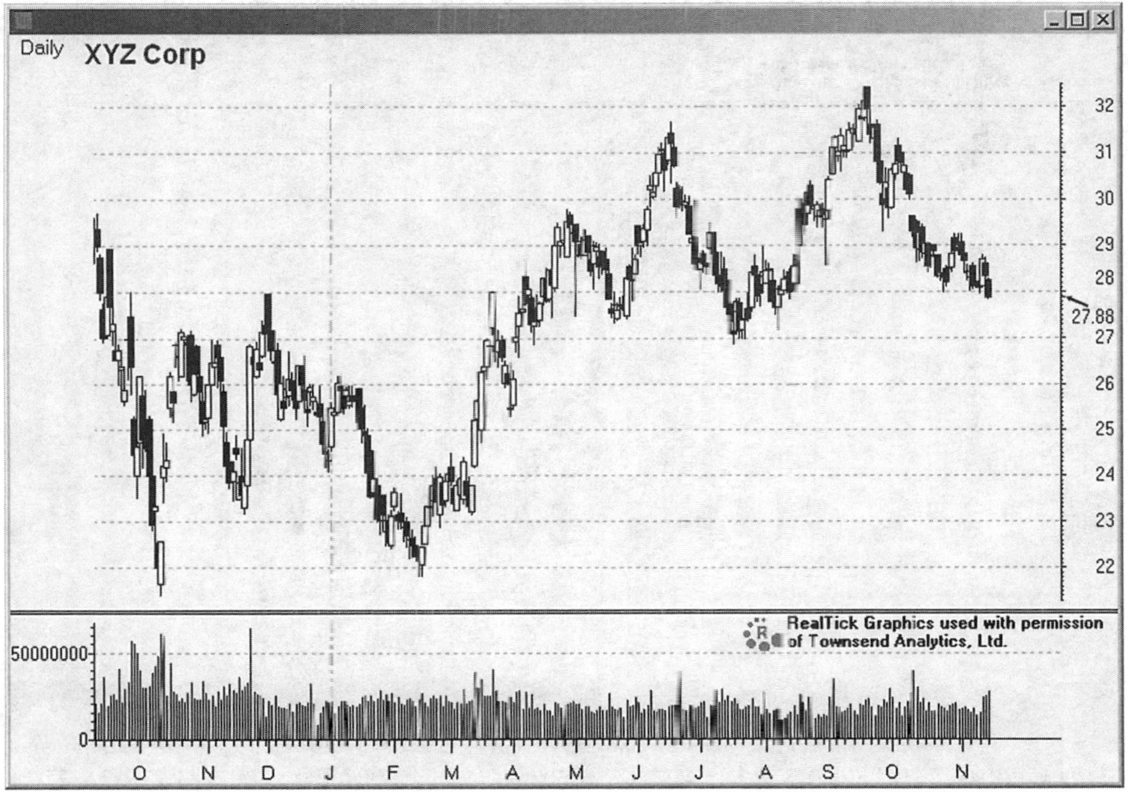
Daily
XYZ Corp
32
31
30
29
28
27.88
27
26
25
24
23
22
50000000
0
O N D J F M A M J J A S O N
RealTick Graphics used with permission of Townsend Analytics, Ltd.

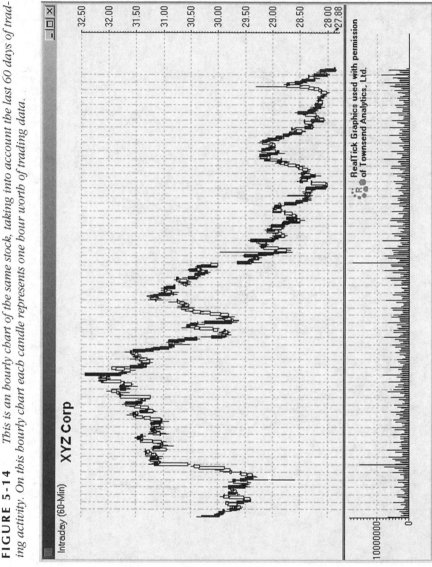

FIGURE 5-14 *This is an hourly chart of the same stock, taking into account the last 60 days of trading activity. On this hourly chart each candle represents one hour worth of trading data.*

the open, high, and low for the period in addition to the close. There is an important psychological feature we receive by using candles and bars—range.

The theory of elasticity is based on the psychology of price range. The high and low of a particular timeframe represents the extent of bullish or bearish sentiment. As a securities price trades up near an elastic high, a battle of emotions (fear and greed) takes place. The maximum strength of the participants who are buying the security is shown by the high of the day. The maximum strength of the sellers is shown by the low of the period. These "tails" as they are called represent the truest forms of support and resistance for the period measured. There is no subjectivity. With this small dose of reality and some common sense, support (lows) and resistance (highs) are best read with the brain, not the computer. See Figure 5-15.

If the general movement of a stock is sideways, meaning little change in price with the passage of time, the stock is in a range oscillating back and forth. The average price of the range is called the *true level of value* within the time being measured. More volume tends to occur within this range since supply and demand are close to equilibrium. Buyers essentially agree with sellers and therefore shares turn over more. It is only when demand exceeds supply that the stock starts to move higher (vise versa for declines). As the rally unfolds, at some

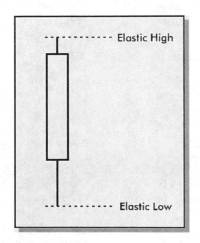

FIGURE 5-15   *The elastic range of a particular period is the range between the elastic high of the period and the elastic low of the period.*

point the selling pressure increases until it equals the buying pressure. It is at this point that the high is marked. As sellers add pressure to the rally, price tends to get pulled back to equilibrium like a rubber band. Elasticity theory describes the condition in which price gets pulled back to a "true level of value." See Figure 5-16.

When a stock trades within a range and ultimately breaks the range with high volume the event is considered significant. This shows a new level of market consensus that is now outside the prior range. Picture the rubber band being stretched tight near the high of the range. If the rubber band is capable of breaking through the prior highs, we can then expect follow-through motion in the direction of the trend. Figure 5-17 illustrates an upside break-out example.

Figure 5-17 demonstrates that the bulls are firmly in control for the day because the second day breaks the range of the first day. The stock price passes right through the point where the selling pressure is equal to the buying pressure (Day one's elastic high). This shows that the psychology of the people trading the stock is bullish and the price at which the bears exert their influence on Day one is no match for the power of the bulls on Day two.

The examples of elasticity that have been given were of bull-ish examples. Elasticity works exactly the same when dealing with a

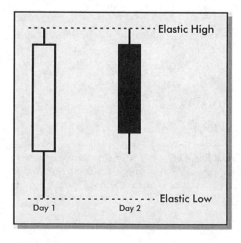

FIGURE 5-16   *Day two has trouble breaking out of the elastic range set by Day one.*

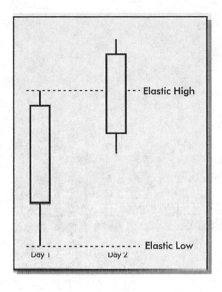

FIGURE 5-17   *As the second day's price breaks the range that the first day set, the rubber band is broken and the price is no longer pulled within the first day's range.*

bearish example. The theory runs true as well when looking at multiple days of data. See Figure 5-18.

In Figure 5-18, the first segment displays the stock trading within a range where the elastically of the price remains within the range. The second segment displays a breaking of the previous range to the downside. Once the elastic range is broken, there is nothing to pull the stock back into the range, so the stock continues lower (Segment three). This is an example of bearish elasticity. This kind of market action will be discussed in more detail, but to satisfy your curiosity now, know that when a range of elasticity is broken, any subsequent rallies should not equal the prior level of support broken. For example, shares that breakdown below prior lows may rally somewhat, but not to the extent of the prior low. If they do, the breakdown is considered a false breakdown. Notice in Figure 5-18, on the fifth day, that the elastic high never penetrated the closing price on Day four. This suggests that bears are in control and the breakdown is real. Selling longs or opening shorts would be where the statistical edge lies. The opposite is true on new elastic highs. If shares break out above prior elastic highs and then pull back or retrace, they can only pull back to a higher low above the prior high in order to be defined as a

FIGURE 5-18 *As the three-day elastic low gets broken the stock continues to lower.*

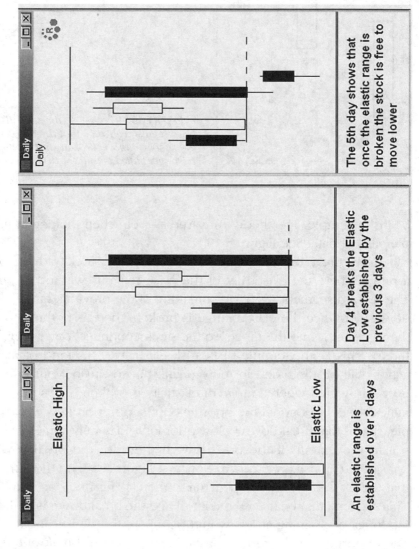

true breakout. Figure 5-17 illustrates that longs should not be affected until shares trade higher than the Day one elastic high (mid-body of the candle).

Now that you know how to display the essential market data, the next step is to understand what influences the data. Everything in the market is based upon this set of essential market data. Analyzing this market data is called *foundational analysis.*

CHAPTER 6

SUPPLY, DEMAND, AND EMOTIONS

B y now you should feel yourself moving through the process of thinking like an analyst. We have a long road ahead of us, but you're doing well. An understanding of basic charting, as well as the important psychology behind it, is vital to good trading and investing. Already in this process you are separating yourself as smart money from dumb money. Most people jump into the financial markets and don't know what they are jumping in to. They simply don't know what they don't know. They don't have the knowledge base needed to understand the nuances of supply, demand, price, time, volume, and velocity—all of which will be discussed in this chapter. Without a solid foundation of knowledge, many people make decisions based on emotions like hope, greed, fear, and even anger, which is a sure path to lost money when engaging in the financial markets.

When a stock price starts to fall, for example, most participants that are long the stock *hope* the price will begin to move higher. The truth is, however, that hope is skewing the decision-making process. Most participants are on the wrong side of the trade and if they had a knowledge base to work from, they would know to exit the position.

Greed rushes the trading process and is the basis of most poor decision making. Even when positions are profitable, greed can turn even winners into losers. Amateur market participants hold on to profitable positions even after market trends indicate they should exit the trade.

Fear may cause people not to trade at all, or trade too much. Fear can influence people to jump into trades because they are afraid of missing a move or exit a position prematurely because they are afraid to lose money. Fear can also lead to misplaced faith as they convince themselves they are in the right trade while the trade moves against them. These amateurs may not even realize that they are being ruled by their emotions, and in this case, ignorance is not bliss. It costs money.

Anger manifests itself as well among amateurs, blaming others for poor advice they should never have consumed. Anger also shows up in other ways such as trying to "get even" in a stock they lost money on. As if the stock itself had something to do with it. This revenge syndrome shows up often among amateurs.

Emotions or combinations of them, although they usually travel together, are the seeds of failure. Once we can reduce their impact, we can improve the edge we seek. Professional traders look to hard data, math, statistics, and experience to influence their trading decisions. History provides another tool of objective analysis to the professional still used extensively today called *normal distribution*. The theory of normal distribution was first published by Abraham de Moivre in the mid 1700s. A bell curve is illustrated in Figure 6-1. If a person measured the heights of a large group of people, they would find the most common heights clustered around the average height. As the height range gets further away from this average, there are less people with that height.

The distribution of heights of many people, when plotted on a chart, looks much like Figure 6-1. Many things that appear to be random occurrences actually take the form of a bell curve when plotted. A good example is rolling a pair of dice. Plotting the number that comes up after rolling a pair of dice again and again looks much like Figure 6-1. The mean value is 7 since there are so many ways to arrive at this number: 1 + 6, 2 + 5, 3 + 4, 4 + 3, 5 + 2, and 6 + 1. In fact, the odds are six times better that you will throw a 7 than other numbers. This is why the game of craps is based on this number and why casinos can build million dollar pyramids in the desert!

FIGURE 6-1 *This is the normal distribution or "bell curve." The number of occurrences is on the vertical axis and the data is on the horizontal axis.*

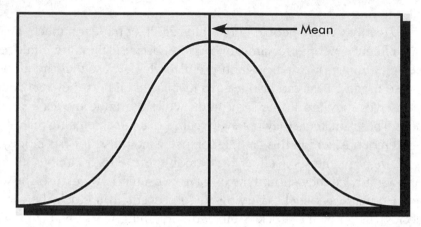

Market participants using technical analysis apply probabilities to market movement not unlike those described above. Technicians apply this probability theory to the psychology behind market movements. The probabilities found through technical analysis allow a statistical edge to be traded upon, instead of relying on emotions, fate, or advice from others. The fact is that mutual funds and other money management services need to index to the market in order to manage large sums of money and compete with other funds. Therefore, they miss the benefits afforded to the small investor who can trade and invest around the wake they leave behind. While we no longer build bell curves to plot averages and deviations from the average as seen in Figure 6-1, we apply the same principles. Having the benefit of managing relatively small sums of money by comparison to funds, we gain the value of the data they create to find an edge and reduce emotions.

SUPPLY/DEMAND—THE EMOTIONAL HEDGE

The concept of supply and demand is a key concept upon which traders base their decisions. Supply and demand fuels both our economy and the world's economy. It is pure capitalism. For example, trade is based on getting goods from where they are built, grown, or mined, to a place where there is a need (or a demand) for those goods. Goods are taken to a place where they are less abundant and consequently sold for a premium. In theory both the buyer and the seller are better off for having traded. This is the basic premise of arbitrage—acquiring or building an asset in one market and selling it in another.

The balance of supply and demand is actually an equation. This equation equals itself at a center point where it balances out. To truly understand how this equation works, it is necessary to understand what supply and demand is and how to use it as a technical trader. Demand is defined simply as the willingness to buy a particular item, good, or service. The key word is willingness. There has to be a desire for the product. In addition to willingness, people must also have the ability to buy the product. For example, if someone wants to buy a black hole, there is a desire for a black hole but there is no supply since a black hole is not for sale. Supply is the amount of goods or services that people are willing and able to sell. There has to be both willingness and the ability to sell a product in order to have a true supply.

As stated earlier, the supply and demand equation is self-equaling, with price as the center point. For example, if there is a demand for llamas, but there are not many llamas available, then llamas are strongly desired and people will pay more for the llamas. High demand combined with low supply drives the price higher. As a llama seller, why would you sell llamas at a lower price when there are people lining up to buy your llamas at a higher price? Consider also the reverse scenario. Why would you buy llamas at a high price when there are 10 different people selling llamas at a lower price? As supply outpaces demand, the price of the product falls. Here is another example. Most people would like to own an expensive high-end sports car. The demand is there, but the supply is small because high-end sports cars are hand-made from expensive materials. This small supply means a very high price. There is also only a small number of people that can afford to purchase the car, so the equation equals itself out. The supply and demand equation is a fundamental principle of capitalism, and the center point, or price, is one of the variables to pay attention to in foundational analysis. We will soon apply this cornerstone of capitalism directly to market analysis to find specific trading and investing opportunities. See Figures 6-2 and 6-3 for an example of how the supply and demand equation works.

FIGURE 6-2   *As demand increases, supply decreases and prices move higher.*

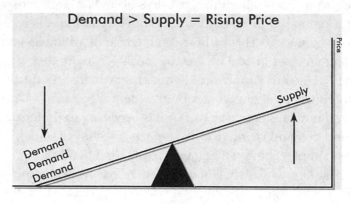

FIGURE 6-3   *As supply increases, demand decreases and prices move lower.*

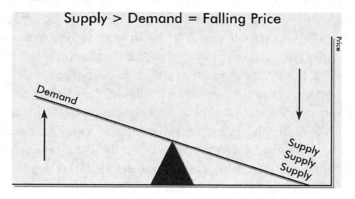

PRICE

Capitalism, in its purest form, is the buying and selling of securities.
Price is the center point of the supply and demand equation, and it
plays a very important role in the movement of a stock. Price is the very
measuring device used to gauge the movement. *Price* is the consensus
of all market participants as the fair value of a security at a certain time.
If buyers are more aggressive than sellers, demand is greater than
supply, and the price goes higher. This is seen when the demand
becomes so great that there is no more stock for sale at a certain price,

and the buyers in essence take up all the supply at a particular price. In this case, buyers would then have to pay up for the stock, which would drive the price higher, regardless of fundamentals. If there are more people trying to sell stock than trying to buy stock, the price decreases. If supply increases to a point where the demand has been filled at a particular level, in order for participants to sell their securities, they have to lower the selling price. This is capitalism in its purest form. There are no premiums on either end; just supply and demand. As the supply and demand equation levels itself, the price moves. On shorter timeframes there are many small movements in price that are smoothed out on longer-term timeframes. These small movements are called *volatility*.

VOLATILITY

There is always volatility or a "choppiness" to stock movement, depending on what timeframe you are observing. On shorter time-frames, volatility is very important. A small change in the volatility could have a significant impact on when you enter or exit a trade. On longer-term timeframes, the overall trend of the market is more important than the volatility of stock movement. A *consensus range* is where the price a security is trading at may seem fair to some but undervalued or overvalued to others. This is why securities trade in ranges. On longer-term timeframes the range can appear smooth on charts. When looking at charts on a small timeframe, the volatility becomes more apparent. Some people are willing to pay a little more for stock or sell their stock a little lower than an average price. In fact, very active traders attempt to trade some of the intraday volatility (volatility that occurs within the trading day). See Figure 6-4.

Referring to Figure 6-4, notice that by looking at the daily candle it looks like a day where the sellers were aggressive and the stock moved lower in price. By looking at the second chart, which is a two-minute chart, notice that there was choppy or volatile intraday. A daily chart shows only one candle with the high, low, open, and close displayed on it. The same day can be charted on a two-minute chart that breaks up

FIGURE 6-4 *Both charts show the trading information for the same day. One is a daily chart and the other is a two-minute chart. Notice that the wide range elasticity is more simply viewed on the daily candle as opposed to the "noise" that can be overanalyzed on the two-minute chart. Traders and investors will do best by seeing the bigger picture, and this picture hedges out some of the volatility that can feed the two-headed monster of volatility and "whip-saw" risk (being shaken out of positions too quickly).*

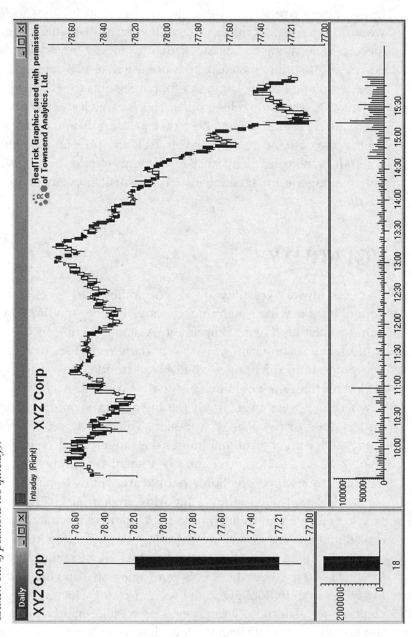

the day into 195 two-minute segments. The daily chart shows the high, low, open, and close, but it doesn't show how the security traded throughout the day. This is an example of how consensus should be seen as an average, but keep in mind consensus varies with time.

When taking the foundational variable of price into account, the psychology of the crowd, meaning all market participants, is seen in the movement of price. Professionals see both the actual price movement as well as the psychology of what is causing the movement.

THE VOLATILITY AND SMOOTHING OF TIME

Time can mean many things in the market. Time can make the market look volatile (short term), or make it look smooth (longer term). Time can be the seeds of rationalization, whereby a short-term trade is turned into a long-term investment. These trades are generally losers. In the most basic sense of the word, it reveals what time a trade happened. Time is also the length you stay in the market per trade or investment. Time means many things and needs to be defined in terms of analysis and risk.

Although there are no definite timelines of market engagement, for the purpose of this book, the types will be defined as follows:

- *Investor*—One to six months is the typical timeframe for our purposes.
- *Swing Trader*—One who takes trades from one day to a couple of weeks.
- *Active Trader*—One who takes several trades per day and also carries position overnight when risk is acceptable.
- *Day Trader*—One who takes many trades per day, typically in and out of the market several times in one day.

These time horizons bring up the subject of position sizing. Sizing a position to time, which is how many shares or contracts are bought or sold, compared to the time spent in the market, is paramount to risk management. The only things that can be controlled in the market are the securities you plan to trade, the amount of shares or contracts you buy or sell, and the length of time you spend in the market.

The two items of risk that can be actively managed are the size and the time you spend in the market. Just by being engaged in the market you are taking on systemic risk—the risk of events happening that you cannot control. *Systemic risk* is the risk of time. The longer a position is held, the higher the chances are of an event occurring. An event is anything that could move the market—world news, national news, or company-specific news. If you are planning on being in the market for a lengthy amount of time, then your share size should be adjusted for the risk of time. In the era of the highly active day trader, we enter and exit trades within minutes if not even seconds, but would enter trades with large size. Time risk was small but position size risk was high. The longer-term trader has to be able to tolerate the volatile swings on the shorter-term charts. The position size to timeframe equation has to be balanced. As you are planning your trade or investment, this must be calculated.

In terms of analysis, the timeframe you observe and study when looking for patterns of the market form another basis of time. When looking for trades you need to know what timeframe you plan on trading on—such as minutes, hours, daily, weekly, or even months. So it becomes clear the value of measuring time and adjusting risk according to your method of engagement. Clearly the investor should look at long-term trends and evaluate the direction of the market or stock, while the active trader pays more attention to short-term patterns. Both methods work well, but neither works when mixing styles. Active trades that don't work out should never become investments, and investments that are influenced too greatly by short-term patterns can destroy conviction.

VOLUME

As stated earlier, volume is the amount of transactions that take place in a certain instrument in a certain amount of time. If you are charting a stock on a daily timeframe, then the amount of transactions that take place during that particular day is the daily volume. If 300,000 shares of stock change hands over the course of a day, the daily volume is 300,000. Volume varies from stock to stock. It is usually dependant on the number of shares available for trading and the particular interest level in the stock at a certain time.

Volume is best viewed as fuel for the fire. It shows the excitement of participants as the security moves either higher or lower. If buyers are excited, the stock will move higher in price, causing the volume to increase. This increase in volume reveals the emotional state of participants. If many shares change hands and the stock moves higher, then the bulls are in control. Volume acts as a confirmation to the movement of a stock. As a security moves higher in a typical, expected way, it increases in volume each time it pushes higher.

The reverse is also true. As a security moves lower on higher volume, the sellers of the security are excited. As a stock moves lower in an expected way on heavy volume, the price moves lower, and volume increases each time the stock rises in price and the volume will be lower. In this way, the strength of the bears can be seen.

If a stock moves either higher or lower on light volume, the strength of the move is suspect. It lacks the fuel to get the fire started. The emotional strength of the crowd is not enough to confirm that they are really aggressive. It signals a lack of consensus. If a stock moves higher on light volume it shows that there are no aggressive buyers jumping in. If a stock moves lower on light volume, it shows that sellers are not being aggressive. When larger players jump in to participate in an emerging trend, then they will typically get in with large positions. These are not your average investors that buy a couple of thousand shares; the large player can buy hundreds of thousands of shares. These large players can be mutual funds, hedge funds, or pension funds, and are referred to as institutions. This institutional buying would show up as volume on a chart. See Figure 6-5.

Notice in Figure 6-5 how each time the stock moves higher, there is a surge in volume. This surge in volume reveals the aggressive sentiment of participants trading this stock. In other words, when stock is aggressively bought at a high volume, the bulls are in control. When stock is aggressively sold at a high volume, the bears are in control as demonstrated by an increase in volume as the stock price moves lower. Each time a stock moves lower, we look for confirmation in the volume. The surge in volume as the stock price moves lower shows that the bears are in control and they are aggressive.

FIGURE 6-5 *When the stock moves higher there is an increase in volume, illustrating the aggressiveness of the buyers. Volume therefore confirms trends.*

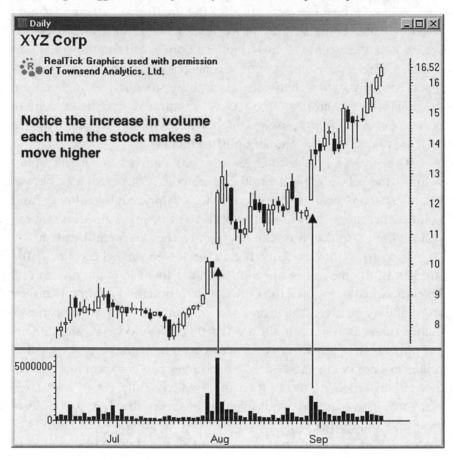

Figure 6-6 demonstrates how as the stock is pushed lower, the volume rises. Each time the stock rises, it shows a decrease in volume. Then as it moves lower again, the volume increases. This is how volume is supposed to look as a stock trends lower.

Since volume is a measure of how many shares exchange hands in a certain timeframe, it is a direct measure of how easily a buyer is found for each seller or vice versa. This is called *liquidity*. Volume is a good measurement of how liquid a stock is. If you had 5000 shares of a particular stock and decided you wanted to sell the shares, if many shares of stock trade hands each day, then you would have no trouble selling that stock.

FIGURE 6-6   *The stock moves sharply lower amid a surge in volume.*

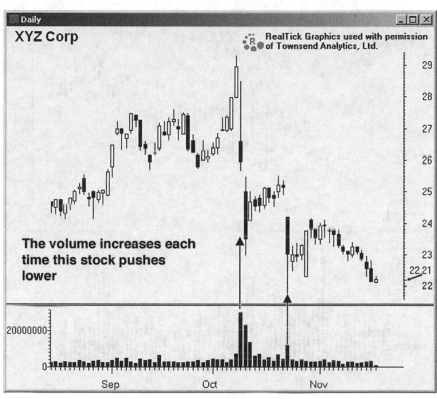

Figure 6-7 illustrates a stock that trades over 20 million shares each day. This stock allows easy entries and exits into positions. The large number of shares exchanging hands makes buying a large amount of that stock easy.

However, if you owned 5000 shares of a stock that doesn't trade very many shares each day, you would be hard pressed to find a buyer for your stock.

Figure 6-8 shows a stock that trades under 10,000 shares on some days. If you owned 5000 shares of this stock, it could be difficult to find a buyer for your stock at a reasonable price. You would have a lot of stock for sale but not very many participants interested in buying that stock. It might force you into a situation where the only way to sell your stock is to sell it below the market, adding to your losses or cutting

FIGURE 6-7   *This is the chart of a heavy volume stock.*

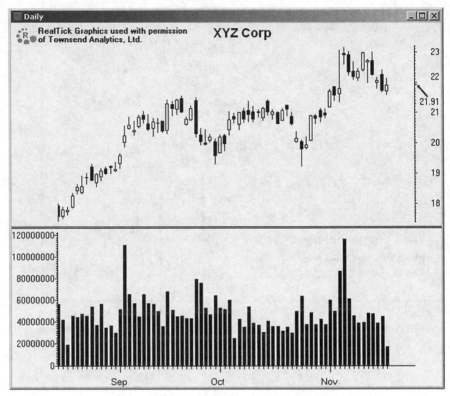

into your profits. The only participant active in the market at this time may be a bargain hunter who will buy your stock, but at a low price.

VELOCITY

The definition of velocity as it applies to the financial markets is the change in price divided by time. If a stock moves $2 in two minutes, it has a high velocity. If a stock moves $0.20 in two days it has a low velocity. Velocity determines whether the stock is moving aggressively or just drifting. Figure 6-9 shows a stock that has a low velocity for several days then increases in velocity toward the last several days. In just a couple of days the stock moved lower by seven points.

FIGURE 6-8   *The stock illustrated below is a low volume stock.*

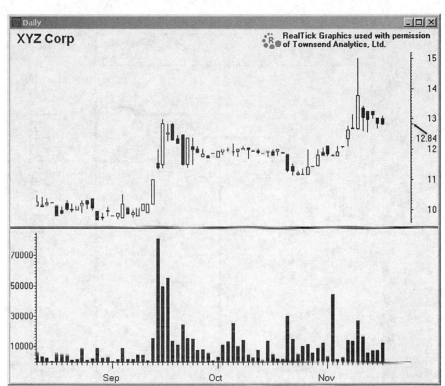

The high velocity shown in Figure 6-9 is caused by people aggressively selling their shares of the stock. High velocity can either hurt you or help you in a hurry, so be prepared to react. People who own the stock see the selling pressure start to increase. This produces fear, and they start to exit their long positions aggressively. In this case, it happens so aggressively that the supply they bring to the market, by selling aggressively, completely overwhelms demand. This causes an imbalance and the price quickly falls. Velocity can be thrilling, especially when the stock goes in your favor. When you are on the wrong end of a trade, conversely, velocity can cause fear. The fear can manifest disbelief and can cause paralysis, which is the worst possible thing at this point.

Often stocks will exhibit low velocity where they don't do anything at all and their price stays within a small range. When actively

FIGURE 6-9 *This is an intraday 60-minute chart that shows a stock that has low velocity suddenly turn into a high velocity downward move.*

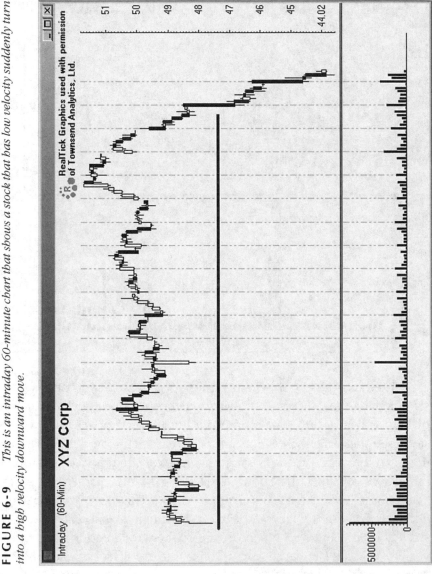

trading and investing, you don't want to be in a stock that does nothing for an extended period of time. See Figure 6-10.

Taking a position in a stock that is trading in a small range simply ties up your trading or investing capital in a market that is essentially flat. The ultimate goal of entering a trade is to take a position just before it makes a large move. Instead of keeping capital tied up in a stock like the one shown in Figure 6-10, wait until the stock starts to make a move. Going back to elasticity, by breaking the elastic range you can then jump into the position. This saves you the aggravation of having a position in a stock that is static.

Understanding the basic concepts of supply, demand, and emotions is a solid start to your journey of learning what you don't know. What we don't know is what fundamental factors are driving the current price condition of the stock (driven by supply and demand). The fact is, the reason we don't know is because the markets see to it that you, the investor, exist at the end of the food chain, meaning that any fundamental information having nutritional value is either extremely rare or illegal to have! The irony is you don't know what you don't know. Therefore, we as technicians rely on market food that is available through the foundational variables of price, volume, time, and velocity, as represented on the charts. These variables tell more about the stock's condition and the next likely move than the news and media ever could. Only after these moves occur will the reasons for the moves be told through the media. Remember that the charts tell the story before the media does. The information leaks and anticipation of the leaked news shows up on the charts and illustrates the supply/demand state of affairs before the information becomes widely held. Therefore, the nature of markets is that we don't know what we are not supposed to know, except we can gain a statistical edge ahead of others by anticipating what is soon to be known by the way a stock "acts" on the chart ahead of its fundamentals or news. These basic concepts apply to every security, every entry, every exit, and every decision you make while trading and on any timeframe. From this understanding, we can see this psychology on the charts beyond the lines they draw. We can understand what draws those lines on the chart. We can learn to see the data behind the lines, and this defines the instincts that cultivate with experience.

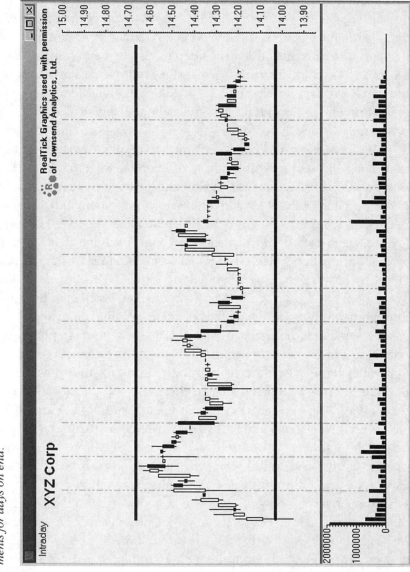

FIGURE 6-10   *This chart shows a stock that is trading in a relatively narrow range, making small movements for days on end.*

CHAPTER 7

MARKET CYCLES AND TECHNICAL ANALYSIS

Now that a strong foundation and understanding of foundational analysis (price, volume, time, and velocity) is set, we can apply this knowledge directly to the charts. As stated throughout the book, the psychology behind market action is the focus, not a literal interpretation of chart patterns. The psychology behind the patterns is often a source of insight most traders and investors miss. This is a strong edge in and of itself. Over time, the collective patterns form cycles as demonstrated by the business cycle. The same caution is warranted; these cycles are not absolutes or literal patterns, but an edge we can use for analysis and risk management. It is important to note that these chart patterns are a reflection of the psychology, not a perfectly literal representation of psychology. While the two are similar, the market is more complex and has no perfect answers. Therein lies the challenge for participants.

Much research and analysis will be done looking for opportunities in the market, only to find that the idea needs to be "let go" when it fails. This can be a difficult task. Subjectivity exists in any form of analysis (including technical analysis), and while this approach gives us the best edge to increase our odds and reduce risk, our opinions can still get in the way. A constant reminder is warranted—do not become emotionally attached even when the clearest set-ups appear. With this in mind, we can now learn how to apply what you have learned thus far to the most enduring method of trading and investing.

MARKET STAGES

The analysis of the stages of stocks is called *stage analysis* and was brought under greater focus from Stan Weinstein in his book *Stan Weinstein's Secrets For Profiting in Bull and Bear Markets* (highly recommended reading). Stage analysis indicates the current direction of the market and the next likely move it will make.

By anticipating the movements of the market, participants time their engagement that will result in making the most profit with the least risk. There are many methods to accomplish this goal. By applying statistical odds, you can anticipate future moves. Stage analysis is an important step to putting together the overall picture of what the market is saying about itself.

Like the business cycle, stocks go through four distinct phases:

- Accumulation
- Markup
- Distribution
- Decline

These four phases can be applied to any financial instrument that you are able to chart such as stock, futures, and bonds. Studying the stages will allow you to decipher which phase the instrument you decide to trade is in, and this is beneficial to your trading in the present and the future. See Figure 7-1.

It is important to note that each stage can be viewed and interpreted on all timeframes (from monthly charts to one-minute charts). Active traders and investors need to analyze the chart patterns on several timeframes, which is part of the top-down method. Multiple timeframes show the larger picture as it relates to the shorter-term picture. The closer and more narrow timeframes represent timing indications while the larger timeframes set directional bias.

FIGURE 7-1   *The four stages of a market cycle.*

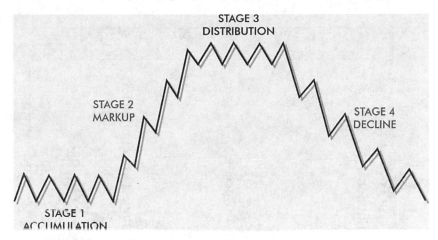

Charles Dow believed that there were three types of stock market movements; a long-term primary trend that may span years, a secondary movement that takes place over the course of several weeks to months, and day-to-day fluctuations. He metaphorically related them to the ocean, where the primary trends represent the tides, the secondary movements are the waves, and day-to-day fluctuations as the ripples within the waves. This analogy serves us well and reminds us not to confuse the outlook of any given trade or investment. Obviously if the analysis uncovered patterns of tides, we would not want to be overly influenced by the ripples. This example would describe the investors' perspective. If the analysis uncovered opportunity patterns within the day, we would remain focused on the ripples within the waves and not remain in positions longer term. When engaging the market, it is essential to know what the different trends are doing and stay true to the time horizon of the analysis. By observing securities in this matter, you are starting from a broad perspective (tides) and working your way down to the more narrow perspective (waves and ripples). The objective is to have all perspectives line up as much as possible. We call this *trend alignment.* Before getting into detail on trend alignment on multiple timeframes, it is necessary to understand each stage in detail. Figure 7-2 is an example of the four stages as they apply to an actual stock.

FIGURE 7-2 *The four stages of a stock's cycle applied to a long-term chart.*

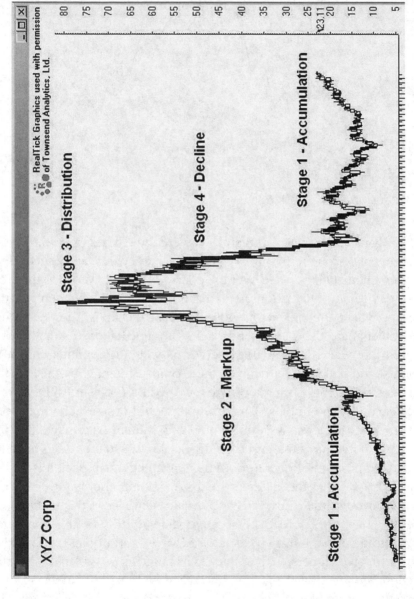

STAGE 1—ACCUMULATION

Stage 1 or *accumulation* is the time during which a stock is near a cyclical low. Bullish participants acquire stock in anticipation of higher prices during stage 1. These participants are able to acquire the stock without pushing the stock higher because this phase follows a stage 4 decline and there is still selling pressure. Stage 1 is a period where there is a fierce battle between the bullish buyers, who are trying to establish large long positions, and the bearish sellers, who are trying to exit large positions from previous stages where the security was higher priced. Think greed and fear, respectively.

A stock in a long-term accumulation phase is in a fairly bullish pattern since the stock is basing, which means that the securities price has been holding near a cyclical low for an extended period of time following a decline. The security is building a base or a foundation from which it will move higher. The risk of owning securities is fairly low at this time. The risk of buying a stock in an accumulation phase is a "time risk" if the stock does nothing. Instead of getting long a stock that is basing, you are better off waiting for the stock to break out of the basing pattern. Otherwise, you might be in a trade tying up your capital a lot longer than you anticipated. It is a drag on capital and elevated time risk to have a position that is going sideways. This is a good time to stand on the sidelines and let other people do the dirty work of providing liquidity. It is during this stage that participants can experience "whip-saw risk." *Whip-saw risk* is defined as small price oscillations due to false moves that can lead to many small losses and account churning. This can be an expensive lesson. The goal of active trading and investing is to keep your money in stocks that are moving, not going sideways. Although buying a stock that is accumulating is usually avoided, some investors choose to enter trades on dividend-paying stocks while they anticipate the markup stage.

For example, suppose a large institution, mutual fund, or major retirement fund wants to build a substantial position in a stock. A stock in stage 1 is the only real opportunity to enter large positions (sometimes as much as tens of millions of shares), without moving the price higher. Buying a stock in an accumulation process gives institutional traders the opportunity to minimize their market impact cost, which is the influence of their buying pushing the price higher (vise versa when selling). These *value players* are traders and investors who buy stocks of companies that have good fundamentals and low prices. They are some of the most patient people on the planet. These kinds of investors conduct forward-looking fundamental analysis on industries or companies and then buy millions of shares from participants who were late to sell during stage 4 decline. Once this market segment begins to realize they have damaged goods in their portfolios, they provide the liquidity for buying during stage 1, hence the basing pattern of support.

As stated before, remember the market cliché, "if they don't scare you out, they'll wear you out." All the participants who ride the stock down through a stage 4 decline, waiting for "just one more rally" that never seems to materialize, get tired of looking at their portfolio statements as a reminder of how stupid they were not to sell. This stage 1 accumulation pattern can last for a fairly long period of time. During this period institutional value players are patiently buying stock as others get tired of the position. This is known as stock moving from "weak hands to strong hands."

While active trading and investing is not suggested during stage 1, monitoring signs of an "awakening giant" is valuable. Analyzing a security in stage 1 reveals some clues as to when a stock will transition into a stage 2 markup phase. Volume can be an early indicator that a transition is eminent. For example, if a stock has been in stage 1 accumulation for a long period of time, and a surge in volume is suddenly seen, the stock may be ready to move from stage 1 accumulation to stage 2 markup. This pickup in volume is often a sign that the buyers are getting more aggressive and depleting the supply of stock at current price levels. This sets up the stock for a transition into markup where prices tend to move rapidly higher. Remember your foundational analysis. Price, volume, time, and velocity are all now represented on the chart. Figure 7-3 illustrates a stock that is trading in a stage 1 accumulation phase.

FIGURE 7-3 *This shows a stock in a stage 1 accumulation.*

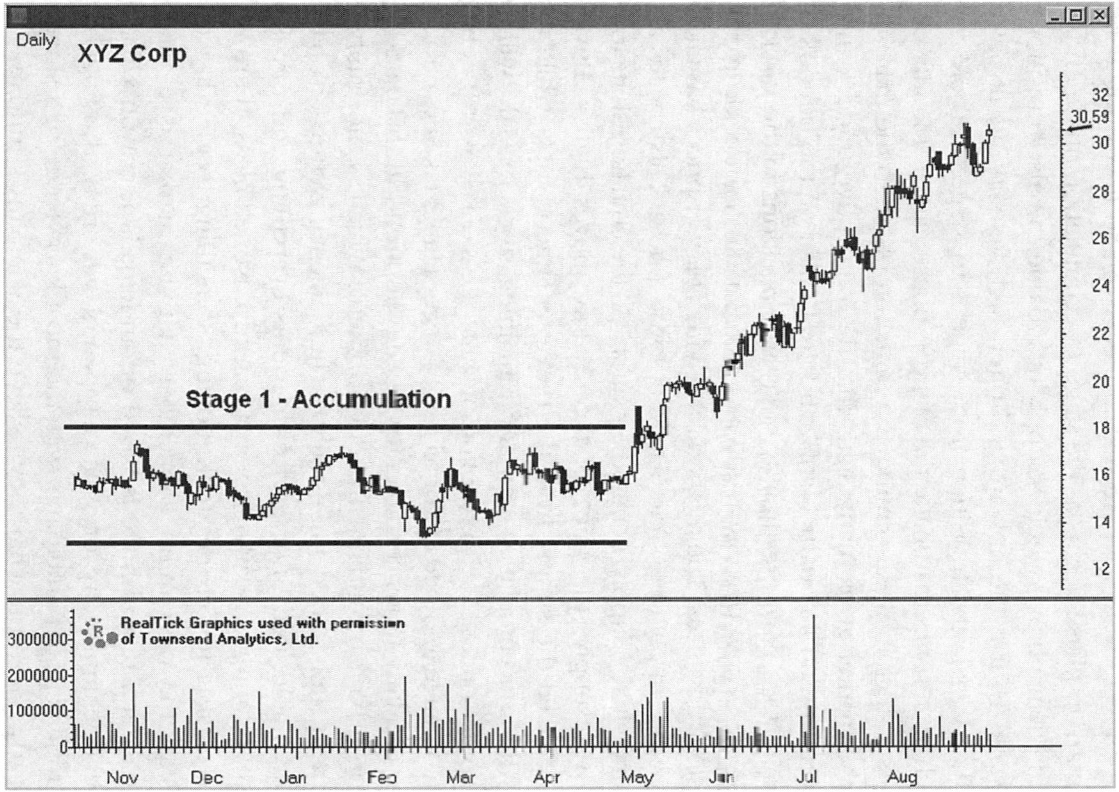

STAGE 2—MARKUP

Stage 2 or the *markup phase* of a stock cycle is the most exciting time for investors. It's where real money is made if you are a bull. The markup phase begins as the stage 1 accumulation phase ends, assuming demand overwhelms supply (stage one can also transition back to stage 4). It is the upward and often high velocity break-out of price that signals the transition from stage 1 to stage 2. There are many characteristics that make the markup phase easy to identify on charts. As a stock moves from the accumulation phase to the markup phase, the market gives many signs that the perceptive trader can pick up on. Institutional participants who are bullish on the outlook of a certain stock have presumably built large positions in the stock at lower levels. They are now ready to participate in the upside gains as the stock advances. The methodical buying at lower prices has taken much of the supply out of circulation at lower prices. This creates an imbalance in the supply/demand equation. As the equation shifts to demand over supply, the price of the security moves higher. Buyers have depleted the supply from the previous large owners while the stock was in accumulation and any remaining stock for sale will demand higher prices. The perception of what the stock is worth is beginning to change and perception is reality once stage 2 takes control.

Many times stocks enter this new uptrend in the markup phase on a bullish fundamental development, which is the catalyst to get the motion started, but usually the fundamental picture isn't particularly favorable. Remember. price discounts everything and prices are still low during the early stages of markup. Nonetheless, there is usually a catalyst to get the stock moving, something to give it a nudge to start the new trend. Remember that the market is a discounting mechanism and price is based on anticipation, not on what may be happening today or what happened yesterday. Buying based on anticipation, participants with the most knowledge of a situation buy early based on what they believe the company's fundamental position will be. Often it is said that the stock tells its own story first. The point is that before a company looks good in the fundamental picture, it will likely have already started its trend higher and look good from a technical perspective. Following the money flow is what technical analysis is all about, and it rewards those who anticipate the good or bad news and disciplines those who react to the news. When a stock moves into a stage 2 markup, it usually does so in advance of any news that gets released. The stock moves higher in anticipation of the news that has yet to come out. This is how the concept of price discounting comes into play, and how stage awareness helps you to anticipate and follow trends.

Besides the obvious upward movement in price, probably the biggest clue that a stock is ready to make a sustained move higher is the volume. The markup phase is driven mostly by greed. As a stock breaks out of the range it has been trading in, many people who missed buying the stock when it was stabilizing at lower levels (stage 1) feel that they should own the stock, so they jump into long positions at higher prices. This too is a form of fear. The fear in this scenario is missing the rally, and the combination of this fear and greed are the ingredients for a powerful rally. Yet this element of fear is far less powerful than what is seen in stage 4 as detailed later in this chapter. The overwhelming demand for the stock causes the price to move with high velocity on heavy volume. Velocity in particular will be seen clearly during stage 2 (and stage 4, to be discussed), represented by the angle of attack. *Angle of attack* is simply the slope of price action. At this point, the move upward has aggressively begun. As an active trader or investor, you need to take notice of high volume breakouts from a stage 1 base since it often signals the beginning of a sustainable move higher.

For an investor this is a good entry point to buy stock near the beginning of a strong move. Substantial gains can be observed while simply monitoring the strength of the stock and exiting the trade when it starts to demonstrate any weakness. For the active trader, the stock can be traded repeatedly as it completes the stage 2 markup phase. Figure 7-4 is an example of a stock transitioning from a stage 1 accumulation to a stage 2 markup phase.

STAGE 3—DISTRIBUTION

The third stage of a securities lifecycle is the distribution phase. The *distribution phase* is the reverse process of accumulation. It is a period when the upward movement of a stock from the markup

FIGURE 7-4   *The stock moves from a stage 1 accumulation phase to a stage 2 markup phase. Notice the increase in volume as the stock breaks out of the accumulation phase.*

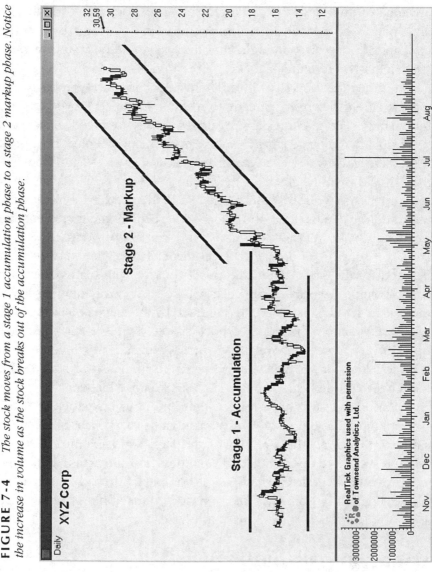

phase begins to slow until it ends up trading in a sideways action, leaving it vulnerable to the inevitable decline (although as stated earlier, it can also restart its uptrend as well). The distribution phase occurs when the previously bullish accumulators of stock begin to dispose of their large positions and their selling gradually equals the buying pressure, leaving the stock stuck in another trading range (consolidation). This is a period where the stock moves "from strong hands to weak hands," demonstrating yet again, the cyclical nature of the market.

The strange thing about the distribution phase is that during this stage, the fundamentals are known to be strong, while during early markup they were anticipated to be strong—a big difference! It's often said that good news comes out at the top of a market cycle. This supports the metaphor we have used in terms of the market's food chain. It is here that the most bullish news becomes known to the amateur, but as stated, also the best indication that reversals are likely since they live at the end of the chain. Remember, by the time this food is known, it is also digested and has little or no nutritional value left. At this point, traditional analysts are extremely bullish and they sometimes compete to see who can set the highest price targets and go on record with strong buys. At the same time the company is often floating more stock to the public through a secondary offering in an attempt to raise additional operating cash, causing the stock to be temporarily overvalued. It is also common to see stock splits, where companies divide each share of stock to make the price look more appealing to investors during this stage of the cycle. The dumb money eats up the advice from analysts who urge stock buying at these exuberant levels. This helps them and their "most favored nation" status customers exit their positions. This is a tactic you now understand and will not again fall victim to!

A decrease in volume and range are two indications that a stock is transitioning into the distribution stage from the markup stage. As a stock nears the end of the markup phase, buyers are not as confident because the stock is often "extended in price," meaning the stock has already moved up from the last significant range and the risks associated with the downside are larger. Although the risk of a stock correcting from these levels is increased, it will often make short-lived moves higher in price on lighter volume (volatility). The lower volume is due to less confident buyers and those looking to ride it up as long as possible, unwilling to offer any meaningful supply. At this point, the stock is ripe for a correction. In other words, the fruit is ready to fall from the tree.

The price movement in stage 3 distribution has much the same action as stage 1 accumulation, except it occurs after a markup period. If the stock were to continue its markup phase, it would have been pushed higher by excited buyers. Instead, it becomes a fierce battle between the bulls and the bears with sellers gradually overwhelming the buyers. This action puts a lid on the stock's price and its action is described as heavy. There are often wide swings in price on large volume during the distribution phase, but the net result is that the stock is unchanged. This action, when there are wide swings in price with heavy volume, is called *churning*. When this action is observed, investors should begin to liquidate long holdings if not out already. For active traders, stocks that appear to be in the distribution stages should be avoided and attention should be moved to stocks that are trending in stage 2 or 4. Figure 7-5 shows a chart of a stock in a stage 3 distribution pattern.

STAGE 4—DECLINE

Once a security has started to top out, the next stage of the securities' cyclical evolution is the inevitable *stage 4* or *decline*. Aggressive sellers further help the decline stage as owners attempt to get out of their remaining shares before the stock gets too far away from them to the downside. The dumb money, who are prevalent in the distribution phase, start to get less anxious in their purchases since they are buying stock that is not moving, therefore, supply gradually overcomes demand. While the bulls find the advancing phase the most profitable, the decline stage is where the bears thrive. The action of a stock in a downtrend is usually quicker and more severe than the slow and steady upward movement that most stocks follow because fear is more powerful than greed as described in stage 2. In fact, the fear in a downtrend is much greater than the combined greed and fear (of missing the rally) in an uptrend. The quick moves found in a downtrend are also appealing to active short sellers, because you can make a lot of money in a short period of time.

FIGURE 7-5 *This chart shows a stock in a stage 3 distribution pattern.*

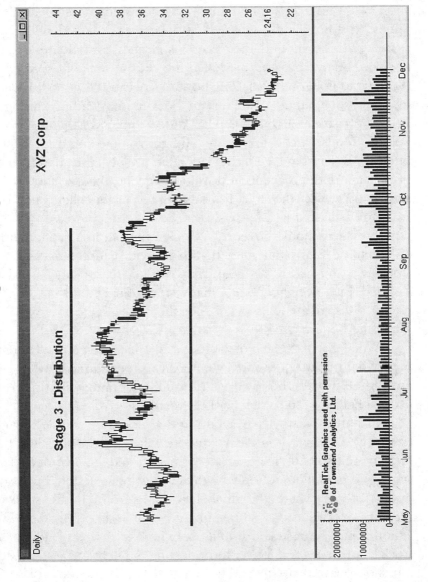

115

A security in a decline phase is marked by brief rallies, usually on light volume, that are soon overwhelmed by selling pressure. Most rallies in this decline phase are short lived and usually fall well short of the previous rally high. These are known as "bear market rallies." It is important to know that once a stock has identified itself as being in a downtrend, there is no justification for holding onto long positions. Many investors are lulled into a false sense of security and continue to hold onto their long positions because the stock is declining on light volume. Volume can be very misleading during the decline phase, so price action takes precedence over trying to predict volume trends. Prices can decline on light volume and these declines often do severe damage to the stock simply because there is a lack of buyers. As the perception of value worsens, there are fewer buyers willing to take the stock from the all too eager sellers, and losses will rapidly mount in long positions.

Investors should never try to pick a bottom in a stock that is in a downtrend, no matter what the fundamentals are telling you. If the stock is going down, it's going down for a reason and should be avoided. Interestingly enough, many stocks finally bottom out when news stories are at their worst, hence the phrase "all bad news comes out at the bottom."

While this discussion of the four stages has been limited to examples of daily charts, it cannot be emphasized enough that these cycles are repeated over and over again on all timeframes, illustrating the cyclical nature of the stock market. See Figure 7-6.

In summary, stocks in stage 1 and 3 should be avoided by most traders and all investors. Active traders will scalp during stage 1 and 3, but until experience is gained, this should be avoided. These stages are identified not only by the current price action, but also by understanding where the stock has come from. If the stock has recently experienced a strong up move, it is likely that sideways action could represent distribution, whereas sideways action in a stock that has seen a longer-term decline is likely to be in an accumulation phase that will lead to eventual upside movement.

Stage 2 stocks should be bought as the stock breaks out of accumulation or on pullbacks in the upward trend. These stocks should

FIGURE 7-6 *This chart shows a stock that transitioned from a stage 3 distribution to a stage 4 decline. Note the volume increase as the stock moves lower.*

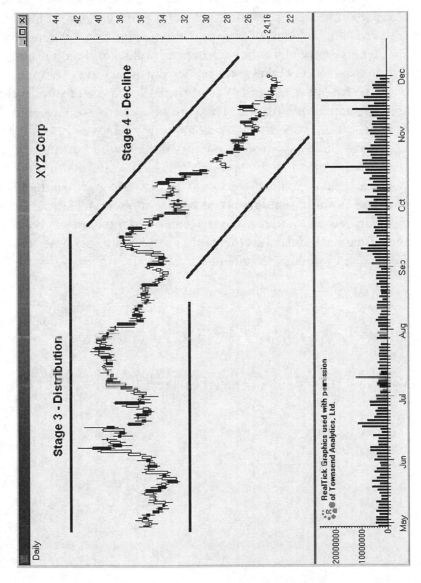

not be shorted because you don't want to fight the trend. Stage 4 stocks should be sold short on a break of distribution or on rallies in the downtrend. Never go long on a stage 4 stock. Although there are times when going against the prevailing trend can be profitable, the odds of failure are considerably higher when fighting the trend. Fading the trend is reserved for the experienced scalper and requires true discipline, which I feel takes most participants years to develop.

The foundational variables of price, volume, time, and velocity are constants in the market. They are timeless as well. Keeping this in focus along with the psychology of what moves prices through each stage builds a powerful edge. We continue to add to the edge and increase our odds by applying the same concepts to other tools available to us. The next step in the process of top-down trading and investing is understanding some of the tools of technical analysis, including support and resistance, trends, and the use of moving averages. Chapter 8 describes the proper application of these tools and their value as timing instruments.

CHAPTER 8

SUPPORT AND RESISTANCE

nderstanding stage development is a natural lead-in to the discussion of support and resistance. Support and resistance are not literal lines on the chart or an exact destination, but are more accurately defined as "areas" of support and resistance. This translates into areas of buying (stages 1 and 2) and areas of selling (stages 3 and 4). Defining support and resistance on the charts will now allow a trader and investor to take the next step in top-down analysis. Our objective in this chapter is to start seeing support and resistance on all timeframes that will lead to actionable trades. This chapter is truly the foundation of technical analysis.

The ongoing battle between bulls and bears is what makes the stock market such a fascinating study of the basic laws of supply and demand. By using technical analysis to study how a stock reacts to these battles, you can be poised to participate in a continued trend. Support and resistance levels are one of the most important forces in technical analysis because they are the building blocks upon which trends are built.

Support levels, are areas where there is enough buying pressure (demand) to offset selling pressure (supply) and provide a temporary halt to declines. Support levels represent the "demand half" of the supply/demand equation. Support levels are like a trampoline. Whenever prices drop to a level of support, buyers overwhelm sellers and the stock bounces higher. Certainly support can also be defined as an area where price declines are halted without the bounce, but strong support and typical market action represents the trampoline analogy versus what some call a "dead cat bounce." Therefore we expect upside elasticity at support, not rigor mortis! Rallies that fail to appear at the expected support call the level into question. It is important to remember that support on longer-term charts tends to be defined as a range in price (area of support), rather than a specific number. However, on short-term timeframes, support is often a very specific price. In both cases, defining support will be very helpful in timing trade entries. By increasing the accuracy of the entry, you not only have greater profit potential, but more importantly, you are assured that if that market doesn't agree with your analysis, then any losses will be small and the discomfort of heat (withstanding a losing position) will be minimized.

Resistance levels are areas where selling pressure (supply) offsets buying pressure (demand) and halts advances in the price of stocks. Resistance represents the other side of the supply/demand equation— the barrier of supply. Resistance levels are like a rubber ceiling where sellers overwhelm the buying pressure and the stock retreats. Much like supply, resistance on longer-term timeframes tends to be an area and not a specific number. Just as shorter-term support levels are often a specific number, the same is true for resistance in short-term charts. Zooming into shorter-term timeframes allows you to find key resistance levels with a greater degree of accuracy. This is because the close-up view can show intraday volatility where the security may have run into support or resistance several times during the day. On a longer-term chart it would be seen as only one test of the level. Figure 8-1 is an example of support and resistance.

The psychology of support and resistance can be defined in many ways, but this example helps make the point. Have you ever bought a stock only to watch it decline in price and wish you could go back in time and get out in time to break even? This type of buyer's remorse shows up on the chart as resistance. Obviously, one person's position will not offer much resistance, but when prices are at a level where many people are involved with the stock, the selling pressure is multiplied and so is the resistance. At these levels we refer to participants as

FIGURE 8-1   *The chart shows an example of support and resistance on an hourly chart.*

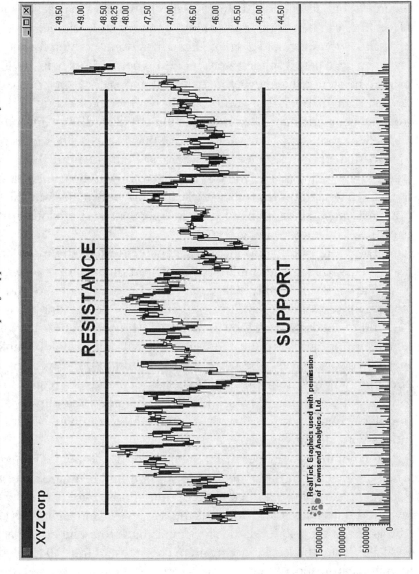

"weak holders of stock." It becomes much harder for the security to work through the increased supply before moving higher. What makes a good support or resistance level? It depends on how much time the security spent at that particular level and how many transactions took place. This can be verified by looking at ranges and volume.

Have you ever sold a stock after it has done nothing for months and then watched it immediately move higher without you, as if the market mysteriously knew you exited the position? Of course this doesn't really happen, but you probably wish you could buy back the stock at your original price. These actions, repeated by many buyers and sellers, form support for a stock price because as a stock pulls back toward that prior resistance level there is demand from those who wished they hadn't missed the first chance to buy at those initial levels. In fact, what often occurs is that stock does not pull all the way back to prior resistance since demand can be impatient and anxious participants respond early (think greed).

The more often support or resistance is tested, the more likely that level is to fail. After multiple assaults on the sellers of a stock at a resistance level, supply will eventually be overwhelmed and the stock will experience an upside "breakout." Put simply, when demand exceeds supply, the stock is free to move higher. The more times support is tested, the more likely it will fail to hold. Think of these levels as fences. The more they get bumped, the weaker they become. When selling pressure exceeds demand, it creates lower lows and a continuing downtrend. Breakouts and breakdowns are a popular way to trade because they often lead to dramatic short-term moves with strong velocity.

One of the better clues that a breakout or breakdown is coming is when an increase in the frequency of support and resistance is tested. For example, suppose a stock in an uptrend finds resistance at the $40 level and pulls back to $35 and tests the $40 level again eight days later. At this test of the $40 level, the stock pulls back to a higher low at the $37 level. Then the stock once again makes a test of the $40 level, only to pull back to the $39 level. The buyers are getting more aggressive each time the stock retraces from each successive test of the $40 level.

The impatience to own the stock shows that buyers are getting control. The buyers show their tenacity not only through price but also through time. The second test of the resistance level comes after four days compared to the first test at eight days. The last test is after only two days (the fence is getting bumped often and with less rest between assaults). Each test of the $40 level reduces the supply offered at that level, making a breakout imminent. The inability of the stock to retrace more than $1 indicates supply (those who drive the price down by hitting bids) is beginning to be removed. Once the passive supply (offered at $40) is freed up, the stock can move higher. At this point there will typically be a large surge in volume as the last of the $40 stock is bought, and the stock experiences a breakout that sees the stock move up to $45 in just a couple of days. It sounds easy—buy support and sell resistance—but if this were not the case, the stock would just go sideways.

What happens when support is broken? Once broken, support becomes resistance. If a stock has been trading at a valid support level for a long period of time and suddenly breaks through that level, then support tends to act as resistance in the future. Many people who bought at the support lost money as the stock broke down. These people have the "just want to get out even" syndrome. Many times these participants do not use protective stops below the support level. They become emotional and hold onto the stock until shares get back to the level where they entered. As they attempt to sell their stock, new supply is created. Refer to Figure 8-2 for an example of a stock that broke support then became resistance.

Once broken, the resistance becomes support. For example, let's say you own stock that has traded within a range for a long period of time. Since the stock is not doing anything, you exit the trade. As soon as you exit the position, the stock breaks out of the range and starts to move higher. In the back of your mind you are angry and think that if it only comes back to that range, you will jump back in, since you want to participate in the move and you want your old price. This thinking creates an underlying demand for the stock as it pulls back to a level that was prior resistance. It is a sort of "revenge syndrome" whereby the participant needs to validate that they were originally right and acted

FIGURE 8-2 *Support, once broken, tends to act as resistance.*

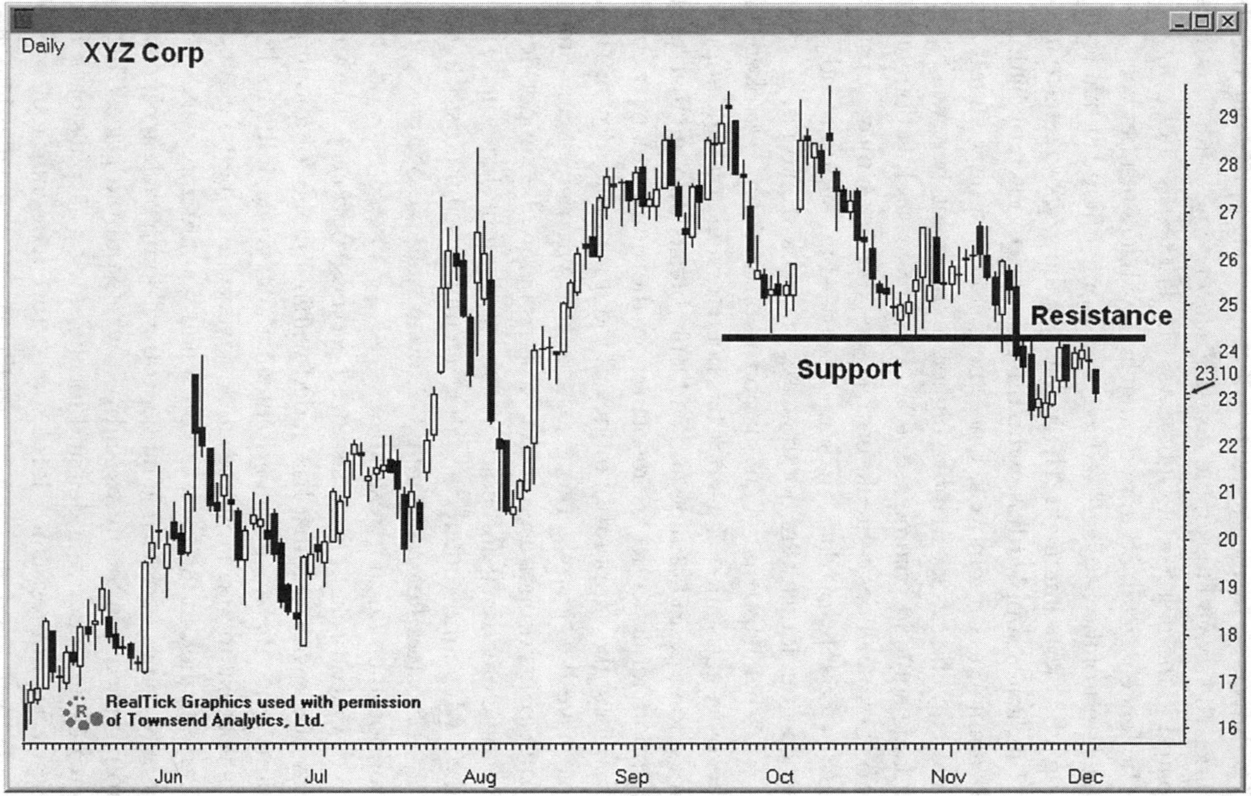

accordingly. We can again apply psychology (personal in this instance) to the market. Another source of demand comes from traders who shorted the stock as it came to the top of the range. As the stock breaks higher from this level, the shorts lose money. As these participants who were short hold onto their positions, they hope for the stock to pull back to the resistance that was previously broken. These people who were short must buy their stock back in order to exit their positions. This creates an underlying demand for the stock at the prior resistance level. This is how resistance, once broken, becomes support as this process is repeated over and over again as the stock moves higher. Figure 8-3 is an example of how once broken, resistance becomes support.

CONSENSUS

Your goal as an investor or active trader should be to take money out of the stock market on a consistent basis. The most important thing you can do to make this possible is to trade with the trend. Trends are another one of the foundations that technical analysis is built upon and should be considered the backbone to developing a directional bias.

If you enter the trade at an appropriate time within a trending stock, a trader then has the greatest probability of making larger profits and at the same time helps to formulate intelligent levels for protective stops. Once a trend is established, the security is more likely to continue in its original direction than to reverse. This is the path of least resistance (different context in the definition of resistance). Even the strongest stocks don't go straight up. They tend to move in a stair-step fashion, defined by a series of peaks and troughs. It is the direction of these highs and lows that determines the overall trend.

When a stock enters the stage 2 markup phase, it is in an uptrend defined by a series of higher highs and higher lows. Each time a stock in an uptrend pulls back after getting ahead of itself, it finds support at a level higher than the last time it experienced profit-taking. Pullbacks in uptrends provide ideal entry points to enter long positions. See Figure 8-4 for a stock in an uptrend.

FIGURE 8-3 *Once resistance has been broken, it becomes support. Typically, the strongest signals occur when the pullback does not equal the prior resistance since anxious buyers act promptly.*

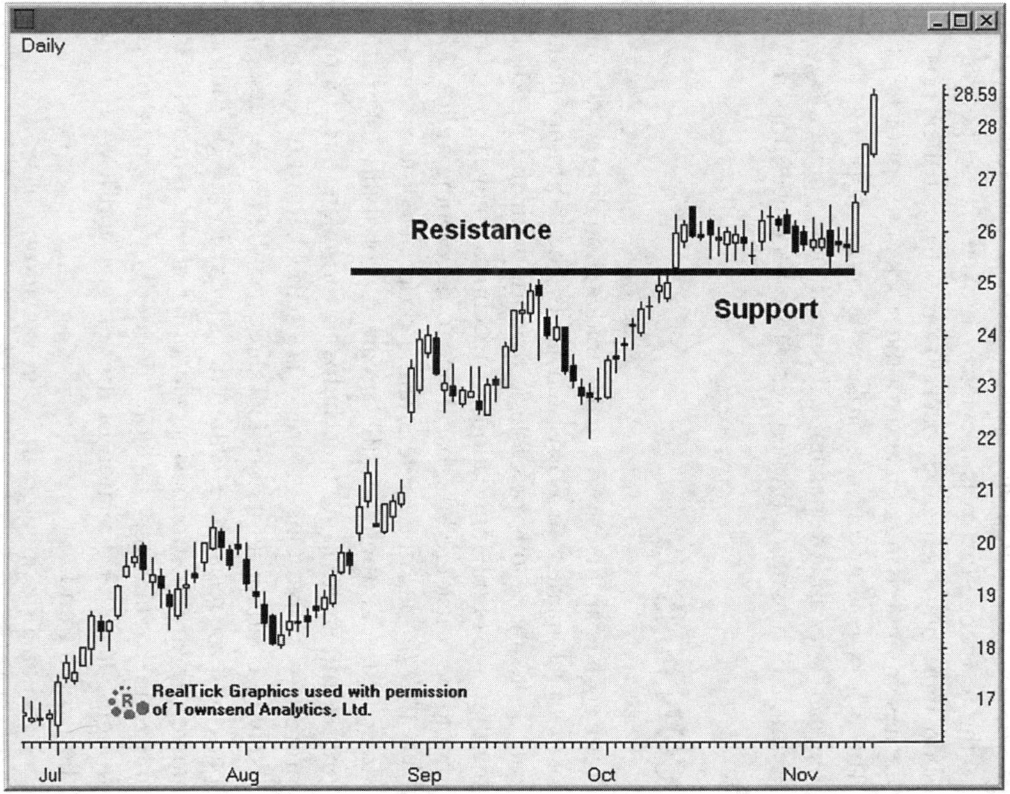

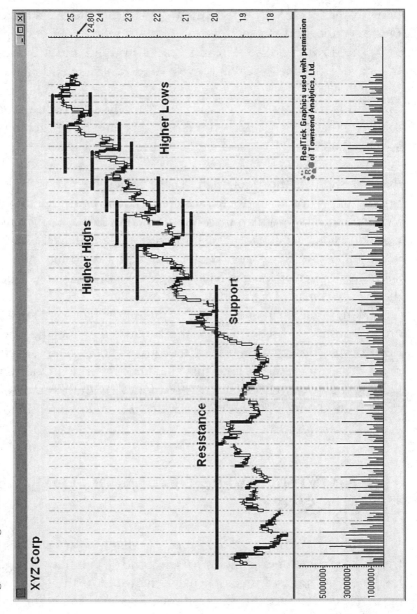

FIGURE 8-4 *This stock broke out of a stage 1 pattern and transitioned into a stage 2 uptrend making higher highs and higher lows.*

It is important to recognize that there are trends within trends and the longer-term trend is the sum of all the short-term trends. As noted earlier, look to long-term trends to indicate the overall direction of the security and the shorter-term trend to refine your entry points.

The downtrend is the reverse of an uptrend and it is found in the stage 4 decline of a stock cycle. A downtrend is defined by a security making a series of *lower highs and lower lows.* When a stock breaks down to new lows, the subsequent rally will take the stock up to a level that does not exceed the previous rally high. Each time the sellers take control, the stock price makes a lower low.

Downtrending stocks show a series of sell-offs followed by rallies that fall short of the prior high. These rallies give short sellers an opportunity to profit in declining stocks. Stocks in a downtrend tend to trade more on emotion than an uptrending stock. This is because people become complacent when things are going well and fearful when things are not. When people are fearful of losing money, the subsequent price action can have a high velocity and this is where all the money is made for the short seller. See Figure 8-5.

Many times market participants attempt to get long stocks that are in a downtrend. They may do this because they feel the stock has been beaten down too much or that it is a good value at this low price. It is important to note that the trend is your friend, and by fighting the downtrend, you will lose money. With that said, there is never a good time to a get long stock that is in a downtrend. The risk is simply not worth it.

THE MOVING AVERAGE—SMOOTHED CONSENSUS

While the market may have consensus in that it has moved with the trend, it is sometimes difficult to see trend if volatility is high. By taking the average of the consensus, the trend of the stock can be easily noted. The tool to smooth out the consensus is the moving average (MA).

XYZ Corp

Lower Highs

Lower Lows

MAs are one of the most versatile and widely used of all technical tools. They are the backbone for most trend-following systems because of the ease of their construction and the fact that moving averages can be so readily tested. The MA is also the basis for many popular oscillators (a tool that will be discussed in Chapter 16) and indicators. A trend-following device smoothes out the noise that price data can produce, and this makes it easier to recognize and gauge the strength of the underlying trend.

Construction of a simple MA is calculated by adding the closing prices of the period being studied and dividing the total by the number of periods being studied. In the case of the daily MA, on each successive day the data for the new day is added to the total after the first day is dropped off, and again divided by the amount of days for which the study is being calculated. Because MAs represent the smoothed trend of the market or security it is following, it makes sense that a rising MA represents a rising trend and a declining MA represents a downtrend. See Figure 8-6.

When you adjust the period of the MA, you adjust the fast and slow MAs. If you shorten the period of the MA, it speeds up since it is more influenced by current prices. This means that it tracks the security more closely because each point of data that gets added and each point of data that gets dropped off now has a greater influence on the overall MA. In the reverse case when you lengthen the period of the MA, you are taking relatively more pieces of data into account. When the MA has many points of data involved in its calculation, one piece of data has less effect on the MA as a whole. If a slower MA is moving higher, the long-term consensus for the stock is bullish. If the faster MAs are trending higher, the stock has near-term strength and there is an urgency to own the stock.

A common way that investors and traders use MAs is to place trailing stop orders (orders that will get you out of a position) just under an MA as the security progresses in an uptrend. The reason for placing a stop under a rising MA is that it is thought that as long as the price remains above the MA it will continue to pull the MA higher and remain in its trend. By practicing this technique, you are able to remain in a position while it is trending strongly. In the case of a short sale,

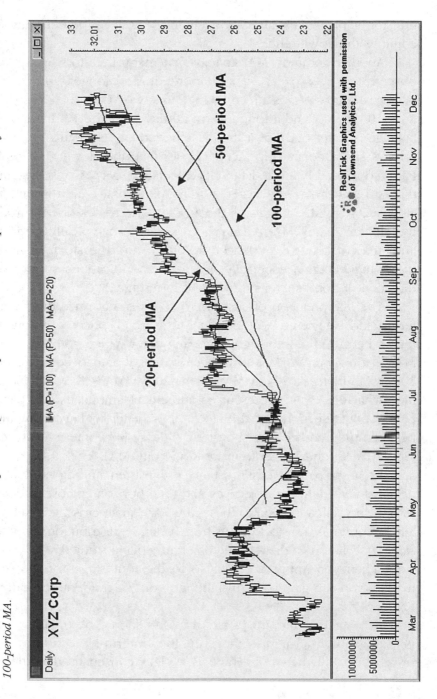

the stop is placed just above a declining MA, since the declining MA confirms the downtrend.

Another common MA strategy that many investors and traders observe are "crossovers" of a shorter-term and longer-term moving averages. A *crossover* is a method that uses two MAs—such as a short-term 10-day MA and a longer-term 20-day MA. The 10-day moving average is faster because it uses less periods in its calculation and it follows spontaneous price action closer than the slower MA, which takes considerably more data in its calculation. A crossover system in theory buys when the faster 10-day MA crosses up through the slower 20-day MA or sells as the 10-day MA crosses down through the slower 20-day MA. A bullish crossover can typically be found after the stock has experienced a sell off and the stock begins to move higher again especially when other indications support the direction of trend such as movement into stage 2.

The interpretation of such a crossover is that once the shorter-term trend has exceeded the longer-term trend, prices can continue higher because the trends confirm each other. When you add a third MA, like a 50-day MA, a bullish crossover would occur when the 10-day MA pierces a 20-day MA and the 20-day MA is above the 50-day MA. What this really represents is agreement among market participants about the trend of the stock. It is better to have agreement between the trends of the short-term (10-day MA), intermediate-term (20-day MA), and longer-term trend (50-day MA). This is because it shows that the path of least resistance is consistent among various participants with different objectives and time horizons whose decisions to buy and sell are keyed to these MAs. A bearish crossover can usually be found as the stock heads from a stage 3 distribution top into a stage 4 decline regardless of the timeframe being studied.

When you apply MA analysis to the four stages of the stock market, you can gain some insight into your stage identification. See Figure 8-7.

In a stage 2 markup phase, the MAs should be trailing higher with the shorter-term MAs above the longer-term MAs and the stock price above all the MAs. There is a clear consensus that there is

FIGURE 8-7 _Notice that while this security is in stage 4 decline, the 20-day MA is below the 50-day MA, which is below the 100-day MA. In a stage 1 accumulation, the MAs are going sideways, and while the stock is in a stage 1 accumulation, the 20-day MA is above the 50-day MA, which is above the 100-day MA._

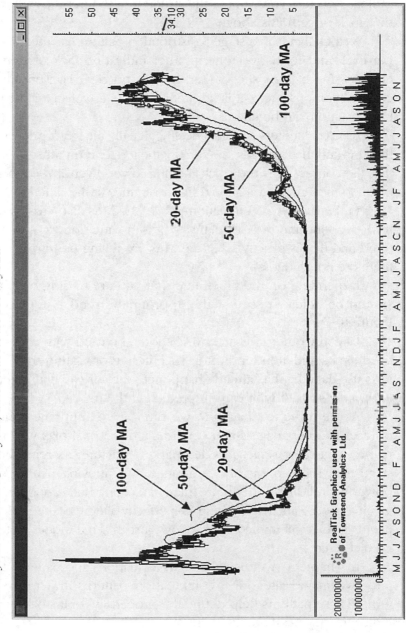

demand for the stock as the price moves higher. If any significant pullback occurs, you can tell the strength of the trend by which MAs the stock price holds above.

A stock that is in a stage 3 distribution pattern has the MAs crossing back and forth over one another indicating lack of trend. The crisscrossing of MAs shows that there is no clear consensus, hence confirmation of stage 3. It is not until the MAs establish a clear pattern before action can be taken.

As a stock enters a stage 4 decline, ideally the stock price is below the MAs and the faster MAs are below the longer-term MAs. This shows that the consensus is the stock moving lower. Even if the stock does begin to move higher, it should find resistance at the different MAs.

In the stage 1 accumulation phase, the MAs also cross back and forth over one another. Since the stock is moving sideways, there is no trend and that is exactly what the MAs are telling us—no consensus, therefore no action.

Depending on the timeframe that you are trading on, the MAs should be adjusted so that the appropriate trend is revealed. See Figure 8-8.

Like any other indicator, MAs should be used with care and not used as a stand-alone indicator for entering or exiting trades. Since MAs use data that has already happened, they are a lagging indicator and must be used with care in predicting the future.

As we move to Chapter 9, we can start to apply the confluence of ideas to form analysis that confirms a directional bias within a primarily stage 2 or stage 4 cycle. Market structure, as represented in stage analysis, support and resistance, and moving averages, form powerful indications of future market action. But caution must be given once again that nothing is perfectly literal. Stage 1 does not mean stage 2 will immediately follow, just as stage 3 does not always predict stage 4.

In Chapter 9, we discover chart formations and patterns that fall into two major categories: continuation patterns and reversal patterns. These patterns help define the propensity for a stock, sector, or indice to either *continue* its prior stage or transition and *reverse*. With

| Recommended Moving Averages for Different Timeframes | | |
Long-Term	Intermediate-Term	Short-Term
50-day	20-day	10-day
100-day	50-day	20-day
200-day	100-day	50-day

FIGURE 8-8   *These are the suggested MA periods for several timeframes.*

this understanding, traders and investors can increase their odds again by understanding when to stay with the prevailing trend or when to expect a new trend to emerge. When these structures within the market all point to the same analysis, we can then act on our plan with clarity and confidence while reducing risk.

9

TRAJECTORIES AND PATHS

ow that you have a basic understanding of the psychology and structure that make up technical analysis, the next step is to see how it all fits in with the overall picture of "directional bias." Remember that in the spirit of top-down analysis and trend alignment, we must learn to see the market from different perspectives. We begin with somewhat of a 30,000-foot picture high above the landscape for the overall picture, and descend lower for a sharper view. In this chapter, we learn to see the market from both altitudes to assimilate the information. Many people who are new to active trading and investing tend to be too myopic and only see the minor picture. These amateurs tend to find one indicator to grasp on to and forget about the overall scope of the market. This is perhaps the most common mistake that leads to whipsaw risk, lack of conviction, and utter confusion if not randomness.

When ballistic experts calculate the trajectory of a cannonball in an attempt to predict where it will land, they take several factors into account. The dominant factors include the size of the cannonball, the size of the cannon, the direction it is aimed in, the angle it is aimed at, and the amount of gunpowder used—all significant factors that dictate where the cannonball will land. Once these factors are integrated and the general trajectory is calculated, other more minor factors such as wind direction and speed, air density, and air temperature should be considered. When looking at the overall picture of the stock market, all factors, both big and small must be taken into account. Some factors have a dominant impact, and other factors have less. We have at this point focused on the more dominant factors that move markets, but we cannot forget the less obvious factors either.

The major factors we have studied so far include the four stages, support and resistance, trends, and MAs. Factors such as chart patterns, oscillators, and indicators are less significant but they are important since they tend to improve the accuracy of the trade and impact the overall picture. While these patterns and trajectories repeat time and time again, when taken in the right context, they can produce profitable trade setups with limited risk.

As stated earlier, charts are a reflection of psychological and emotional patterns that repeat over and over again. Most patterns are separated into two groups—continuation patterns and reversal patterns.

CONTINUATION AND REVERSAL PATTERNS

Patterns are not to be confused with trends. Patterns are merely indications in a trend that help to define if the trend will continue or reverse.

Because trending stocks are where the substantial money is made, you need to be able to recognize patterns that favor the odds of a trend continuing or reversing. Investors can benefit from interpreting these patterns by having a way to judge whether their positions are acting healthy or if there is a potential problem. Active traders benefit the most from these patterns because they allow traders to identify low-risk areas and enter strongly trending stocks.

Even the strongest trends do not continue uninterrupted, however. Investors run into profit taking, support and resistance levels, and periods where the trend must simply consolidate or stabilize after a large move. Seeing the patterns within the trend will improve all participants' edge.

CONTINUATION PATTERNS

The first continuation pattern to be covered is the consolidation pattern. The *consolidation pattern* is where energy builds up for another move in the direction of the trend. It is a continuation pattern that is a pause in the current trend. For the most part, securities will consolidate through price or time. When a security consolidates through price in an uptrend, the price will drift lower, usually on light volume. When a security in a downtrend consolidates (also referred to as stabilization) through price, it drifts higher on light volume before making another push lower. It is also possible to consolidate through time. After a security makes a large move in either direction, it pauses and trades sideways in a tight range where shares trade hands before the security becomes poised for another move in the direction of trend. In an example of an uptrend, a consolidation through time is usually indicative of a stronger stock since the sellers are only strong enough to keep the bulls at bay, even after a strong move when the bulls should be tired. Consolidation patterns are one of the most basic continuation patterns and one that you should always watch for. Figure 9-1 illustrates a stock in a consolidation range continuation pattern. Notice how the stock continues its previous trend higher after consolidating.

Flags

Flags are one of the most reliable continuation patterns. They provide the active trader and investor trade set-ups with good risk-to-reward ratios. It is very common for flags to form after a violent breakout from a base or other important area of consolidation. These patterns typically allow you a safe entry point in a rapidly moving stock that has temporarily paused after getting ahead of itself. Flags are formed, as a big move in either direction temporarily stalls out, and buyers become less excited while sellers become tempted to take their profits. Whenever a stock moves sharply in either direction, it attracts the attention of more participants, and inevitably brings short sellers to any strength and bottom fishers to any weakness. It is often that these contrarians add fuel to the fire once the original trend resumes, thus increasing the strength of the move.

The two main characteristics of flag formations are large increases in trading volume on the original breakout, and a low volume pullback with lower highs and lower lows as the stock consolidates. The shape of the formation takes on a slight downward slope for a bullish flag and

FIGURE 9-1 _This shows a stock trading in a consolidation range, acting as a pause to the overall stage 2 markup phase._

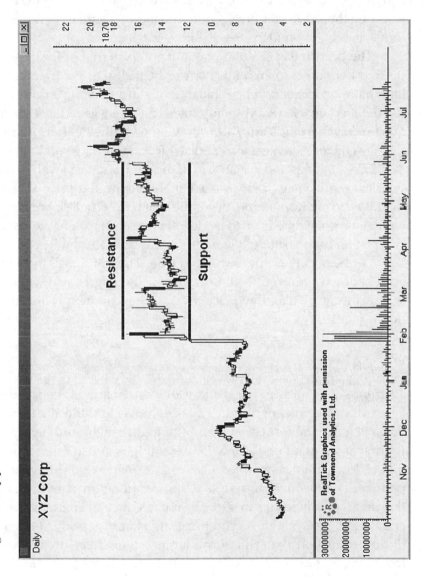

an upward slope for bearish formations. It is very common for a flag to pull back to one of the shorter-term MAs, with the 10-day MA the most common on daily charts. The easiest way to initiate a trade from a flag is to buy the stock as it breaks out past the descending trend line that forms its upper boundary. See Figure 9-2.

The bearish flag is also a continuation pattern, but for the stage 4 decline period or downtrend. For the bearish flag you need to be a little more anticipatory when initiating a short trade to ensure getting the required uptick. (Short selling rules can be reviewed in *How to Get Started in Electronic Day Trading*, written by this author.) Once the trade is entered, the most logical place for a stop is just under the support level for longs and just above the upper resistance level for shorts. Price targets for flags can be reached by taking the price where the stock broke out from to the top of the flag for the bullish scenario and adding the point difference to the level where the stock broke out upon completion of the pattern. Figure 9-3 is an example of a bearish flag.

For bearish flags, the reverse is true. The difference from where a breakdown occurred to the bottom of the flag is subtracted from where the flag breakdown occurred and subsequently resumes its downtrend.

Pennants

Pennants are similar to flags, and they share many of the same characteristics. Pennants occur after a large move, and the stock consolidates in a triangle formation with both higher highs and higher lows. By drawing a trend line along the lower highs and another along the higher lows, it is easy to see how the formation got its name. The pennant is generally viewed as a shorter duration pattern than the flag and typically results in stronger moves once the pattern has been completed. As with most continuation patterns, study the volume during formation that will show larger volume on up moves and lower volume on pullbacks in the bullish example. In the bearish example, it will show higher volume on the downward moves and lighter volume on the rallies. Price targets can be reached using the same method used for flags. See Figure 9-4.

FIGURE 9-2 *This stock has a bullish flag continuation pattern, providing a brief pause within the bullish trend.*

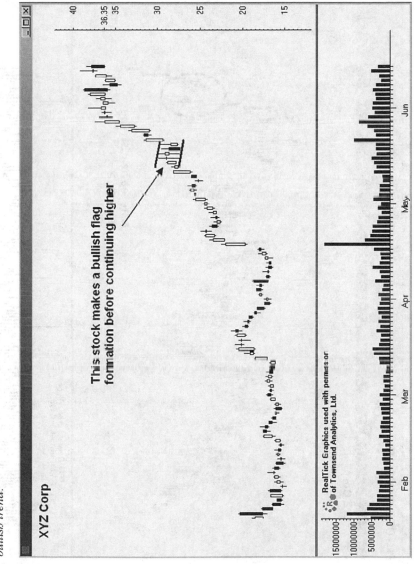

141

FIGURE 9-3 *This stock forms a bearish flag before continuing its trend lower.*

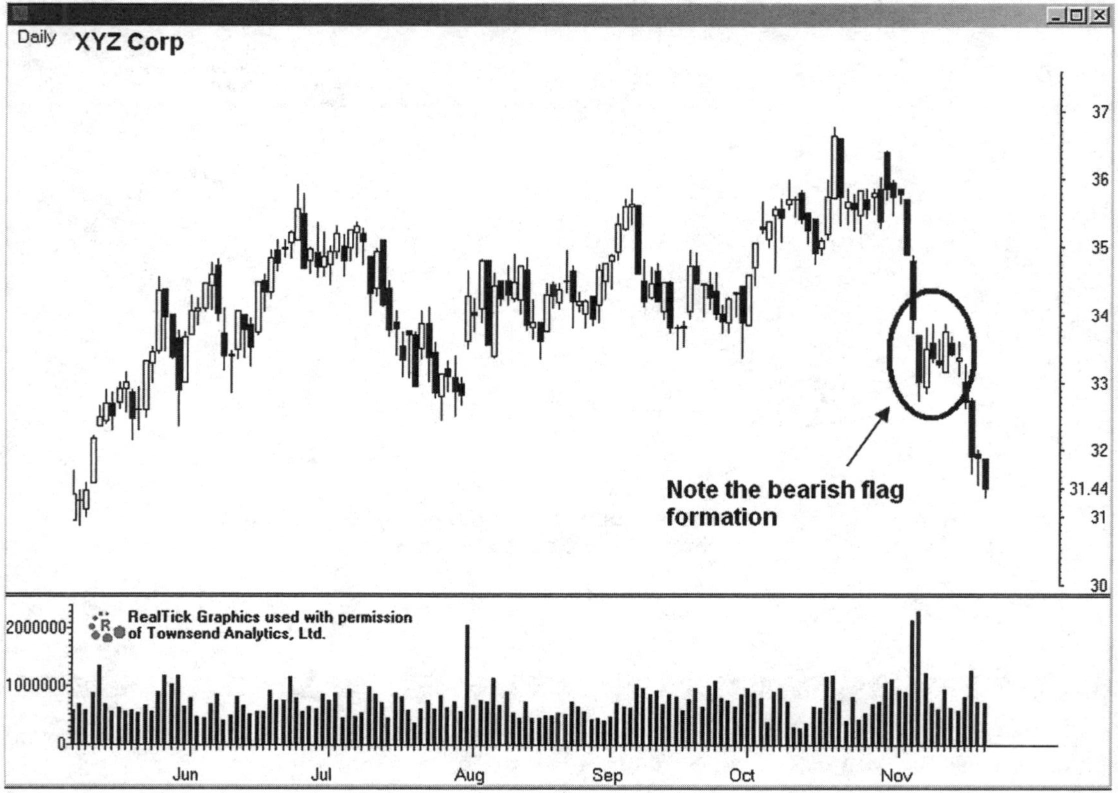

Daily
XYZ Corp
37
36
35
34
33
32
31.44
31
30
Note the bearish flag formation
RealTick Graphics used with permission of Townsend Analytics, Ltd.
2000000
1000000
0
Jun
Jul
Aug
Sep
Oct
Nov

FIGURE 9-4   This stock makes a bullish pennant pattern as it consolidates in its uptrend.

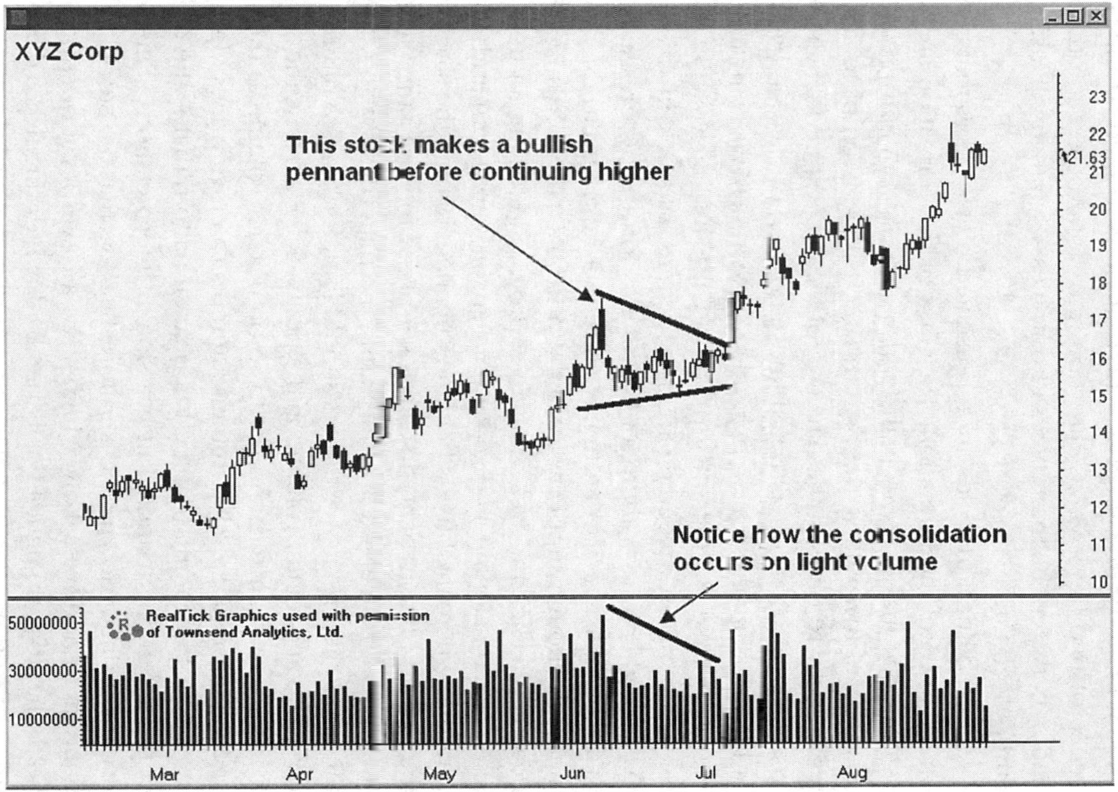

Triangles

Triangles are continuation patterns formed by the constriction of a trading range for the security. The triangle is formed by the convergence of two lines whose direction and slope determine the designation between the three types of triangles—symmetrical, ascending, and descending.

Symmetrical triangles are represented by two lines that converge on the apex of the formation. The lines of this formation are formed as the stock makes lower highs and higher lows. When prices break past one of these lines, the pattern is considered complete. This pattern usually resolves in the direction of the original trend. Symmetrical triangles can occur on all timeframes and are not classified as bullish or bearish. Figure 9-5 is an example of a symmetrical triangle.

A horizontal line on top and an up-sloping lower trend line form the bullish ascending triangle pattern. A stock in this pattern makes higher lows with upper boundaries formed by a resistance line that the stock must overcome. Each time it rallies up to this line, it is met with enough supply to force the price back down. These sell-offs become weaker and weaker as they progress, creating an up-sloping line. The up-sloping line represents an increased demand on each pullback where the buyers become impatient to own the stock. When the demand finally overcomes the supply at the resistance level, the stock breaks out above it, completing the pattern. As with other continuation patterns, active traders should look for bigger volume on the rally days and lighter volume on the pullbacks. Each time the stock rallies up to resistance, it should do so on heavier volume as the buyers become more aggressive in their attempts to move prices higher.

The descending triangle is a bearish pattern that is the opposite of the ascending triangle but has similar interpretations. This pattern occurs during a downtrend and foreshadows that the stock will continue its trend lower. Lower highs and a lower level of support that holds the stock up until it finally breaks down distinguishes this pattern from the other triangles. The descending line marks lower highs for the same reason. This downward sloping line is formed as the sellers become more aggressive selling bounces and buyers become

FIGURE 9-5 *A symmetrical triangle pattern is completed before the stock continues higher.*

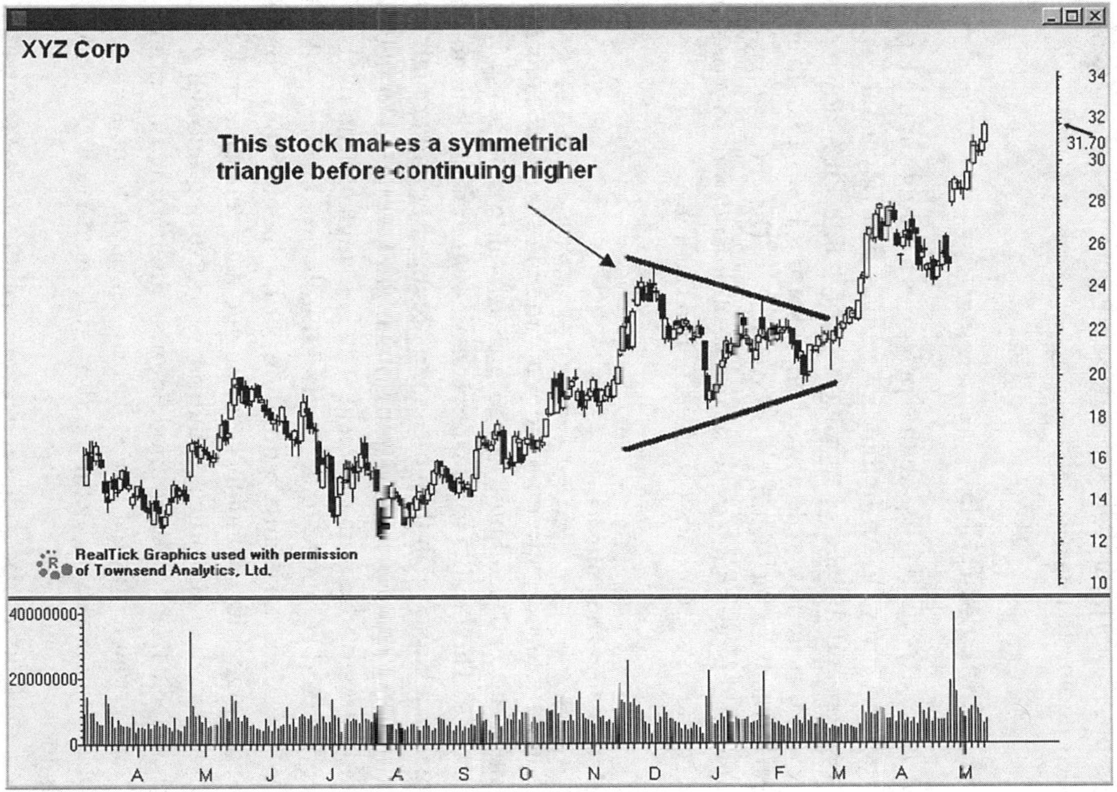

XYZ Corp
This stock makes a symmetrical triangle before continuing higher
RealTick Graphics used with permission of Townsend Analytics, Ltd.
34
32
31.70
30
28
26
24
22
20
18
16
14
12
10
40000000
20000000
0
A M J J A S O N D J F M A M

less willing to chase prices higher. Each successive lower rally up to the descending line generally occurs on less volume than the previous high. As sellers overwhelm buyers, there is a large pickup in volume as prices break through support. See Figure 9-6 for an example of a descending triangle.

REVERSAL PATTERNS

A *reversal pattern* is a path that precedes a change in the larger trend of the security. In an uptrend, it signals that buyers are starting to weaken and a stage of transition is probable. In a downtrend, the reversal pattern signals a weakening of the bears and an increased probability for the security to move higher. The reversal pattern goes against the prevailing trend so use caution and wait for confirmation that the new trend has occurred before acting.

Double tops and bottoms

The double top pattern provides a valuable sign that stage 2 is coming to an end, leading to stage 3 distribution and possibly stage 4 decline. The double top pattern occurs when a stock in an uptrend makes a higher high then tries to make another higher high but only manages to get back to the previous high. If you draw a neckline on the bases of the highs, it creates two triangles. This pattern is not considered complete until the neckline is broken on the downside. As the bulls take an up-trending stock higher, they continue to make higher highs until they don't have the strength to make another higher high. This indicates the bears are strong enough to prevent the stock from making another push higher. At this point, if the bears are able to push the stock low enough to make a lower low below the neckline, the uptrend is broken and downside movement is more probable.

   The double bottom is the reverse of the double top pattern. The bears have a stock in a downtrend, and the stock continues to make lower highs and lower lows. At a certain point, the bulls are strong

FIGURE 9-6 *This shows a descending triangle pattern, indicating the pause within a lower trend.*

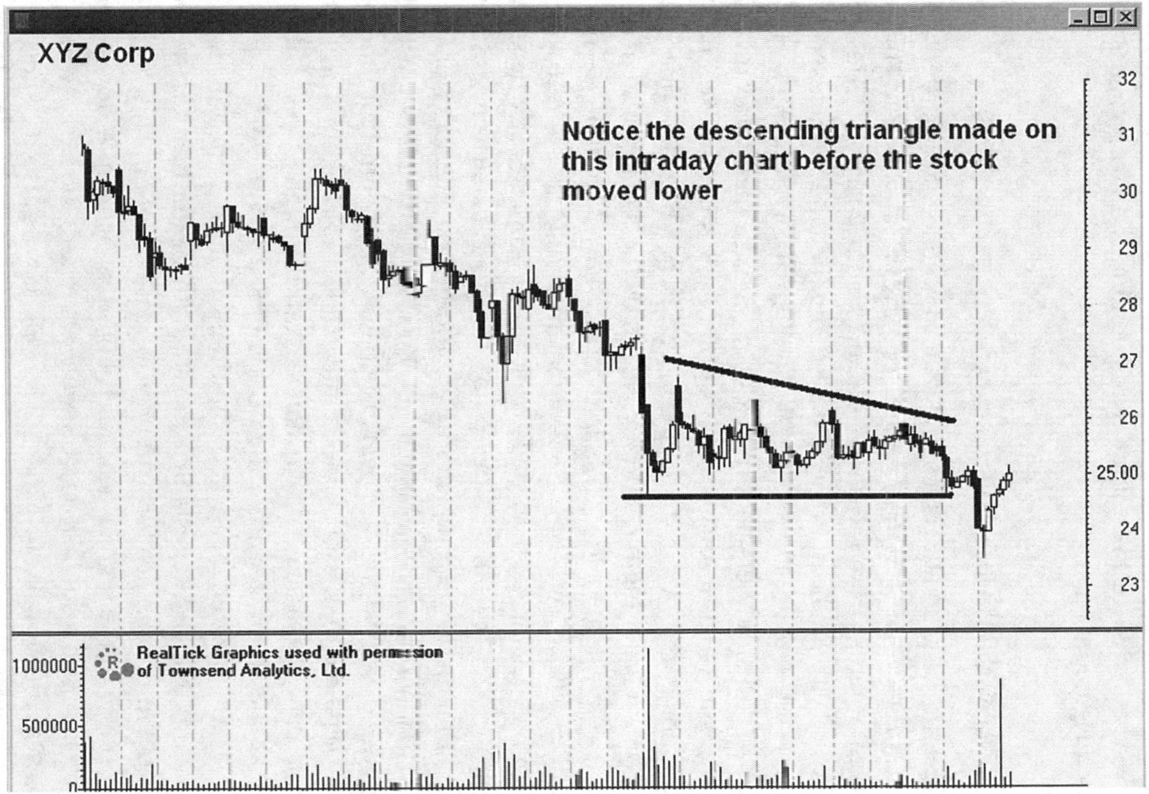

XYZ Corp
Notice the descending triangle made on this intraday chart before the stock moved lower
32
31
30
29
28
27
26
25.00
24
23
RealTick Graphics used with permission of Townsend Analytics, Ltd.
1000000
500000
0

enough to stop the bears from making a lower low and when the neckline gets broken; the bulls create a higher high and stop the downtrend. This typically occurs as a stock transitions from a stage 4 decline to a stage 1 distribution and continues on to a stage 2 uptrend. See Figures 9-7 and 9-8.

Head and shoulders patterns

The head and shoulders reversal pattern is generally regarded as one of the best known and most reliable of all reversal patterns. This pattern gets its name from the shape it makes on a chart—a series of three peaks with the head in the middle being the tallest and a shoulder on each side that are lower than the head. In an up-trending security, the head and shoulders pattern is a warning sign that the trend is losing strength. The price action at this point begins to slow and the forces of supply and demand are considered in balance. The first peak is a normal higher high in an uptrend, but as the stock pulls back, it fails to make a higher low. This is the first sign of trouble. As the stock rallies off the low, it makes a higher high but has no follow-through buying. The stock then pulls back to the same level where it got a bounce the last time. At this point, the stock makes one last attempt to continue its uptrend and makes another run higher. This last peak is usually on lighter volume as the bulls are getting tired. As the stock trades down off this last peak, the bears take control and the pattern is complete as the neckline of the pattern is broken. The target on this pattern is usually the distance from the highest peak above the headline subtracted from the neckline. See Figure 9-9.

An inverted head and shoulders pattern is a bullish reversal pattern, which suggests that the strength of the bears is weakening and the probability for a trend reversal is higher. This is the exact opposite of the regular head and shoulders pattern. A down-trending stock makes a succession of three lows where the first low is a lower low in the downtrend, and the second low is also a lower low, but the third low is a higher low. The down-trending stock makes a series of lower highs and lower lows. At some point the bears start to lose some of their strength, and the stock makes a lower low but

FIGURE 9-7 *This chart shows a stock that has a double top reversal pattern, bringing the prior uptrend to a halt and signaling the downtrend.*

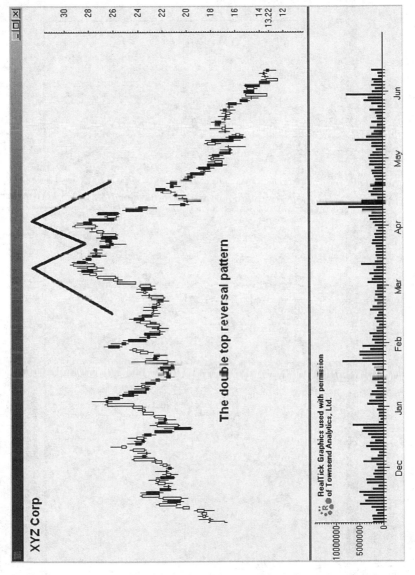

FIGURE 9-8   *This is an example of a double bottom reversal pattern, bringing the prior downtrend to a halt and signaling the uptrend. Pay close attention to the volume pattern as the formation takes shape.*

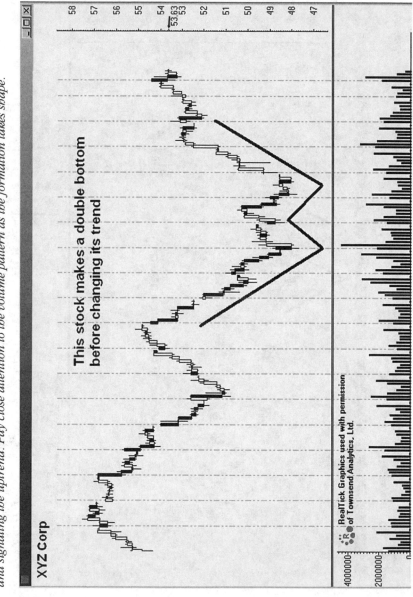

XYZ Corp

This stock makes a double bottom before changing its trend

RealTick Graphics used with permission of Townsend Analytics, Ltd.

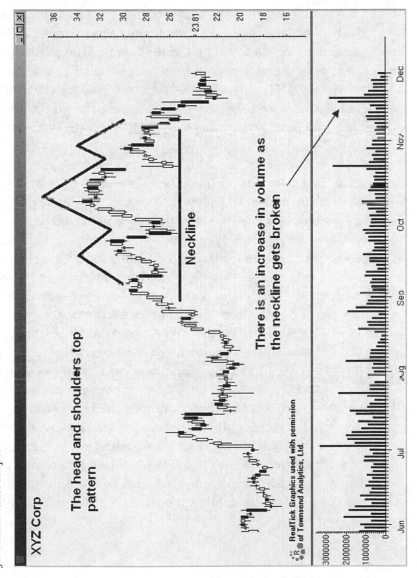

XYZ Corp

The head and shoulders top pattern

Neckline

There is an increase in volume as the neckline gets broken

RealTick Graphics used with permission of Townsend Analytics, Ltd.

fails to make a lower high due to the increasing strength of the bulls. The bears then try to take it lower again on strong volume. At this point, the stock usually makes a lower low, but the bulls step back in and the stock bounces back to the neckline. The right shoulder is formed when the bears make a final attempt to move the stock lower. Most of the time this happens on lighter volume. The strength of the bulls has increased, and they take the stock through the neckline, completing the pattern. The target on this pattern is calculated the same as for the regular head and shoulders. The distance from the neckline to the peak of the head is added to the neckline to project a target. See Figure 9-10.

The highest peak of the head and shoulders pattern and the lowest peak in the inverted head and shoulders pattern is a unique peak. This peak usually occurs on heavy volume and is a defining point.

The patterns and trajectories of the market offer outstanding pictures of the crowd psychology in terms of consensus, and also signals when trends may grow tired. To use a continuation or reversal pattern alone, without the bigger picture, would be akin to waxing the car before washing it. These patterns are compliments to the analysis done prior, not replacements. Top-down analysis requires the trader and investor to continually work their way down from the top, staying aware that the broad market picture feeds the more narrow perspective.

Our next step in the process provides a very well regarded method of applying charting techniques to top-down analysis. Chapter 10 covers the essentials of an ancient form of analysis called *Japanese candlesticks*. Candlesticks are well regarded and deserving of your attention, but they need to be viewed in context to the big picture. I have found that candlestick techniques work best when used also in conjunction with oscillators, which are also covered in Chapter 10. The combined benefits of candlesticks and oscillators will contribute greatly to top-down analysis.

FIGURE 9-10 *This demonstrates an inverted head and shoulders reversal pattern.*

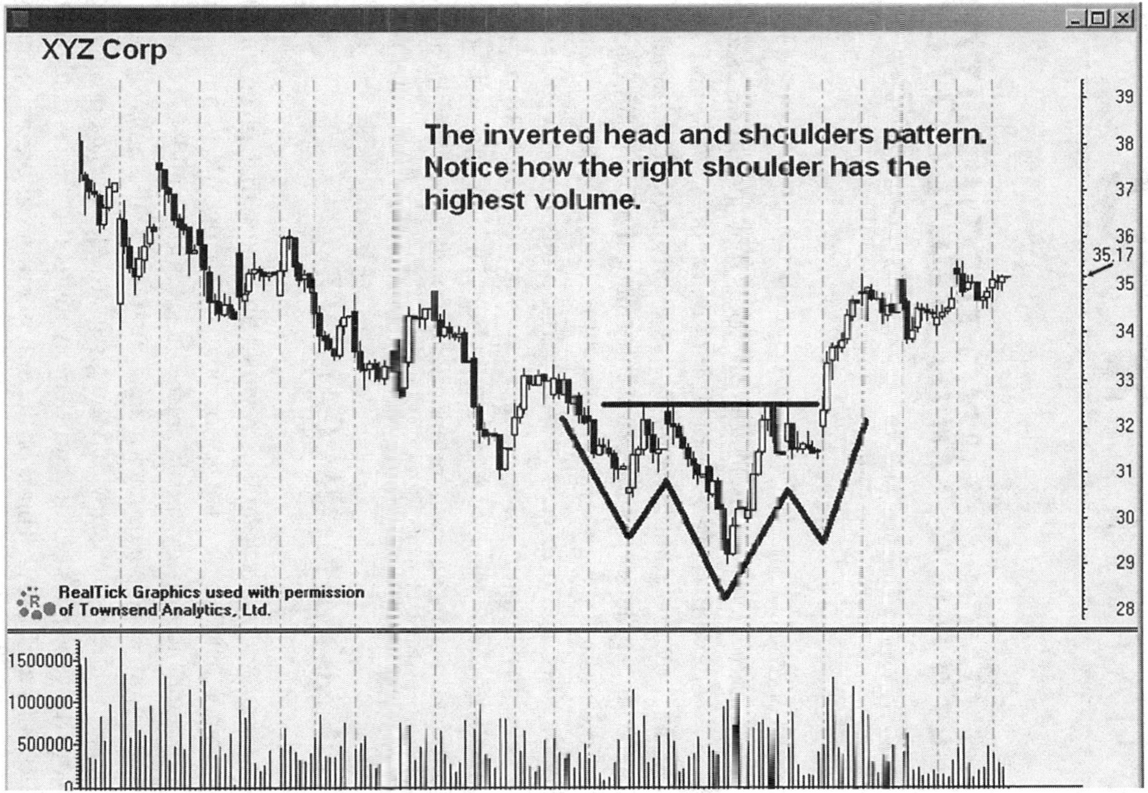
XYZ Corp
The inverted head and shoulders pattern.
Notice how the right shoulder has the
highest volume.
RealTick Graphics used with permission
of Townsend Analytics, Ltd.
39
38
37
36
35.17
35
34
33
32
31
30
29
28
1500000
1000000
500000
0

CHAPTER 10

CANDLES AND OSCILLATORS

C andlesticks and oscillators are tools that should be used in concert with stages, support and resistance, MAs, and patterns. They are complements to the charts, not stand-alone indicators. The candle shows the same information a bar chart does in that the open, close, high, and low are illustrated, but the format allows another visual aid in color. Many participants prefer candles for this reason. In Chapter 16, I cover a favorite approach using both the candle and stochastic oscillator together. This chapter will serve as a foundation to using each independently or in concert with each other.

THE MOMENTUM CANDLE

The *momentum candle* is a reversal indicator that gives investors a warning that the trend has potential to change. It is much like the important high or low peak on the head and shoulders patterns. The momentum candle illustrates a final push where the bulls or bears exert the last of their strength within the given trend. This last push is accompanied by heavy volume and demonstrates the fierce battle between the bulls and bears. Think of the momentum candle as an emotional outbreak whereby the tails (elastic highs and lows) represent the extreme range in either direction within the period being measured by the candle. In a bearish example, the momentum candle often occurs during the later stages of an uptrend. Typically the stock will gap open and make a higher high, but then close down, creating a long dark candle. The bulls initially take the stock higher but the bears ultimately take control which overwhelms the bulls. This price action closes the period much lower than the highs.

The momentum candle can be interpreted as a turning point in the trend, where control was taken from a bullish market by bears. The clear indication of the momentum candle is also represented by the vertical range or height it exhibits. The taller the candle, the greater the elastically or stretch of emotional range. This represents the "out break" of emotional range. I am sure if Sigmund Freud were alive today, he would describe the market as a child, capable of schizophrenic outbreaks and irrational behavior. The market is not a mature adult who has learned to control their emotions, but a loose cannon of emotion capable of extreme behavior. Comparative examples include the madness of crowds and the behavioral characteristics that mobs exhibit when challenged in difficult situations (fires, soccer games, concerts, and riots). Mature adults rarely act out in this manner unless under the influence of others. See Figure 10-1.

In the bullish example, the momentum candle will come at a point where sellers push the stock to a lower low but buyers exert their strength and close the stock much higher, creating a large white candle. Like the bearish example, this takes place on heavy volume, illuminating once again the fierce battle between the bulls and bears. Note Figure 10-2.

CANDLESTICK PATTERNS

There are several candlestick patterns that tell the collective psychology of the participants, and there is an entire area of study devoted to identifying these patterns. The candlestick reader relates market psychology to various individual candles. A few candles are shown in the pages that follow.

The *doji candle* is the most popular candlestick formation. This formation signals indecision in the market since the opening price and

FIGURE 10-1 *A bearish momentum candle signals a clear reversal situation as closing prices are near the lows of the period, following a bullish trend.*

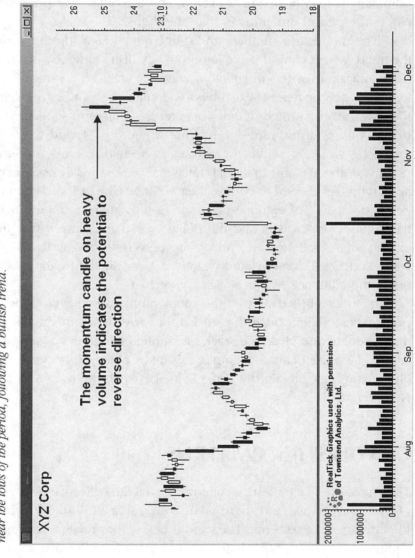

XYZ Corp

The momentum candle on heavy volume indicates the potential to reverse direction

RealTick Graphics used with permission of Townsend Analytics, Ltd.

FIGURE 10-2 *This demonstrates a bullish momentum candle. Following a bearish trend, if closing prices are near elastic highs, the bulls begin to show their presence and strength—a strong sign of the strength reversal to come.*

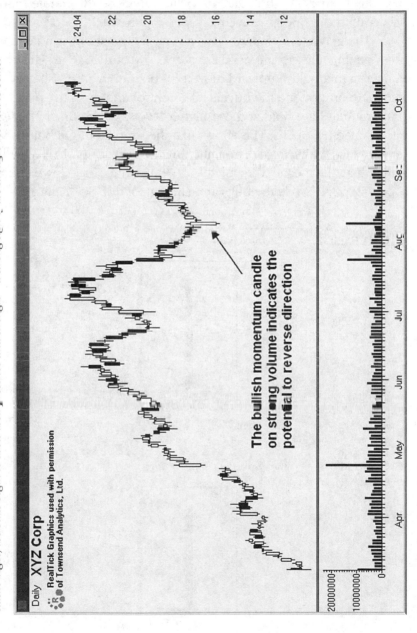

Daily **XYZ Corp**

RealTick Graphics used with permission
of Townsend Analytics, Ltd.

The bullish momentum candle
on strong volume indicates the
potential to reverse direction

the closing price are the same. Psychologically, the bulls and bears are battling, but neither the bulls nor bears can close the candle higher or lower than the open, respectively. See Figure 10-3.

The gravestone doji candle is a special type of doji candle in which the opening and closing price are at the low of the range. This can signal a top in a bullish upward move or a bottom in a bearish downward move. In an uptrend the buyers take control and push the price higher but are unable to hold at these higher levels, where finally the candle closes where it opens. This shows that the strength of the bulls is weakening while the bears are strengthening. In a downtrend this candle signifies that the bears were unable to push the stock lower than the opening price, while the bulls are gaining control. See Figure 10-4.

FIGURE 10-3   *The doji candle.*

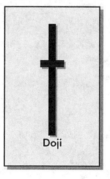

FIGURE 10-4   *The gravestone doji candle.*

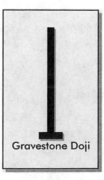

The classic hammer pattern indicates that a potential bottom may be eminent during a falling market. When a hammer pattern occurs, the bears are able to stake prices lower, but when the candle closes near the top of its range, this shows that the strength of the bulls is increasing. This "changing of the guard" represents a potential change in trend. Note Figures 10-5 and 10-6.

The shooting star pattern is the opposite of the hammer pattern. This candle warns of a potential reversal in an uptrend—the bulls are able to take the price higher, but unable to keep it higher. The shooting star candle shows that the bulls are weakening in strength. See Figures 10-7 and 10-8.

FIGURE 10-5   *The classic hammer candlestick pattern.*

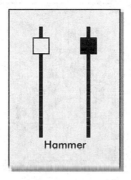

FIGURE 10-6   *The hammer pattern often signals a reversal from a minor downtrend to an uptrend. Keep in mind candles are short-term tools, as a rule.*

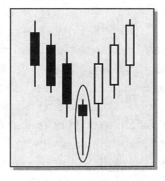

FIGURE 10-7   *The shooting star pattern.*

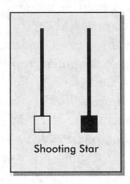

Shooting Star

FIGURE 10-8   *Many times the shooting star pattern signals a reversal in an uptrend.*

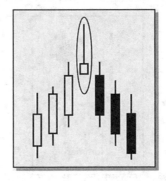

There are countless candlestick formations each made up of complex patterns involving several different candles. Each formation has a unique name (such as the bullish concealing baby swallow pattern and the upside tasuki gap pattern). The study of all the different patterns could easily fill another book. To aid in this study, there is no better reference than *Japanese Candlestick Charting* by Steve Nison.

Although candlestick patterns can help you to see the psychology of the market participants, like any other formation pattern, it is necessary to use these patterns as a tool and not a crutch. To many followers of candles, the insight to supply/demand imbalances through visual reference is invaluable. Like many other aspects of human diversity, some people are analytical and some visual. Candles seem to appeal more to those who prefer pictures.

OSCILLATORS AND INDICATORS

In addition to the continuation and reversal patterns discussed in Chapter 9, there is another important analytical method to measure psychology—oscillators and indicators. Oscillators and indicators are a group of tools that measures the foundational variables in order to gauge the sentiment of the market. In Chapter 6 we discussed the bell curve, the concept of standard deviation, and regression of mean. These are conditions in which a particular stock, sector, or indices may move sharply in one direction or another on high velocity. The rapid rise or fall of the security deviates from the historical mean price to the point where a correction back toward (not necessarily to) the mean price is expected. Standard deviation measures a number of levels beyond the mean. At some point, determined by mathematical formulas that vary greatly, the security is considered "overbought" or "oversold." Keep is mind, these terms are considered strictly statistical vernacular and have nothing to do with fundamental value. It is at these levels we expect the correction. The bell curve is a long-standing way of illustrating this standard deviation. The oscillators are another variation of a bell curve. The indicators are some of the less significant factors that should be considered when trading or investing, although they can increase the accuracy of your trades through timing. They do not measure trend as well as stage analysis, but can be strong tools to confirm the trend. Take caution when using these mechanisms, and be sure to focus on the overall picture rather than making decisions based solely on smaller factors.

Oscillators and indicators include the stochastic indicator, the relative strength indicator, and the average directional indicator, to name a few. These indicators give you a measurement of the sentiment of the market or a particular stock. The sentiment that an indicator can demonstrate may be compared to a football player attached to a rubber band that is held by a stake in the center of the football field. As the player runs toward the end zone, the force that the rubber band exerts gets stronger and stronger. In the stock market this relates to a stock, sector, or index that runs toward the bullish or bearish end zone. As the market moves to a given end, the chances for a reversal are increased. It does not tell you exactly when a move will happen, but it does indicate when securities are potentially overextended.

The stochastic indicator is a good example as to how an indicator can be used to assist in making trading decisions. The stochastic indicator was created by George Lane. It is based on the observation that in an up-trending market, the closes of the periods tend to be near the high of the period and in a down-trending stock, the closes of the periods will be near the low of the period. This means that there are many white candles in an uptrend and many dark candles in a downtrend.

The stochastic indicator puts this observation in a mathematical form. The oscillator identifies areas where the stock is stretched too far to the upside (overbought) and conditions where the stock advances too fast to the downside (oversold). Once again, keep in mind, overbought and oversold are strictly technical terms and have nothing to do with the fundamentals of a stock. They instead speak to the regression of a mean and other standard deviation metrics of reading stock prices. When the stochastic indicator gives an overbought indication, the security being measured is mathematically exhibiting the signals that it is ready for a correction or decline. When the stochastic indicator gives an oversold indication, it simply means the security has the mathematical traits of an increased potential for an upward corrections. Stochastic numbers are usually plotted below the stock chart and consist of two lines, %K and %D. On the grid (usually a 100 point scale), there is a zone at the high that indicates an area where the stock gets overbought and an area to the downside where the stock appears oversold. As the %K and the %D lines cross in the overbought territory and exit the overbought zone, the stock has a higher probability of moving lower. If the %K line crosses the %D line in the oversold territory, the buy signal occurs when the lines exit the oversold territory. When this happens the stock has a propensity to go higher. In many cases, the security moves lower after a sell indication is given and higher when a buy indication is given. Stochastic indicators are covered in greater detail in Chapter 16. See Figure 10-9.

The other indicators and oscillators act in much the same fashion. For more information about the strategy of using several of the indicators, refer to *Market Evaluation and Analysis for Swing Trading* where my co-author and I explain in great detail the mathematical and psychological implication of each.

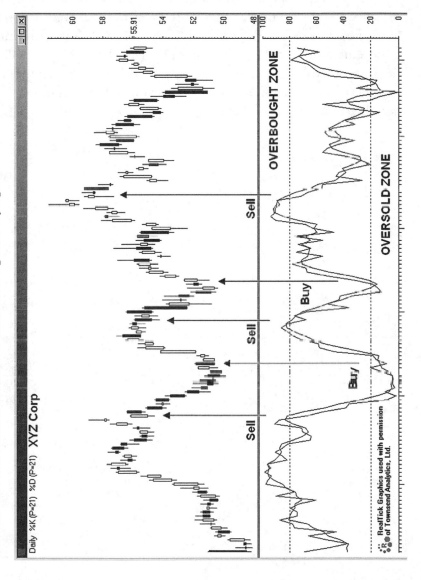

We are approaching the point where we need to start pulling the information from the prior chapters together, but before doing so, we first must spend some time on fundamentals and the quality of market information. Traders and investors will want to consider fundamentals to some degree, and Chapter 11 will focus on only the important components of this method of analysis. As you will soon discover, I explain fundamentals with a fair dose of skepticism due to the frequent manipulations that occur at the corporate, institutional, and even government level.

11

FUNDAMENTALS OR FINANCIAL FANTASY

FUNDAMENTALS ANSWER WHY, NOT WHEN

Throughout this book you have learned how to analyze securities from an objective technical point of view. By carefully analyzing charts and other indications, you should now be able to make educated trading decisions regarding risk and reward based on the technicals and the psychology behind them. If you are a very active trader, technicals provide a framework to base most trading decisions. But when taking positions for a longer period of time—a few weeks to even months—it is helpful to research and understand basic fundamental information about the company.

While technical analysis is used to time *when* a particular price move will likely occur, fundamental analysis can be used to understand *why* price moves occur. But know that the understanding of why prices move cannot directly help you in making trading decisions about the future, because the fundamental information that is current is anticipated and already discounted through price. This we know, but indirectly, it can be useful, because other large-sized market participants place a significant emphasis on fundamentals when making trading and investment decisions. If a stock you are trading is appealing to other market participants both technically and fundamentally, it adds to the probability of being profitable. The large institutions that build positions based on fundamentals often look to buy pullbacks as stocks make higher highs and higher lows as the stock trends higher. Armed with the knowledge that the stock is appealing to institutional traders and that they will likely buy pullbacks, you can buy technical pullbacks as well and have the peace of mind that institutions are likely to support the stock. This should be evident technically as light volume pullbacks and high volume rallies. The active trader can use fundamental analysis to get into the minds of other market participants that can move the stock in the direction that makes you money.

WHAT IS FUNDAMENTAL INFORMATION?

Industry analysis and other factors that affect the individual company itself are the domain of the fundamentalist. The fundamentalist believes the market value of a stock is a function of how well the company is managed and measured through financial indicators such as earnings, financial ratios, the economy as a whole, and the performance of the company's industry.

To ascertain a company's ability to compete within its industry, analysts examine the company's current and probable future market share. It seeks to measure whether it is a leader within its industry and introducing new product lines that might increase its market share. Fundamental analysts are concerned with the growth and stability of a company. They look at the quality of the firm's management and historical earnings trends. They plot how its projected growth compares with that of its competitors, and whether its growth is stable or erratic. Analysts also examine a corporation's capitalization and use of working capital. They try to pinpoint stocks that afford the investor maximum potential for growth, stability, and profits. The bottom line with a fundamental approach is that the price of a stock will move based on the profitability of the company. The fundamental approach leaves much room for corporate manipulation, trickery, and subjective analysis, as we have explored in Part I. This information can be so alluring and market-impacting that it requires a deeper understanding before we move into actionable trading and investing.

MANIPULATION OF FUNDAMENTAL INFORMATION

Basic fundamental information is the driving force behind many aspects of supply and demand in the market. As touched on in Chapter 1, the crash of the stock market in 1929 wreaked havoc on investors, causing them not only to lose money but to lose confidence in Wall Street. As a result, several laws were created to help squelch these feelings of mistrust. The Securities Act of 1933 was passed to regulate the securities industry. This required registration and disclosure. In 1934 the Securities Exchange Act was passed, which created the Securities and Exchange Commission (SEC), the primary federal regulatory agency for the securities industry. The SEC is made up of four basic divisions. The Division of Corporate Finance makes sure that publicly traded companies disclose the required financial information to investors. The Division of Market Regulation takes care of the legislation involving brokers and brokerage firms. The Division of Investment Management oversees mutual funds and investment advisors. The Division of Enforcement is charged with the investigation and enforcement of securities regulation.

The information that a publicly traded company must file to the SEC must also be made available to the public. This fundamental information includes information released by the company, such as earnings, annual reports, and quarterly reports.

Earnings are the primary focus of all analysts. Also known as net income, earnings are defined as the company's revenues minus cost of sales, operating expenses, and taxes over a given period. Many investors value earnings information because they give an indication of the company's expected future dividends to stockholders and its potential for growth. Earnings are stated in both quarterly and annual reports. Earnings are to the fundamentalist what price and volume are to the technician. Obviously, regardless of earnings and forecasts, current price is the market's final word on the company's perceived value. As we know, perception is reality in the markets.

Annual reports are audited documents required by the SEC. They are sent to a public company's shareholders at the end of each fiscal year. The report includes a balance sheet that contains information about the company's financial condition. The balance sheet can be analyzed to give you some idea of what would be paid to the shareholders if the corporation was liquidated. Annual reports also include an income statement that accounts for sales, expenses, and net profit for a given period. Each annual report contains a cash flow report that shows the cash receipts minus the cash payments for the fiscal year. Very similar to the annual report is the 10-K report that is filed to the SEC each year. The 10-K report contains more detailed information about the company than the annual report and is available for free from the SEC's Web site.

Quarterly reports are un-audited documents required by the SEC that report the financial results for the quarter and note significant changes that occurred during the quarter. The quarterly report includes a financial statement with an income statement, balance sheet, and many times a cash-flow statement on a per quarter basis. The quarterly report is also referred to as a Form 10-Q and is also available from the SEC Web site for free.

By utilizing this fundamental information, you can see how the company actually performed in the past and view predictions by the company for their future performance. From a fundamentalist's point of view, if a company is growing and further growth and profits are expected, then the company's stock should go higher. Most all market movement has some base in fundamentals, but remember it is not profitable to base your trading decisions off this fundamental information. As stated earlier, price discounts everything, meaning the current and anticipated fundamental information available is already factored in the stock price. This is basic human nature since participants know that in order to profit, others must buy the shares behind them. Acting on anticipated fundamentals drives prices ahead of actual fundamentals. The technician believes this is where practice trumps theory. In theory, fundamentals should reflect stock prices, however, in practice, perception reflects price (supply and demand).

In my opinion, the very nature of fundamental information makes it a conflict of interest between the entity that is releasing it and the public that is receiving it. The releaser wants to put out information that looks good to the public, in order to further attract investors. The SEC is charged with ensuring the quality of these reports but manipulation is possible. Let's face it, in many cases (not all), publicly traded companies use the stock market like some people use dating services. Participants in dating services want to show themselves in the best light possible. If the dating service is analogous to the stock market, I argue why even use the dating service. If you can't get a date on your own merits, something is wrong! In other words, the healthiest companies fundamentally are private companies, who are not interested in public scrutiny, nor need the hype often associated with the stock market.

If picking good stocks were as easy as researching a company's financials and making trading and investment decisions based on this knowledge, anyone with this knowledge could be profitable. As you know this is not the case. It takes more than just an understanding of the company's data since this information is subject to subjective interpretation, and yes, even manipulation.

DISTORTION FROM THE COMPANY

The data a company releases passes through many hands. Any time information goes through human hands there are some bad apples that will manipulate the data to further their own ends. Manipulation is possible from a variety of places, but history shows most scandals involve those with the most to gain—high-level executives. It is an old cliché in politics that says, "if you want to find the corruption, follow the money." If corruption is to be found, the path leads to the boardroom. For example, in 2002 WorldCom disclosed that it had hidden $3.8 billion in expenses from investors to inflate earnings. The Chief Financial Officer (CFO) and the Chief Executive Office (CEO) were blamed for the scandal. The manipulation at these high levels is truly alarming and brings to light the conflict of interest that occurs in company reports. The CFO is responsible for the financial planning and record keeping for a company. They also want the company and the stock itself to appeal to investors. When putting this information into a company report, the CFO has an opportunity to use tricky accounting to exaggerate earnings. If there is any manipulation by the CFO, in most cases they don't work alone and others in high positions within the company take part in the deceit. Most executives in publicly traded companies own a considerable amount of stock in the company. They are hurt financially if the stock price moves lower.

The reason for these manipulations is because no company wants to report poor fundamental information to the public, since that would decrease stock price and tarnish the company's image. Thereby, through tricky accounting these companies are able to hide expenses and make the company look more profitable than it is. This does not mean that all companies operate at this level of malice, but I do believe all publicly traded companies put their very best foot forward with a few inches to spare.

While there is regulation in place to prevent market-wide manipulation, it's always there to one degree or another. Throughout the 1990s there was plenty of creative accounting taking place. One piece of trickery that companies used was reporting earnings on a pro forma basis. These earnings reports were released to the public in press releases. Some companies selectively excluded many expenses that would have reduced earnings in order to boost their stock price and company image. Later these companies filed a more complete and accurate set of numbers quietly to the SEC. The reports that were given to the SEC included expenses that were excluded in the pro forma earnings. The public rarely responds to the restated financials until it's too late. There are many other tricks used by companies to boost earnings, and who better to explain them than one of the market's best friends (as Warren Buffet put it), former SEC chairman Arthur Levitt. I highly suggest reading his tell-all book, *Take on the Street.*

The point to all of this is that the only annual reports filed to the SEC have to be independently audited. The astute researcher could have discovered things weren't quite right if they went through the annual 10-K report and not the press releases handed out by the company. The difficulty is that 10-K reports can be long and complex, while the press releases are flashy and easier to read. It comes down to the need to get your hands dirty and dig through the quarterly and annual reports filed to the SEC. Most investors simply do not want to work that hard. This contributes to our advantage as hard-working self-analysts.

MANIPULATION BY FINANCIAL INSTITUTIONS

The market analyst's job is to give objective advice about companies and make buy and sell recommendations to investors to help them make investment decisions. Throughout the 1990s the analysts developed unique relationships with the companies they covered. As companies perform creative accounting to boost earnings, they often leaked the earnings information to the analysts. The analysts are paid to do objective research on the companies that they are covering. Instead of being objective, they fed off the scraps of information thrown to them by the company's CFOs. In the previous WorldCom example, the company was rated as a buy just days before the company announced its accounting scandal. Where does that put the investor on the market food chain? This is just one of many examples. History has plenty more examples of manipulation at both the corporate and institutional level.

As these types of situations escalated, some analysts began to upgrade and downgrade securities based on information leaked to them. Even if the analysts uncovered creative accounting and rated the company a sell, the brokerage that they worked for would be punished by a loss of investment banking business from the company. It worked the other way around as well. Analysts would pressure CEOs and CFOs to leak fundamental data to them. If the company was small they had a tough decision to make since if they didn't pre-release data to analysts, they would be threatened indirectly with a sell rating. This was the leverage the analyst used to get information. They are in a position of power, and like most politicians, they use it. This shouldn't be any real surprise; this is also the nature of people who are influenced by greed. Not all people operate this way, but remember what we said. If you want to find corruption, follow the money. Put another way, a famous bank robber was asked why he robbed the banks, and he said, "Because that's where the money is." Wall Street is also where the money is, and to quote Don Henley of the Eagles, "a man with a briefcase can steal more money than a man with a gun."

In the late 90s, analysts began to release the numbers that companies leaked to them and then the company preceded to beat these analysts' estimates. It was a circle of corruption that left the investor without a leg to stand on when the market entered into a decline. As companies filed for bankruptcy protection, a closer view of their financial statements took place and the deceptions started to emerge.

THE BIAS OF THE GOVERNMENT

Whether the Republicans or Democrats are in office, every administration in office (the administration on the out seems to want the opposite during election years) wants to see the economy in an expansion phase along with a healthy stock market. This makes the public believe that they are doing a good job. In fact, the Government is like a very large company. The fundamental numbers released by the Government are on the economy of the entire nation. Much like the annual and quarterly reports that companies release to show how well they are doing as a company, the Government releases numbers on how well the economy of the country is doing. Politicians are notorious for trying to take credit for the economic prosperity of the nation. When election time comes around, they look back and show a track record of what the economy did while they were in office. The downside to this is that the Government is permanently biased toward trying to show an improving economy.

The Government releases many economic numbers to the public on a regular basis. Every Thursday, the initial jobless claims number is released. Every month employment numbers are released. Every quarter GDP numbers are released. Every administration wants to stay in office, and political forces play a part in public perception of economic data.

One example of an economic number that has been suspected of being manipulated is the Consumer Price Index (CPI). The CPI is an inflationary indicator that measures the change in the cost of a basket of products and services that remains fixed. As prices of goods in the basket move higher, the buying power of the dollar falls since people can't buy as much as they previously could with the same dollar. The board that oversees the Federal Reserve Banks (Fed) pays close attention to the CPI. The Fed adjusts money flow through interest rates to keep inflation around 2 to 3 percent. As long as inflation is under control interest rates can remain low. By lowering short-term interest rates, the Fed makes money less expensive to borrow (loosening the money supply), which in turn stimulates economic growth.

The Fed is an independent committee that sets the monetary policy of the nation but gets their data from the Government. The Government, on the other hand, dictates fiscal policy, which sets the federal tax and spending policies influenced by Congress and the President. If the CPI were to indicate that inflation were rising, the Fed would likely step in and raise interest rates to reduce the money supply, helping to support the value of the dollar (supply and demand). Though the Fed makes its own decision, based on information from the Government, there exists the real possibility that political interest interferes with the checks and balances system described.

The administration in office would like to have interest rates low to help boost the economy and show what a good job they are doing running the country. If the Fed were to raise interest rates, it's like putting the brakes on the economy, which no administration wants to happen. Presidencies associated with runaway inflation are tarnished in the eyes of history, Jimmy Carter being a prime example. Therefore, modern politicians are even more influenced by the position the Fed takes. In a world of global economics and exponential complexity, government officials are more influenced by fiscal policy than at any other time in history.

Since the Government is much like a large company, the politicians, like the CEO, also have an incentive to "put their best foot forward" and show economic numbers that will help the economy and allow the administration to continue to run the country.

This overview of fundamental analysis as applied to our capitalistic system explains procedurally how information is disseminated to the public. Even in a perfect world, the system itself puts the investor at the bottom of the food chain. The hierarchy of the system identifies why other sources of market food must be sought. Technical analysis quenches the appetite, but because present fundamentals are already priced in, there are trends within a company's financial information that can be useful, especially when entering the market for longer periods of time. Traders and investors alike should use this information with caution since it is easy to become emotionally attached to your analysis and opinions especially when a company has good fundamentals. Trading decisions should not be based on fundamentals—only to add confirmation to decisions that are made through technical analysis.

HOW TO FILTER THROUGH FUNDAMENTAL DATA

The study of fundamental data encompasses a very large area. There are several trends that you can look at to get a quick idea about the fundamentals of the company. A review of the basic fundamentals of a company that you want to buy should be that it is making money or on the way to earnings. There are many sources for fundamental data, but the best source comes from 10-K reports. The 10-K report and the 10-Q report are the logical places to start from when beginning the journey into fundamental analysis. Remember that the 10-K report is subject to less manipulation (not immune to) since it must be certified by an independent auditor before going to the SEC.

When looking for long candidates, you want to find securities that are good technically, but if you are planning to be in the trade for a longer period of time, you want to know that the fundamentals are also sound and therefore appealing to institutional clients. By checking the trend of net revenues, net income (earnings), and the earnings per share, you can get a good idea of whether a company looks good from a fundamental standpoint. Many times buying a stock that is breaking out of a stage 1 accumulation to a stage 2 markup will have lagging fundamentals that do not yet look stellar. The important aspect to look for is the fundamental trend of improvement in revenue, earnings, and EPS. In other words, we need to be fishing where others are not, but where the fish are likely to be.

You are only limited by the amount of time you have available when delving into fundamental research. But, there are several important things to look at on a company's 10-K statement. The first thing is to note whether the net revenues are increasing or decreasing year to year.

In Figure 11-1, the highlighted revenues have increased every year for the last four years. This is a quick way to check to see if the company is making money before any expenses. If this number is increasing then the company is doing more business and pulling in profits. Revenues minus expenses and taxes is the net income—the same as net earnings. When looking to go long, make sure these numbers are increasing year over year and quarter over quarter. Institutional participants that trade in large size are looking at the same data, yet most average participants are not. Additionally, fund managers typically don't want to hold positions they cannot justify to their investors, hence the term "window dressing" the portfolio. Many times, funds will move into fundamentally strong issues as their fiscal year ends in order to report quality companies in the portfolio. During the year when they are outside the 10-K spotlight, funds tend to take more risk in issues with less desirable fundamentals but more potential for explosive upside. This desperate method of trading allows fund managers lagging the S&P 500 an opportunity to catch up. Then as the end of the fiscal year approaches, they clean up their act with more fundamentally sound companies—window dressing.

Another component of fundamental data is the price-to-earnings ratio. The P/E ratio is a common measure of how expensive a stock is. The *P/E ratio* is the stock's price divided by the after-tax earnings over a 12-month period. The higher the P/E ratio, the higher the participant will pay for each dollar of annual earnings. One reason the P/E ratio is important is because it is part technical and part fundamental. The stock price component is at least in part derived from technicals, while the earnings component is purely fundamental. By tying a technically

FIGURE 11-1 *This shows the net revenues, net income, and the net income per share highlighted in a 10-K statement from the SEC Web site.*

	Year Ended December 31,				
	1998	1999	2000	2001	2002
	(In thousands, except per share data)				
Consolidated Statement of Income Data:					
Net revenues	$ 86,129	$224,724	$431,424	$748,821	$1,214,100
Cost of net revenues	16,094	57,588	95,453	134,816	213,876
Gross profit	70,035	167,136	335,971	614,005	1,000,224
Operating expenses:					
Sales and marketing	35,976	96,239	166,767	253,474	349,650
Product development	4,640	24,847	55,863	75,288	104,636
General and administrative	15,849	43,919	73,027	105,784	171,783
Payroll taxes on stock option gains	805	1,145	2,337	2,442	4,015
Amortization of acquired intangible assets	—	4,359	1,433	36,591	15,941
Merger related costs	—	—	1,550	—	—
Total operating expenses	57,270	170,509	300,977	473,579	646,027
Income (loss) from operations	12,765	(3,373)	34,994	140,426	354,197
Interest and other income (expense), net	1,799	23,833	46,337	41,613	49,209
Interest expense	(2,191)	(2,319)	(3,374)	(2,851)	(1,492)
Impairment of certain equity investments	—	—	—	(16,245)	(3,781)
Income before income taxes and minority interests	12,373	18,141	77,957	162,943	398,133
Provision for income taxes	(4,789)	(8,472)	(32,725)	(80,009)	(145,946)
Minority interests in consolidated companies	(311)	(102)	3,062	7,514	(2,296)
Net income	$ 7,273	$ 9,567	$ 48,294	$ 90,448	$ 249,891
Net income per share:					
Basic	$ 0.07	$ 0.04	$ 0.19	$ 0.34	$ 0.87
Diluted	$ 0.03	$ 0.04	$ 0.17	$ 0.32	$ 0.83
Weighted average shares:					
Basic	104,128	217,674	251,776	268,971	287,496
Diluted	233,519	273,033	280,346	280,995	292,820

based piece of information in with the earnings, you remove some of the subjectivity from the equation, making it less subject to manipulation. The price is what it is. The P/E is a barometer used to measure the price of the stock by comparison to earnings per share.

P/E is calculated by using the following equation:

$10 current market value per share (CMV)/$1 EPS = 10:1 P/E Ratio

In this example, this stock is trading at 10 times the earnings per share. This is often an acceptable ratio for many stocks to trade at and still not be considered overvalued.

However, many growth stocks will trade higher than 10:1 because of the anticipation that future returns will be explosive. For example, if a company earns $1 per share, keeps the money, and then invests it back in the company as opposed to paying it out in dividends, the company should grow by more than $1 next year. If the company earns $2 per share next year, and the average P/E for similar companies is 10:1, then the stock should be valued at $20 for the next year as well ($2 × 10). Instead of the shareholder getting the $2-per-share dividend, the benefit comes in the form of market appreciation. This is one of today's most important valuation techniques used by fundamentalists and other market players. Most mutual fund managers use this tool to help make investment decisions regarding growth companies.

The P/E ratio is also a lagging indicator because it is calculated over the past year on a quarter-by-quarter basis. The P/E is actually akin to a moving average as a forecasting tool since it calculates the current quarter with the data of the prior three quarters. As time advances, the newest quarter's data is added and the oldest quarter is dropped off. Therefore, based on the price discounting mechanism of the market, many companies are not profitable during stage 1 accumulation. Like the moving average, the P/E will lag the market since a company with negative earnings will have no P/E. As prices rise into stage 2 markup, the market is telling you to expect improving fundamentals. As the stock price moves higher and company earns a profit, the P/E will start to rise. Remember, the market often anticipates itself, therefore the trader cannot wait for the P/E ratio to come alive anymore than a moving average before acting.

Conversely, because fundamental information and P/Es are closely watched by institutional investors and mutual funds, healthy P/E ratios do not always mean strength. These participants usually enter the market with large-sized positions and cannot enter and exit these positions quickly without impacting the market. Therefore, their large size forces them to be more reliant on eroding fundamentals. If a company has declining revenues and earnings, the risk is higher to institutions since the company could release news that is negative such as lower guidance. In this case, the risk of investment is higher even if the technicals look good.

In the introduction, Bernoulli's insight regarding the logic behind taking risk stated that if the satisfaction of each new increase in wealth is smaller than the last, then the "disutility" of the loss (risk) will always exceed the positive utility of the gain of equal size.[1] This timeless insight applies to the logic of avoiding high-risk situations such as buying a stock on good technicals and eroding fundamentals. Clearly the satisfaction gained in a winning trade (wealth) does not justify the disutility of the loss (risk), since the risk factors are disproportionately higher. This is the lesson regarding fundamentals. If they are to be considered in your trading and investing decisions, they must support the technicals and vise versa.

Doing your own research is the key—especially when you trust your own judgment over the advice of others. This does not mean that all fundamental information is untrustworthy, no more so than it means that all fundamental information is trustworthy. The lesson here is to be your own filter and not let any one piece of fundamental data disproportionately influence your trading decisions. It is the confluence of several independent sources of data, and your analysis of this information that will lead to the lowest risk, highest reward trades.

Remember, the amateur blindly follows the advice of the other people with no filters to determine if the information is nutritional or poison, and even if you don't actually manage your own money, you must research what is handed to you. If your broker recommends a stock to you, you can take an objective look at the technicals and

---

[1] Bernstein, Peter L., Against the Gods (New York: John Wiley and Sons, 1996), 112.

fundamentals of the stock and have a reasonable process for filtering the stock's information and then make your own informed decision. If you have money in mutual funds, you can look at the overall market on a technical basis and move your money between mutual funds depending on what stage the market is in and the direction of the trend. The amateur believes there is not much he can do about the market; he is at its mercy. Smart money puts some time and effort into research and takes responsibility. Now that you have a general idea of the two major forms of analysis, it is time to pull it all together, with the greatest emphasis on technical analysis.

Technical analysis, the business cycle, stage analysis, support and resistance, consensus, moving averages, continuation/reversal patterns, and oscillators/indicators can be used to paint a picture of the psychology behind the market. Now it's time for action. In Chapter 12 we pull together the top-down approach using multiple timeframes to form decisions. The trend alignment of these timeframes is vital before acting on the analysis.

CHAPTER 12

BECOMING YOUR OWN ANALYST

At this point you fully realize the importance of your involvement in trading and investment decisions. This is not to say that everyone who manages money or gives advice is not honest. Perhaps your broker or money manager is receiving bad or biased information for the reasons stated in the prior chapters, but regardless, blind faith never will get the job done. Whether you actively manage your capital or oversee those who do, acting as your own analyst to some degree is only prudent. It is also apparent that another nemesis exists to seeing the market objectively—you! Being your own analyst requires that you not only know how to filter exterior influences and market noise, but also your own subjective views of the market. You can be certain your own intentions to effectively manage your capital are pure, and perhaps your broker's intentions are pure as well. But as the cliché goes, "the road to hell is paved with good intentions." The only thing we can do to mitigate un-pure motives or actions is to remain as objective as possible.

In today's Web-enabled society, there is a massive amount of information available that was once difficult to obtain. What was at one time a market associated with not enough information has become information overload. There are thousands of Web sites and media sources that give technical and fundamental views of the market. These services can be tempting to new participants, and they can be excellent teaching aids. But the crucial point to stay centered on as an analyst is, unless you understand the basis behind the analysis, you cannot understand the natural risk embedded in it. All forms of trading entail risk, and the first question you want to ask yourself in any trade is "where am I wrong." This piece of information is very personal and different to all participants. Therefore, no one definition of risk applies to everyone.

What may be defined as tolerable financial risk to one person, may be intolerable risk to another. While position sizing can help balance personal risk tolerances, the fact that stock prices can be volatile may limit your ability to adjust the risk. For instance, suppose you received advice to act on a $100 stock, with a technical reward target of 0.30 on the trade. Based on the metrics of risk in the setup, the trade requires a minimum of 1000 shares in order to justify the risk ($100,000). Those without the capital to make this trade, or an unwillingness to risk this large a percentage of their available capital, would incur more risk than others in a dissimilar position, since a larger reward target would be required as position size is reduced. The technical setup may not support a higher reward target, therefore, many dynamics play into the analysis beyond the technical setup. Perhaps you would need to margin (the borrowing of capital) to make the trade. The use of options, or other forms of leverage obviously would elevate the risk of the trade, based on the same technical setup. Clearly this would demonstrate a different trade for one party compared to another, hence the need to analyze and develop trades that meet your own individual parameters for risk/reward.

REVIEWING THE TOP-DOWN APPROACH

There are two major ways to research the market—top-down and bottom-up. The top-down, as you now know, is when you start with the overall market and move inward toward particular stocks. Researching a particular stock fundamentally and moving upwards to compare it to its industry group or even the entire market is called the bottom-up analysis. Most mutual funds follow the latter, opening the door to more subjectivity and un-pure information. The former approach is clearly more objective and a better source of "nutritional market food."

TOP-DOWN AND TREND ALIGNMENT

The process of top-down research starts with a macro view then narrows into a micro view. This enables you to get the larger picture of what is happening and allows you to use the trend to your advantage. By trading with the trend, your odds of being profitable are highly increased. It is based on the idea that a collection of stocks tend to move in the same direction of the overall market. The top-down approach fits well with technical analysis because you begin with the overall market, determine what stage the market is in, and generally trade the trend with individual stocks that reflect the market well. Although the market is a collection of many securities, crowd psychology suggests strongly that it is better to trade with the trend as opposed to fading it. This is sometimes referred to as the "Herd Effect." In other words, if major stocks are moving higher, they tend to pull other stocks with them. If the overall market is in a stage 2 markup, then the trend is moving higher and odds are that more stocks will be moving higher instead of lower. The same is true if the overall market were in stage 4 decline. A declining market pulls stocks lower, and the odds are with trading with the trend. As proof of this concept, take a look at market internals on strong up or down days. The advancers to decliners tell the story outright. If the overall market has a very strong day, most likely you will see advancers completely outpace decliners. The reverse is also true. If the overall market saw large losses, you will likely see decliners outpacing advancers. It seems obvious, but remember, the simplicity of the market is its greatest disguise. Too many participants overcomplicate the process, or believe the market has some evil intelligence beyond their comprehension. Fading the primary trend elevates risk dramatically while surrendering part of the edge we strive to achieve. See Figure 12-1 for an example of top-down analysis.

To begin, you should look at the major indices on multiple timeframes. As an investor who plans to trade long term, you should look at daily and weekly charts as a rule. The weekly chart shows the movement of the market on a long-term time frame, and the daily chart shows what is happening on a relatively shorter-term timeframe. A

FIGURE 12-1   *This shows the top-down approach to market analysis whereby you seek to become an expert with a handful of stocks or investment products. This approach is the approach of specialists on the New York Stock Exchange, Nasdaq Market Makers, and exchange traders such as S&P 500 pit traders on the Chicago Mercantile Exchange (CME).*

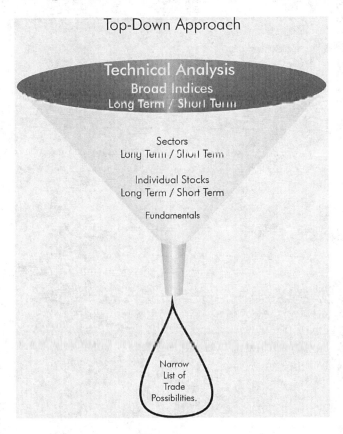

Top-Down Approach

Technical Analysis
Broad Indices
Long Term / Short Term

Sectors
Long Term / Short Term

Individual Stocks
Long Term / Short Term

Fundamentals

Narrow
List of
Trade
Possibilities.

good analogy is our solar system. Our solar system is floating through the Milky Way at a certain speed in a certain direction. The movement of the earth around the sun does little to stop the movement of the whole solar system. Consider the weekly chart of the solar system and the daily chart of the earth and the sun. If you are in the market for a long period of time, the overall direction of the weekly chart is highly important, so you would monitor its movements more carefully than daily fluctuations. See Figure 12-2 for a weekly chart of the Nasdaq

FIGURE 12-2 *This shows a weekly chart of the Nasdaq Composite Index.*

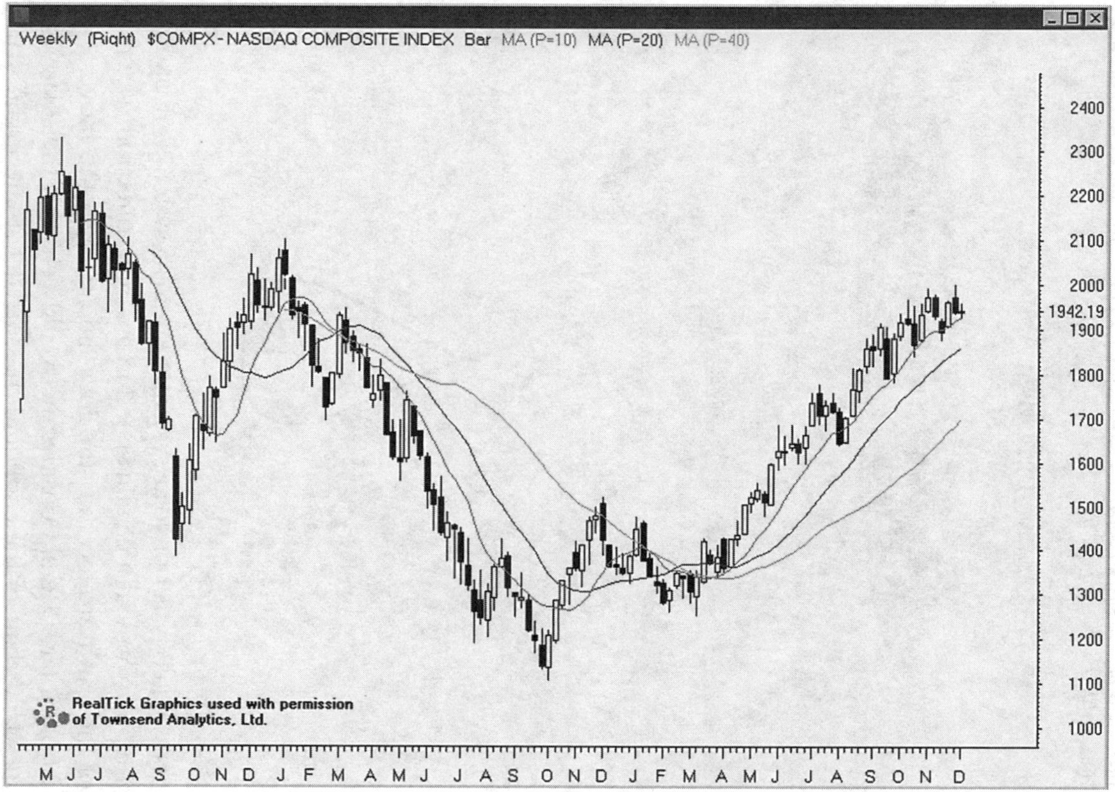
Weekly (Right) $COMPX - NASDAQ COMPOSITE INDEX Bar MA (P=10) MA (P=20) MA (P=40)
2400
2300
2200
2100
2000
1942.19
1900
1800
1700
1600
1500
1400
1300
1200
1100
1000
M J J A S O N D J F M A M J J A S O N D J F M A M J J A S O N D
RealTick Graphics used with permission
of Townsend Analytics, Ltd.

Composite Index—representing the overall solar system in the analogy. The trend of the broad market should be observed by both the trader and investor.

If you are in the market for a shorter period of time, then smaller movements are more carefully monitored. As a general rule, investors should pay more attention to daily and weekly charts while the active trader is more aware of the daily and hourly charts. Figure 12-3 shows a chart of the Nasdaq Composite on a daily timeframe. Notice how the right side of the weekly chart zooms in to the daily chart.

In Figure 12-4 the hourly chart of the Nasdaq Composite Index shows the smaller trends within the larger trend seen on the daily and weekly charts. Since the investor is concerned with the larger trend, the hourly chart will likely be too microscopic and prone to whipsaw volatility. Depending on your level of activity, such as the active trader, the hourly magnification can be amplified once more to see even more subtle trends in the market by viewing a 10-minute chart. See Figure 12-5.

The top down approach begins with getting a feel of the overall market by checking the technicals of the major indices. Keep in mind that this includes the S&P 500 as well, even though it's not used in the example. In fact, many professionals feel more amateurs are attracted to Nasdaq activity by comparison, but regardless, broad market focus is important. The next step is to take a look at market sectors. The market is divided up into many groups, or sectors, of similar stocks in a particular industry. The major indices contain different sectors. Looking at technicals of individual sectors gives you a behind-the-scenes look at what is influencing the overall market. One obvious example is the Nasdaq Composite Index. Many times this index is pulled higher or lower by a specific sector, such as semiconductors or biotechnology. There are many days when the semiconductor sector leads the entire Nasdaq Index. Even though many stocks may be seeing sizable losses, the strength of the semiconductor stocks can hold up the entire index as a whole. The reverse is true as well. If the semiconductor sector moves sharply lower, it can pull the Nasdaq into negative territory even when many other stocks in

FIGURE 12-3   *This is a daily chart of the Nasdaq Composite Index.*

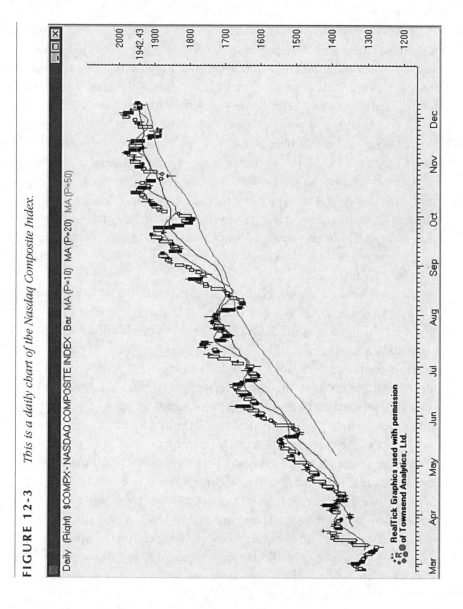

Daily (Right) $COMPX - NASDAQ COMPOSITE INDEX Bar MA (P=10) MA (P=20) MA (P=50)

RealTick Graphics used with permission
of Townsend Analytics, Ltd.

FIGURE 12-4 *This is an hourly chart of the Nasdaq Composite Index.*

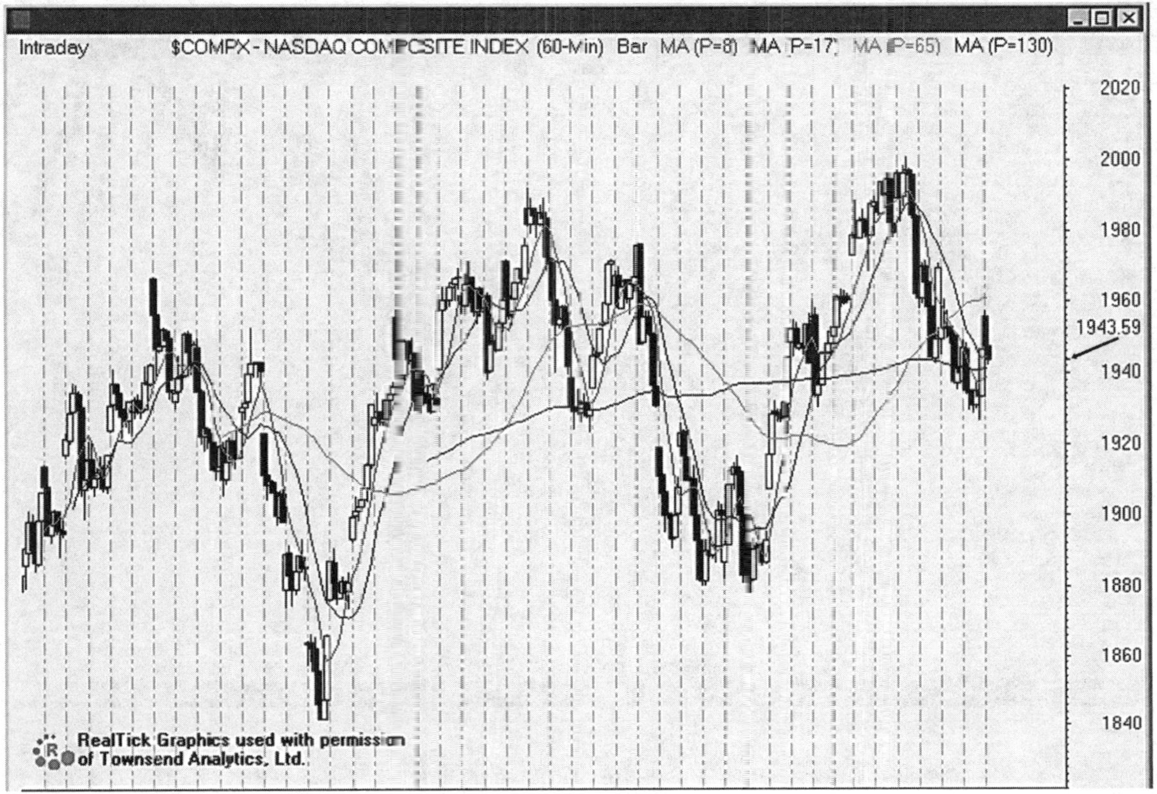
Intraday
$COMPX - NASDAQ COMPOSITE INDEX (60-Min) Bar MA (P=8) MA (P=17) MA (P=65) MA (P=130)
2020
2000
1980
1960
1943.59
1940
1920
1900
1880
1860
1840
RealTick Graphics used with permission of Townsend Analytics, Ltd.

FIGURE 12-5 *Here is a 10-minute chart of the Nasdaq Composite Index. Notice the trends within the trends.*

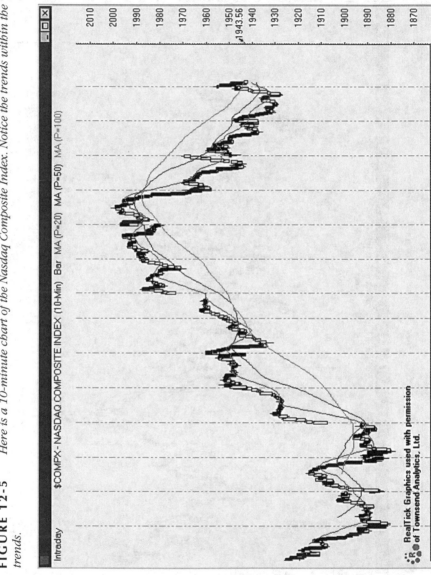

RealTick Graphics used with permission of Townsend Analytics, Ltd.

the Nasdaq show positive strength. How can you use this to your advantage? If you start your research and see that the overall market is in an uptrend, then you should research the individual sectors to find out which sectors are strong. If the overall market is moving higher, then a strong sector in a strong market will usually continue to be strong. If the overall market is strong, but there is weakness in a sector, then that weak sector would not be the place to look for long candidates. If you choose a long stock in an underperforming sector, then you are going against the market and limiting your edge. As with market indices, be sure to look at the charts of sectors on different timeframes. This way you can determine the long-term and short-term trends, which will allow you to better time your trade entries. Look to Figures 12-6 through 12-9 for a top-down example of the Semiconductor Index.

If you have a strong market and a strong sector, then you can look at the stocks within a sector to find stocks that would make good long candidates. This is when you can focus on the individual tree because you already know what the forest is doing. Be sure to note what stage singular stocks are in for both the long term and short term. If you like the hourly chart of a particular stock, check the longer-term daily chart so you know what the big picture is. A stock may look good in the near term, but if it is in a long-term stage 4 decline, it's a good idea to look for other candidates. This would not be the time to try and catch a falling knife. The ideal situation to look for when opening a long position is for the market indices and sector to be in an uptrend while the individual stock has pulled back into support. Many other scenarios exist, but the lesson is, "the trend is your friend."

An often overlooked metric of stock analysis to new participants is volume. Until experience is gained, I suggest trading stocks with a minimum daily volume of 500,000 shares a day. This will afford you liquidity to enter and exit positions without being subject to unreasonable price swings, called *Market Impact Cost*, or the cost of slippage. We will cover more on slippage in Chapter 13 when we discuss types of orders and proper entry and exit techniques.

The following is an example of using top-down analysis on the other side of the market. If the overall market were in the mature

FIGURE 12-6 *A weekly chart of the Semiconductor Index. Notice the overall trend of this sector.*

Weekly $SOXX - PHLX SEMICOND SECTOR INDEX   MA (P=10)   MA (P=20)   MA (P=40)

RealTick Graphics used with permission of Townsend Analytics, Ltd.

750
700
650
600
550
496.65
450
400
350
300
250
200
150

M J J A S O N D J F M A M J J A S O N D J F M A M J J A S O N D

FIGURE 12-7 *A daily chart of the Semiconductor Index. Note that the trends within the long-term trend are visible.*

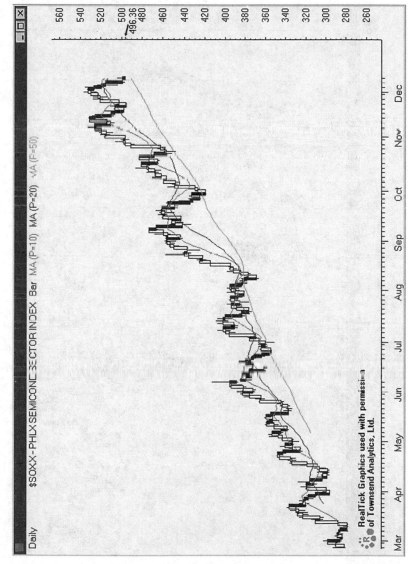

FIGURE 12-8 *An hourly chart of the Semiconductor Index.*

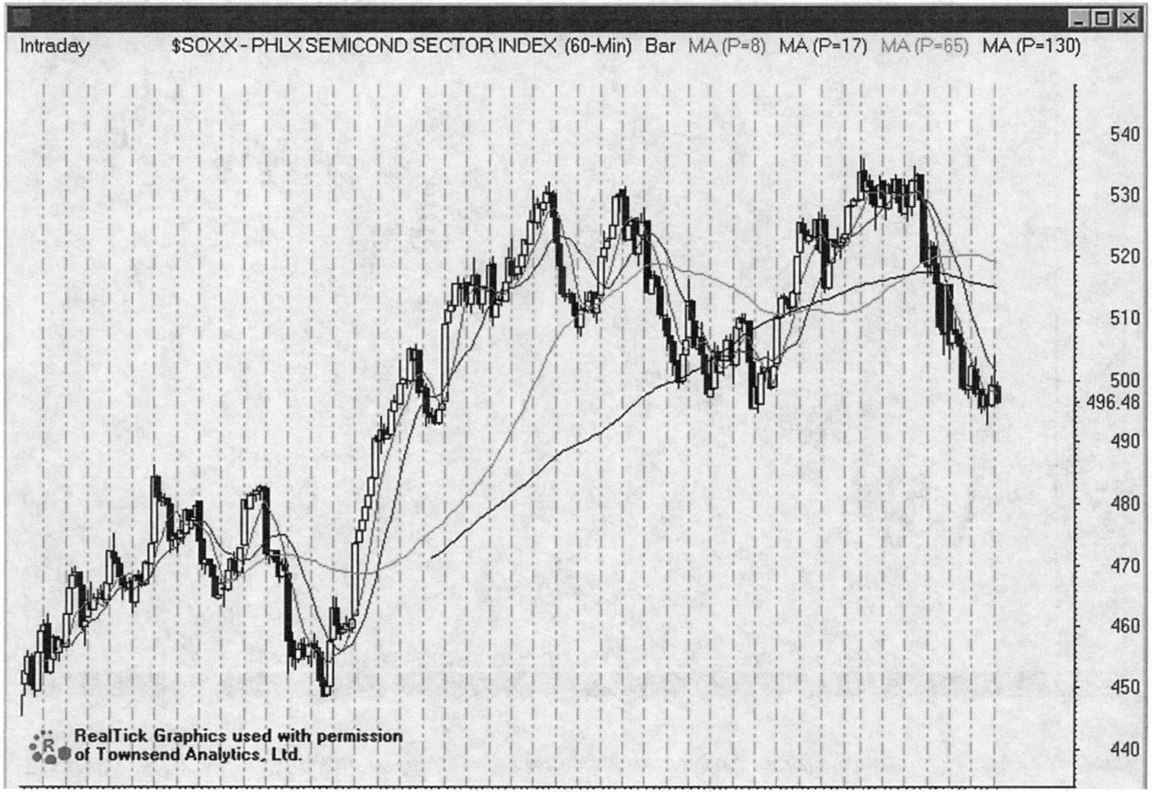
Intraday
$SOXX - PHLX SEMICOND SECTOR INDEX (60-Min) Bar MA (P=8) MA (P=17) MA (P=65) MA (P=130)
540
530
520
510
500
496.48
490
480
470
460
450
440
RealTick Graphics used with permission
of Townsend Analytics, Ltd.

FIGURE 12-9 *A 10-minute chart of the semiconductor sector. Notice that what looks like a pause in a strong uptrend on a weekly chart, looks like a four-stage cycle on a 10-minute chart.*

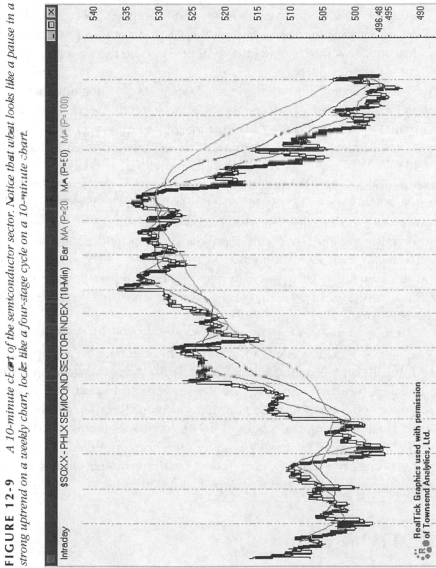

stages of three or early stage 4 decline, then the higher probability trade would be to the downside. Look for sectors that are weak, transitioning from a stage 3 distribution to a stage 4 decline. To improve the edge, also look for weak stocks within the weak sector to short. The same principles apply; trading with a primary trend as opposed to forcing a low percentage trade will prove to be the lowest risk and highest reward approach.

If the overall market trend suggests a stage 1 accumulation or stage 3 distribution pattern, there is no overall trend, therefore, consider sitting on your hands. As experience grows, you can go to the sector level and find a sector that looks strong or weak. If a particular sector looks strong, then find individual stocks to go long within the sector. On the other hand, if a sector looks weak, look for stocks to short within that sector. This kind of situation can be a time of opportunity, but risk factors are elevated. If the sectors look fairly neutral, you can then consider individual stocks, but once again, risk levels increase. At this point it becomes a market of stocks instead of a stock market. Essentially, stocks are doing their own thing, and the market is likely in stage 1 or 3. See Figures 12-10 through 12-13.

Once a stock meets all the technical criteria using top-down research, it is still prudent to consider the company's fundamental reports. If you are biased to the long side, look for the stock to have appealing fundamentals, such as: If you were an institutional participant, would the stock make your radar screen? In other words, buying a weak fundamental stock on strong technicals is still a bad idea, especially to an investor with a longer time horizon. Perhaps this scenario would not alarm a day trader, but day trading should come only after experience and developed discipline.

BOTTOM-UP

Bottom-up analysis is fundamental. It is the complete reverse of top-down analysis. Start with a stock or a company that you like and

FIGURE 12-10   *Notice the larger trend of XYZ, which is a stock within the semiconductor sector.*

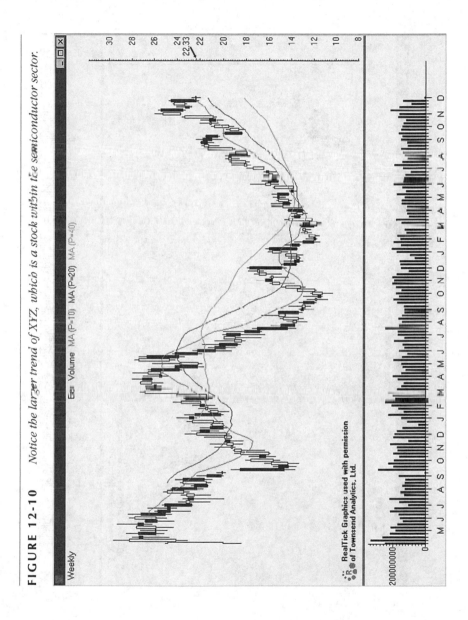

RealTick Graphics used with permission of Townsend Analytics, Ltd.

195

FIGURE 12-11 *A daily chart of stock XYZ, which is within the semiconductor sector.*

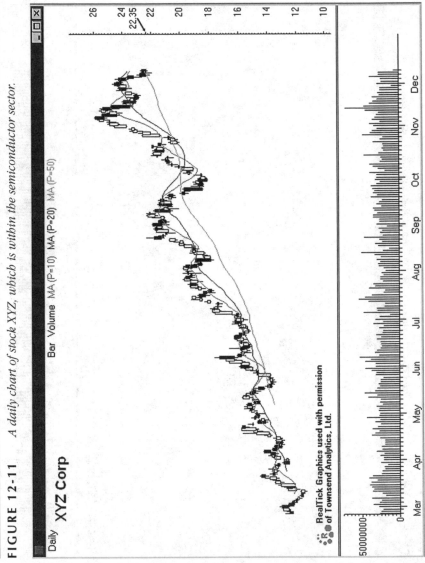

FIGURE 12-12 _An hourly chart of XYZ, which is within the semiconductor sector._

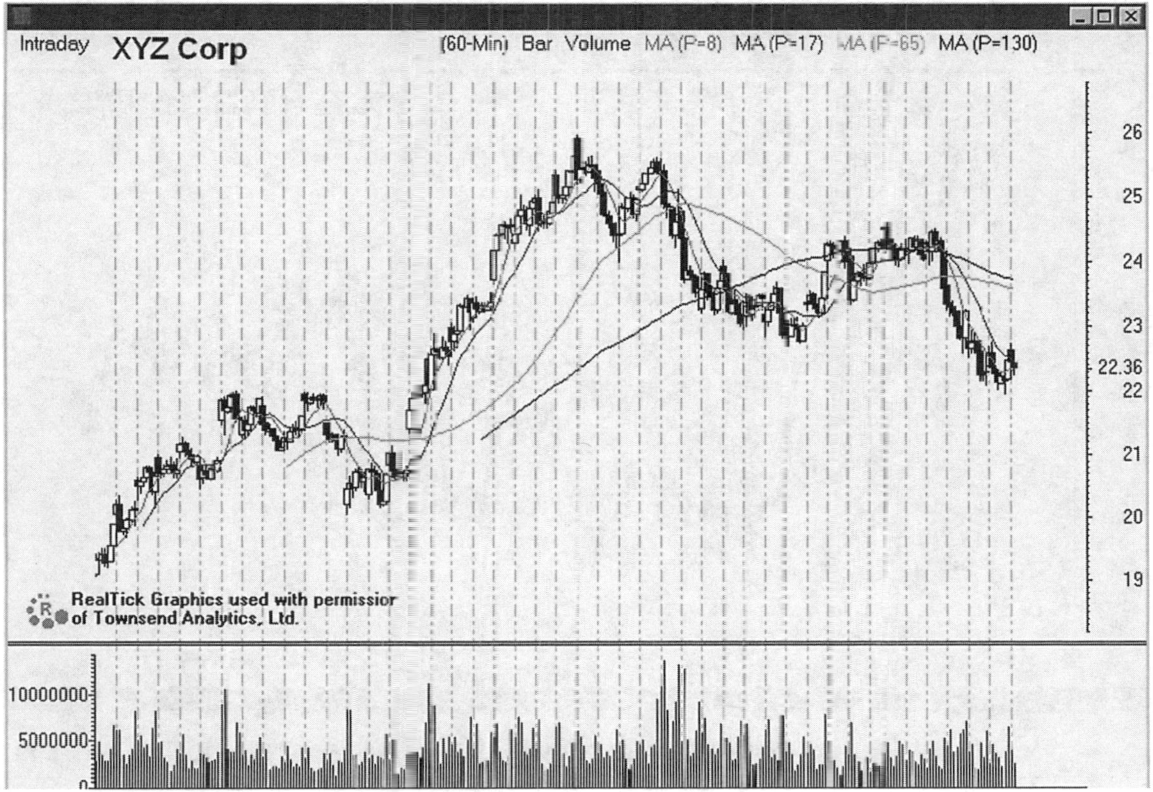

Intraday **XYZ Corp**

(60-Min) Bar Volume MA (P=8) MA (P=17) MA (P=65) MA (P=130)

RealTick Graphics used with permission
of Townsend Analytics, Ltd.

FIGURE 12-13 *A 10-minute chart of a particular semiconductor stock.*

research the fundamentals about it. Then look at the sector and the overall market condition. In other words, look at the tree branch, then the tree, and finally the forest. Mutual fund managers use this approach—they visit with the management of companies testing products, and find every bit of fundamental information they can find, before putting a dime into the company. This approach is more micro-focused on single stocks. It requires a careful research-oriented analysis. Many "half-baked" versions of bottom-up analysis enter the media and mediums of information (Web-portals, newspapers, television, chatrooms, etc.). The worst form of this information comes in the deadly stock tip, whereby a person hears partial information and, based on hope, passes on a tip to anyone who will listen or even pay for it in the form of chatroom prophesies. Remember, this is not your trade. It's someone else's trade and it is rarely profitable.

Other dangers to this approach appear when people find a company that they like based on a certain product, technology, or service they believe will sell well. This is bottom-up thinking. Be careful. This method can skew your judgment. Many people are lured into buying a low-priced, undiscovered stock they subjectively feel is fundamentally sound. If the fundamentals were that good, chances are the efficiency of the market would have already reflected it through price. This would be confirmed by the charts. In the absence of confirmation on the charts, the market likely knows something you don't. In other words, "if the market doesn't believe this stock," why should you? Keep in mind, the mutual fund industry has the best research money can buy. If they cannot consistently beat the S&P 500 using this approach, how will a generally less-educated, less-experienced, part-time fundamental analyst (the amateur) compete? Odds are they will not, as the statistics prove. Therefore, it is our opinion that this approach, used solely on its own merits, is inherently flawed.

DIRECTIONAL BIAS VERSUS NO BIAS

Every trade an investor or trader makes is influenced by bias. There are four kinds of bias—long, short, neutral, or volatility. The important thing is to form your bias on objective analysis, not opinion based on subjective inputs. From all perspectives of the overall market, sectors, or individual stocks, you will form a bias. No matter how hard you try to not have a subjective bias, it will exist. The best thing to hedge this inevitable opinion is to first recognize the bias exists and then test it against data on the charts. Bias can form many ways. For instance, if you have a strong opinion of a company based on macro events, such as the economy, or war for example, before jumping in and buying the defense stock it would be prudent to apply the top-down approach to confirm if the bias still exists. Perhaps your bias is shaped due to a call from your broker, who is pitching a stock. Before acting on any advice, it takes little time to filter the bias using the approach noted. This simple task reduces risk dramatically and takes a quantum leap toward being smart money.

The information contained in this book merely teaches you how to read the signs that the market gives us. So far, it has been a step-by-step plan to help you make good trade decisions. Inevitably, through experience you will also develop market bias based on gut instinct. This can be an invaluable sixth sense if you will, but regardless, you must always employ diligence and filter these impulses. The market goes through stages that can throw rationality out the window. At other times it can be perfectly rational. A market that is going through stage 2 markup and stage 4 decline can be very emotional. These emotional states can cause irrationally. Reading the signs (the four stages, moving averages, trends, and patterns) gives you a better understanding of the temperament of the market, and therefore better methods to temper your own emotional reactions. Many methods exist to help ease these emotional pangs, be it top-down analysis or other simple techniques. For example, a simple approach that I often employ is to clean out my entire portfolio—cover all trades and get liquid. This act forces me to see the stocks objectively again. If I still like the issue, I move into it again with very little frictional cost of commission given today's cost, affording me this little "acid test" whether or not I really want the trade. You would be surprised how many of those positions do not get re-opened.

The value of top-down analysis is that it applies to all tradable instruments and on all timeframes. There is a world of investment products that meet the demands of almost any participant, speculators, arbitrageurs, hedgers, investors, scalpers, day traders, trend traders, options, and futures traders. The product mix of liquid tradable instruments is enormous. Whichever product mix one decides to trade, the top-down approach applies. Let's now move to actionable trading with an understanding of orders. Action in the market requires the placing of orders in securities you choose to trade. Chapter 13 is an important chapter to discover how to act on your analysis like a professional. If you went to work for Goldman Sachs, before you ever pulled the trigger, you would first learn how to place the proper orders to find liquidity and avoid the unnecessary slippage and cost that hurt so many amateur traders and investors. This chapter can help save you thousands of dollars a year.

13

TACTICAL TRADING AND INVESTING

Now that you know how to begin researching the market as your own analyst, we must bring the analysis to the market through actual trading. There are many different investment vehicles and methods of execution that allow you to place yourself in the market in the direction of your bias. Regardless if your bias is long, short, neutral, or volatility, you must have a strong understanding of how to act on your analysis. The first step toward acquiring this skill is an understanding of order flow.

Order flow is defined as the routing process of orders from participants to destinations of execution. Traditionally, these destinations were strictly the physical exchanges and/or communication networks that only brokerage firms could access. In early 1994 this began to change, and by late 1996, technology and rule changes opened execution portals that changed traditional Wall Street forever. Yet most of the public have not embraced the quantum leaps forward the securities industry has enjoyed. Because most participants fear making their own decisions they still also rely on antiquated methods of execution. The twin-headed monster of biased market research from traditional firms and the methods in which they process order flow devours many apathetic investors. By understanding order flow, you learn how people are often manipulated, not just in terms of the release of market information but also actual order processing. That said, we explain how the so-called professionals (analysts, brokers, and market makers) have used customer order flow as a source of liquidity for which to trade against.

THE ROAD TO HELL IS PAVED WITH GOOD INTENTIONS

Many self-directed participants find that their good efforts toward research can be thwarted due to poor execution when using traditional means. But also remember, the road to the market is paved with bad intentions as well. The path your orders take are numerous, as is the flow of institutional orders, but the common variable stands—if you want to find the corruption, follow the money! Let's begin with the individual participant—the dumb money—and first understand where that term came from. It was given to us from Wall Street Insiders and "upstairs" executives who run the Wall Street firms. They're called upstairs executives because every runner and clerk on the exchange floor wants to graduate up to being a trader on the floor. If they accomplish that, the trader targets their sights upstairs at the executive offices where the firm's decisions are made. "Poor man wants to be rich, rich man wants to be king, and the king ain't satisfied 'til he rules every thing," sung Bruce Springsteen in his song "Badlands."

The first rule learned regardless of whether you clerked or ran the firm from upstairs was to trade the public's order flow. In other words, the entire system of floor trading was predisposed to "fading" the public's orders. The entire system is fed from the research of these firms—from the analyst ratings, to the brokers who pitched the story to drive public reaction and orders to the exchanges. The liquidity the public provides is met with the professionals' contra reaction (fading). When the public buys on greed and recommendations, the floor traders and market makers sell. When they sell on fear, they are ready to buy up all the misery and capitulation. What a racket! To finish you off, they laugh about us among their peers at the bar, calling us dumb money! This fact alone has been my greatest motivation to help change Wall Street.

Prior to electronic direct access or in the absence of using it, when you called in your stock orders to brokerage firms, your order went through a variety of potential routes. The orders either go through the hands of the specialist who trades listed stocks on the New York Stock Exchange or other regional exchanges across the nation or through the hands of Nasdaq market makers. Both are paid sharks who get paid to eat you. These participants rely on their research and analyst departments to cause the public reaction, but once the frenzy starts and orders flow, they use every advantage to make money on your orders. To help the process, they rely on the amateur to use different types of orders to misguide their intentions, relying on the fact that most participants don't understand the monopoly they have guarded for over 200 years.

Tactically, the specialist and market maker want orders during times of volatility and excitement because price swings are exacerbated due to emotion. The range or elasticity of these swings is where they get you. The "market order on open" is a classic winner during these times. Unless used properly, this type of order is an amateur trade that generally occurs as a reaction to news. The market loves the combination of volatility and unprotected orders which feeds the sharks. If you feed them market orders, they will execute your trades at the lows during sell-offs and highs during rallies. When the public gets excited about trading, the specialist and market makers sell greed at highs and buy fear at lows, expecting and influencing a quick correction in their favor. This inefficient price execution is often referred to as *slippage*, and it costs the pubic billions of dollars every year.

SLIPPAGE CAN DESTROY ANALYSIS

The reasoning is simple—with excessive slippage, the risk/reward parameters determined through the analysis must mirror the actual execution of your trades, otherwise the parameters of risk and reward change. The solution is to control the order just as you control the analysis. When you allow the professionals to control the order or your emotions, the result is the same. You slip farther down the market's food chain. To act on analysis, you must also become your own order desk. The goal is to enter the position as close to the desired price as possible and in a timely fashion. This can almost always be accomplished by using aggressively or passively placed limit orders.

AGGRESSIVE ORDERS

When trading there are times when you want to enter/exit a position quickly and you don't mind "lifting the offer" or "hitting the bid." This vernacular simply describes buying what is offered at a given price and selling at a given bid price, respectively. These orders tend to be more aggressive since you are taking liquidity from the market. Orders that take buyers and sellers from the market remove liquidity. Orders placed in the market that are away from the current price where the security is trading add liquidity. For example, if XYZ is *bid* at $25 (those willing to buy) and *offered* at $25.05 (shares offered for sale), the difference between them is the *spread*. If you place a lower bid to buy or a higher offer to sell shares at that moment, your prices are *away* from the current market and *adding* liquidity to the market. Conversely, given the same market condition, if you buy the shares offered at $25.05 or sell shares bid at $25, you are *removing* liquidity. As an aggressive order, you take liquidity, while a passive order adds to it. The decision on which approach to take depends on your motivation to make the trade at that moment in time as well as the type of order you will use. Sometimes you want to be aggressive entering positions such as when you buy breakouts past resistance or sell breakdowns through support. For example a security has been range bound for a while and is consolidating near a resistance level. Then volume flares up and you anticipate that it is about to break out of the price range to the upside. As the analyst in this example, you decide to buy the first-up tick-in price above resistance, believing once this occurs that prices will accelerate higher on strong velocity (demand over supply). Under these circumstances you need to be aggressive and *lift the offer,* to avoid chasing the security as the market moves higher. The same reasoning holds true for breakdowns at support levels. The act of chasing a security in one direction or another is what we briefly introduced last chapter as a market impact cost (MIC)—a cost most of us have experienced. MIC is the cost of poor prices when entering and exiting positions. Industry research shows that MICs are on average 10 times more expensive than commissions! Here is a simple example of the MIC. Your analysis shows that you want to own 1000 shares of XYZ as soon as it trades above resistance at $25.25. It trades $25.26 and suddenly the market gets very fast and the price starts to rally quickly. You send an order with no price parameters or protection (market order) and shares are filled at $25.40. You just experienced a MIC of $140 ($.14 × 1000 assuming you could have bought the shares at $25.26). The commission on the trade may have cost $10.00. Obviously the MIC was far more expensive, and some market maker who received your order likely made most of the $.14 in slippage. Fourteen cents sounds like only a little money, but over the course of a year for even the semi-active trader or investor, these costs can become huge and have immediate impact on your analysis, confidence, and profitability. These are precisely the costs that specialists and market makers make a very good living on. The reality is, they are not any smarter than you are, they simply give that illusion by stacking the odds in their favor, not unlike a casino. The question is, are you willing to play their game or yours?

When exiting trades there are also times you want to place aggressive orders as well. A good example is when your limit for risk has been met (protective stop) and you come to the conclusion that you are wrong in the trade. You must limit your loss by just getting out of the trade, and using an aggressive order is the fastest way to do it. It comes down to the fact that being aggressive in fast-moving markets increases your chances of actually getting your order filled at your defined price. This won't occur by accident or luck, only through the skill that develops by becoming your own order desk and analyst.

PASSIVE ORDERS

There are situations when you may want to enter/exit a position only at a certain price, which is the *away* market price. The orders placed in these situations are called *passive orders*. When the need is not there to be aggressive, you typically place passive orders in order to get a fill closer to your desired entry/exit point based on your predetermined analysis. When trading relatively illiquid stocks, for example, you may not want to pay the spread or move the market due to its thinly traded nature. Other reasons for passive orders could include placing resting orders to buy at support and sell orders at resistance. Regardless of the analysis behind the reasoning, passive orders have their place in the market as well. This type of order is used more often by the investor who expects the market to meet their price at some point in the day. The limit order is the most common order for passive orders. The limit order introduces price into the order equation and indicates the price at which you are willing to trade. This order can be either passive or aggressive. If XYZ is trading at $25.50 at the present time and you place a limit order to buy the stock with a limit of $25.40, then the order is passive and you will only be filled if the market retraces to that limit price. If you bid $25.61 (above the market) you are aggressive and will buy any shares available, starting at $25.60, but no greater than $25.61. Even if suddenly stock became offered at $25.45, the limit order affords you price improvement. This assumes once again you are not giving the order to a market maker who has an incentive to fill you at the worst possible price. In both examples, you gain limit order protection in price. This is why technology of direct access is vital. The ability to control the route of the order directly to the exchange is the central theme of taking control of all orders, regardless if they are aggressive or passive.

STOP ORDERS

One of the most important types of orders is the stop order, which is an order to enter or exit a position if a transaction occurs at a certain price. For example, if you are long and the stock trades below a certain price level specified in the stop order, an order goes out to sell your stock. When you short a stock, a stop order is an order to buy the stock back if the price goes above a certain specified price level.

There are three major types of stop orders, the first of which is the *protective stop*. The protective stop should be placed as soon as you take a position. It defines the maximum risk you are willing to tolerate in the trade. Before entering a position you need to have a price level in your mind where you will get out if the trade goes against you. This level is the protective stop. Protective stops will keep your losses small and predefine risk. The protective stop should never be moved. Many undisciplined traders and investors move their stops in order to give them more room, but this changes the original risk/reward equation and therefore the analysis. For obvious reasons, this is a poor practice.

The second type of stop order is the *technical stop*. The technical stop uses technical analysis, i.e. psychology, to help place a stop that will ensure profits. Once the trade turns profitable in the long situation, place the stop just below levels of potential support. As the stock continues to make higher highs and higher lows, keep raising the stop so it is just under the low in each successive higher low. If the stock breaks its uptrend by making a lower low, the stop will trigger and the trade will be exited. Once a profitable level is reached when trading from the short side, place the stop just above each lower high as the trend makes lower lows and lower highs. When the stock breaks its trend by making a higher high, you will be stopped out. By placing stops in this way, you will never be stopped out at the very high or very low of a move. Amateur participants generally lose. Experienced participants are content to take the middle third out of a move. The technical stop doesn't let a winner turn into a loser. There are many investors who buy stocks and become very profitable in their trade only to watch their profits turn into losses as the stock price falls back down. The technical stop prevents this situation.

The third type of stop is called the *trailing stop*. There are times when stocks move with a high velocity in a short amount of time. At these exciting times when you are on the right side of the trade it can be very difficult to know exactly when to exit the trade. The trailing stop is a stop that trails the price of a stock by a specified amount. In a long example, if a stock is moving upward rapidly, then a trailing stop can be placed to trail the price by a specified amount—let's say by $0.20. As the stock trades higher, the trailing stop will automatically trail the stock higher staying $0.20 below the price. When the stock starts to pull back, the trailing stop remains at the highest level it got to. In the long example the trailing stop only moves higher if the stock moves higher. It never moves lower. This stop is effective for high velocity trades where it is difficult to place technical stops. The trailing stop ensures that the winning trade will not turn into a losing trade, assuming you enter it with less desecration ($.20) than current profitability in the trade. Like the technical stop, the nature of the trailing stop ensures that you will never sell at the exact top or buy at the exact bottom, but it does give you a chance to participate in the overall move. The different stops work in a variety of situations but the most important point is to use a stop.

INSTITUTIONAL ORDER FLOW

The institutional order flow we are referring to is on mutual funds, pension funds, banks, hedge funds, and other buy-side firms that manage large sums of money. We are not referring to sell-side firms that provide services such as traditional Wall Street brokerage firms. Institutions moving many shares through the market also are subjected to order handling manipulations from sell-side firms who execute trades for them.

For example, when a fund wants to do large share transactions, they often give the order to sell-side firms with market making and sales trading operations who execute trades. They have traders and relationships on the floors of major exchanges as well as market making operations for electronic markets. Through the process, these funds recognize they have so much size to trade that they can easily move the market even in the biggest name stocks. The sales trader's job is to work the order to avoid as much detection as possible in terms of order intentions and size. This means that a fund wanting to sell one million shares of IBM would not want to announce its intentions to the market anymore than you would announce to the local poker game that you need kings! The sales trader is then charged with ridding the fund of the million lot with minimal market impact. In doing so, the sales trader will be given latitude to work off the position for the fund. Let's use a $2 discretion as an example, meaning they are "not held" for $2 under the current market. *Not held* means not held responsible for prices within $2 of the current market during the act of offing a million shares. The sales trader then has a tremendous incentive to impress the fund by doing better so he gets future orders. This is the theory. But through the process, the sales trader is also expected to make a profit for the firm he works for as well as himself. They can do so by acting as a broker and/or a dealer, meaning they can charge a fee for the service of selling the shares (acting as broker), while also in a position to buy shares from the fund (acting as dealer), with hopes of then selling the shares to public buyers at higher prices. The sales trader, acting in either broker or dealer capacity (and sometimes both), has the same interest to make money from the institutional fund as he does from the individual, but with bigger size. Regardless of who the client is, order flow is the name of their game, and order flow is profitable to them.

While much more can be said about the techniques used by traditional firms to make money on order flow, sales traders, specialists, and market makers are not your friends. Receiving order flow, big and small, is the lowest risk form of trading there is, and this is why I would never send my order flow to a shark who gets paid to eat me.

Technology provides every reason not to send orders to the market via phone or to professionals who want your orders. It is also important to note that many firms, including online trading firms, still route orders to market making operations through the guise of technology, whereby the applications which you use to enter the trades act merely as transport vehicles to these market making operations. It is important to ask the firms with which you trade if they are true direct access firms and if they in fact sell or route order flow to trading desks and operations. If they do, move your account!

SINGLE SOURCE LIQUIDITY INVESTMENT VEHICLES

One method to reduce order flow manipulations while also trading the broad market is to use products with single source liquidity where no human intervention is present. The E-Mini futures products offer such a product and work well for the analysis we have taught thus far. Before discussing the products in detail, let's first explore the nature of futures contracts.

FUTURES

Futures are standardized, transferable, exchange-traded contracts that require the delivery of a commodity like a bond currency or stock index, at a specified price at a specific date in the future. Unlike options, futures convey an obligation on both parties to the contract. The risk pattern is very close to that of owning stocks. Futures contracts can be tracked back to the twelfth century when wheat futures were traded in England. At certain times of the year, the market was overwhelmed by an excess supply of wheat. At other times, there wasn't enough wheat to go around. By paying farmers in advance for future delivery, it helped smooth out imbalances in the supply and demand.

In the U.S., commodities (grain) futures started trading actively in 1848 when the Chicago Board of Trade (CBOT) was established. During the 1970s there was an explosive growth in futures trading activity when futures on financial instruments began trading in Chicago. Since then, futures have been introduced on interest rate instruments, stock market indexes, and more recently, on singular stocks. There are many other futures products available on underlying instruments, but for our purposes, we will focus on stock index futures.

Index futures were introduced in 1982 by the Chicago Mercantile Exchange (CME). Since their inception, the popularity of index futures has grown exponentially. Index futures are futures contracts based on an underlying index. As the basket of stocks that make up the index move upward or downward in price, the index futures respond likewise. If you want to trade the fluctuations in the overall market, index futures are an ideal instrument. You can be positioned long or short on these contracts based on your anticipation of what the underlying index will do. Index futures allow you to trade one instrument, instead of trading the whole basket of stocks individually, cutting down on the commission costs and the hassle. Some of the more popular indices that have derivative futures products are the S&P 500 Index, the Nasdaq 100 Index, and the Dow Jones Industrial Average.

Why should you trade equity derivative futures? To begin with, futures have the same risk profiles as stocks. If you are long and the price goes up, then you make money. If prices decline, you lose money--very simple. Vice versa with a short. Remember, investing in futures means separating the pricing of the stock from the time when you actually buy and sell it. At the time you put on your position, you are not actually buying or selling any stock—you are merely controlling it. Since you are only renting the contract, you are only required to post a sum called the *initial margin*, which provides the assurance you can meet your obligations if the position goes against you. Most of the time you will be trading on margin when trading futures. This initial margin can be as low as 10 percent, but many brokerage firms require a larger percentage due to their own risk toler-ances. The small margin required to trade equity derivatives can be your best friend or your worst enemy. The margin enables you to take large position sizes with less money than would be required by purchasing the stock outright. This can amplify both gains and losses. If you are fully leveraged and don't use good risk manage-ment, you can lose more than your initial margin deposit.

Another difference between trading stocks and their derivative counterparts is that unlike stock trading, futures don't require an up-tick to allow you to get short. This is a nice benefit when trying to short a stock that is already moving lower. Without an up-tick bid to deal with, you can immediately get short in the futures market by hitting the bid.

An added benefit to trading futures is that gains on equity derivatives (futures) are taxed differently than regular securities. Index futures contracts are taxed at a blend of 60 percent long-term and 40 percent short-term capital gains rates, regardless of your holding period. If large gains are realized in a short amount of time, then the tax savings from trading futures can be substantial over the short-term stock trader who is taxed at their normal income tax rate. This tax advantage is not realized by single stock futures traders because they are taxed the same as securities.

Finally, it is important to note that futures trading is a zero-sum game. Unlike the underlying securities which have a defined number of shares available to trade (the float), futures have no set number, but they do have a fixed lifespan. In the futures market, the number of long contracts outstanding minus the number of short contracts is equal to zero. This means that when you go long in the futures market, someone is short. In futures, when someone makes money, someone consequently loses money. Much more can be said about the general futures market, and classes are available to help understand our strategies, but knowing that a product exists to trade in an entire index without any human intervention suggests strongly that traditional Wall Street has changed forever (and for the better).

E-MINI S&P CONTRACT

The E-Mini class of futures contracts was introduced on the CME's GLOBEX trading platform by way of the E-Mini S&P 500. It was the first futures contract designed specifically for online trading and the first electronically traded stock-index contract. The term *E-Mini* applies generically to contracts that have been specifically tailored for electronic trading. The *E* stands for electronic and *Mini* stands for contracts downsized to the needs of a diverse global market. Because E contracts are typically smaller than their pit-traded counterparts, they tend to attract a wider following, which effectively increases the depth and liquidity of the markets.

In the case of the E-Mini S&P 500, the contract is one-fifth the size of the regular S&P 500 futures contract. This evidently was an ideal size since the product has been a huge success and now ranks as one of the most heavily traded futures contracts on earth.

Being one-fifth the size of the pit-traded contract ($50 per point vs. $250), the E-Mini S&P 500 (trading symbol = ES) contract has attracted a large audience that clearly appreciates the scaling of the contract for relatively small traders. Fluctuations are in 0.25-point increments (minimum tick), meaning that if the E-Mini contract ticks from 800.00 to 800.25, the holder of a single contract will have made $12.50.

WHO TRADES THE E-MINI S&P CONTRACT?

A diverse group of participants have gravitated toward the E-Mini, including hedgers and speculators, with the former seeking to minimize and manage price risk of an underlying product and the latter seeking to trade futures for profit. With the business environment continuing to evolve toward globalization and greater complexity, the use of futures has become a necessity for many business models. Traders and investors alike appreciate the single electronic source of execution that the E-Mini products provide, while eliminating the possibility of manipulation of order flow. Other E-Mini products track and include the Nasdaq 100 (NQ) and the Dow (YM), available for review at www.cme.com and www.cbot.com, respectively.

14

PAY RAISES BECOME EFFECTIVE WHEN YOU DO

APPLYING WHAT YOU HAVE LEARNED

The techniques mentioned thus far are timeless methods for consistent profitability. Transforming theory into practice can be a challenge, but realize these techniques are not theory—they only appear to be because you have yet to apply them. The challenge is to remain disciplined to the system and not let emotion take control. This will only come from time and experience. These are aspects of the market that can only be learned by participating. The following example will apply much of what has been learned to this point and explain how to apply your newfound knowledge.

Searching for suitable securities can be a time-consuming process, but it becomes more intuitive after you give it some practice. Just remember, when finding candidates to invest in for a longer period of time, you want to look at the big picture first—top-down.

The first step is to analyze a long-term chart of the overall market. This allows you to see the trend of the market and where it has come from. Figure 14-1 shows a weekly chart of the broad market S&P 500 Index.

FIGURE 14-1 *The S&P 500 Index on a weekly timeframe.*

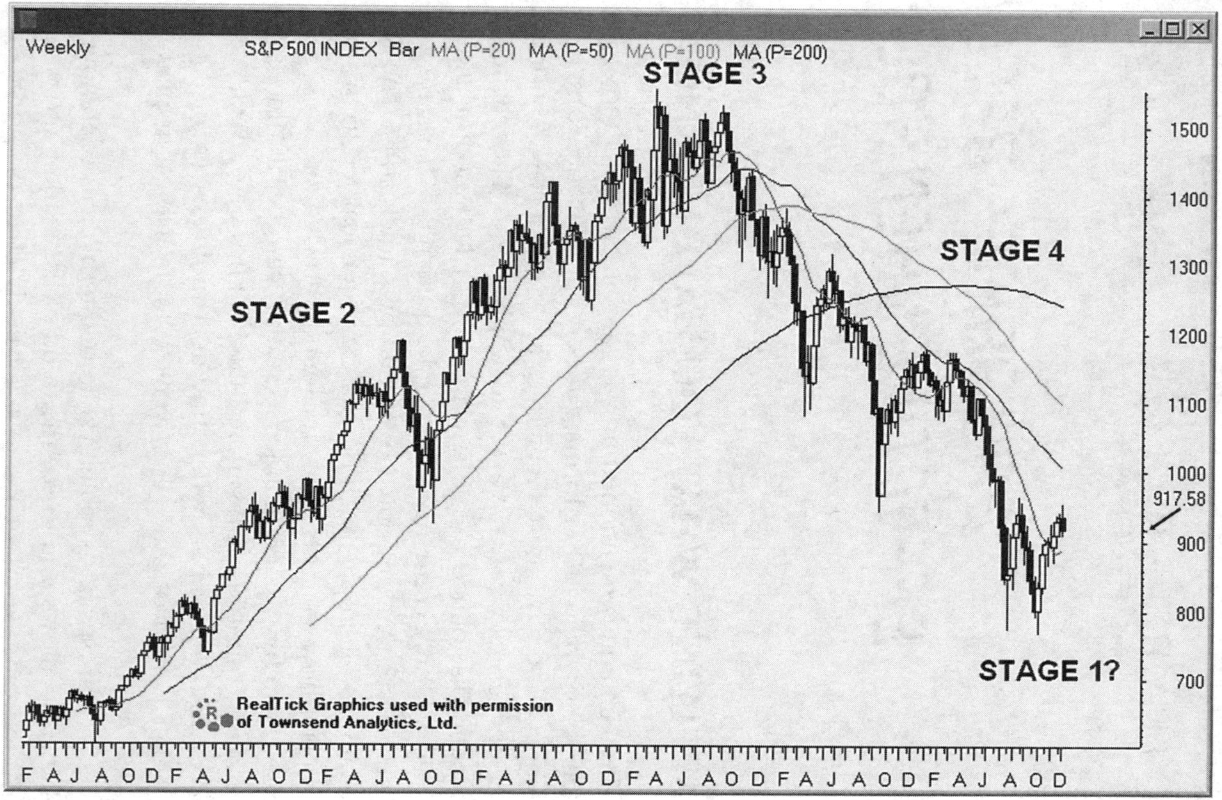

216

In analyzing the overall market, we want to identify what stage the market is in currently as well as the previous stage it came from. Refer to Figure 14-1, and know that each candle represents one week worth of trading data. Although stage analysis can be a form of art, on longer-term timeframes, the stages are typically easily identified. The MAs allow you to easily identify the trend. In Figure 14-1, stage 2 markup, stage 3 distribution, and stage 4 decline are fairly obvious. On the far right of the chart, known as the "hard right edge," we have the present moment and the purpose of our analysis. What is the probable next leg for the market? When you are doing your analysis, take note that the broad market is still in a stage 4 decline but may be beginning to base, developing the start of stage 1 accumulation. Keep in mind, opinions are expensive to harbor, so this has yet to be confirmed. That is why the stage 1 on the right side of the screen had a question mark next to it. The larger picture you should see is that the overall broad market had a huge run-up (stage 2 area), then went sideways (stage 3), and ultimately declined and lost over three-fourths of the gains established in stage 2.

As we now focus on the hard right edge (see Figure 14-2), we notice the two weekly elastic lows (tails) that find support at approximately the same level, yet the candles indicate that the bears do not close the week on a lower low. This calls the stage 4 downtrend into question. The fact that the sellers couldn't push the index significantly lower indicates that the sellers are becoming weaker and the buyers are beginning to gain strength. As buyers gain strength, your attention to a potential stage 1 accumulation period may be near. Although all the MAs are moving lower, the 20-week MA is showing the first signs of a change in trend by beginning to move higher. This long-term weekly chart gives you the long-term bias and trend of the overall market. Remember, history repeats time and again represented by the cyclical nature of markets.

With this potential development upon us, we must filter our early subjective views of potential stage 1 accumulation by now focusing on various market segments—the next step in top-down analysis. By reviewing the shorter-term chart of the Nasdaq Composite Index, we

FIGURE 14-2 *Notice how the S&P 500 gave back most of the gains it made during its run-up. Also pointed out are the elastic lows near the hard right edge.*

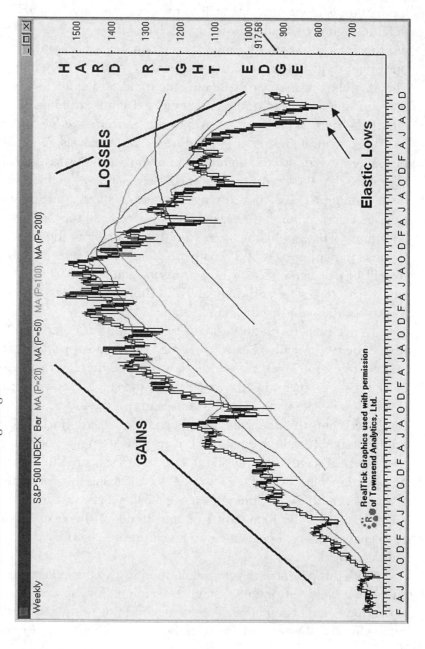

218

review a heavier technology weighted index than the overall market as seen through the S&P 500 in Figures 14-1 and 14-2. Figure 14-3 illustrates a daily chart of the Nasdaq. Though not a sector, it consists of many high-tech stocks that often lead the entire market higher due to its higher beta.

Figure 14-3 shows approximately 1500 days worth of data. When comparing the Nasdaq Composite Index to the weekly chart of the S&P 500 Index, note that the Nasdaq looks like it has progressed farther toward a stage 1 accumulation phase. The Nasdaq has a stronger looking chart at this time. This is important to note because if the over all market begins moving higher, you would expect the Nasdaq to exhibit more powerful upward strength (beta) since it appears to be in a more mature basing pattern of stage 1 accumulation.

After looking at the broad market and Nasdaq on the long-term timeframe, take a look and see what's happening on a shorter time-frame. Figure 14-4 illustrates a shorter-term daily chart of the Nasdaq Composite Index.

The daily chart of the Nasdaq in Figure 14-4 gives you a closer look at what the more recent trend of the market is. It clearly illus-trates that the index has mellowed out its decline in the stage 4 area, and it now appears to be drifting sideways. Also note that on the hard right edge, the index made a higher high from the prior high as shown at the 20 period moving average. This confirms what we saw on the weekly S&P chart in Figure 14-2 where the later stages of stage 4 illustrated the potential transition to stage 1. Remember, the S&P 500 failed to make the lower low, indicating the bulls are gain-ing strength. Couple that with Figure 14-4, and it indicates that there was a break in the recent downtrend, represented by a higher high. These are two strong clues that confirm the same bullish bias. You already know that the broad market looks like it is basing into a stage 1, and the Nasdaq looks even stronger since it is already based and now showing signs of potential breakout. It would be reason-able to expect that if a move higher for the overall market occurred, it would be led by the Nasdaq Composite Index. There-fore, we can take many steps, but the lowest risk approach would

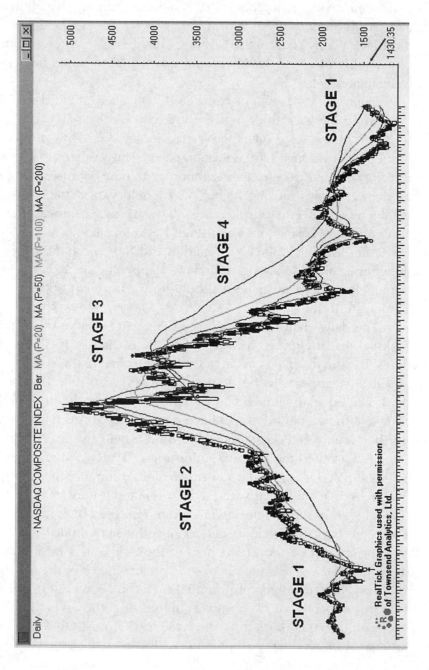

FIGURE 14-3 *A long-term daily chart of the Nasdaq Composite Index.*

220

FIGURE 14-4 *A daily chart of the Nasdaq Composite index showing approximately 600 days worth of trading data.*

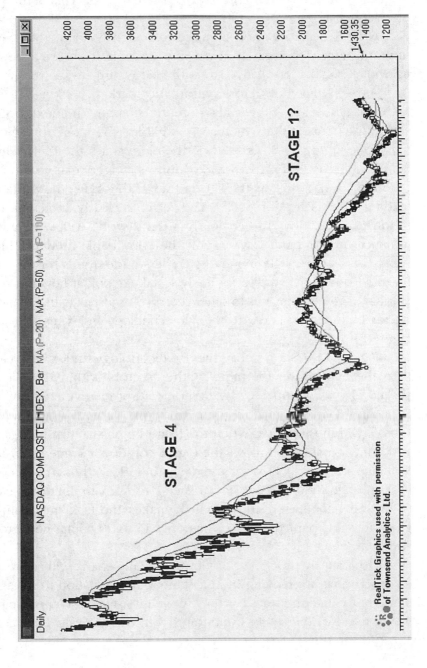

Daily

NASDAQ COMPOSITE INDEX Bar MA (P=20) MA (P=50) MA (P=100)

STAGE 4

STAGE 1?

4200
4000
3800
3600
3400
3200
3000
2800
2600
2400
2200
2000
1800
1600
1430.35
1400
1200

RealTick Graphics used with permission of Townsend Analytics, Ltd.

be to narrow the search criteria to Nasdaq stocks. This is the path of least resistance.

Now that the decision is made to search Nasdaq stocks, continue to narrow the search down into tradable ideas by reviewing individual sectors for relative strength. See Figure 14-5.

As we scan the sectors within the market, it is easy to see technology is leading the bulls' potential charge. The next thought should be figuring out which sectors exhibit the most upside elasticity. See Figure 14-5. As seen on the daily chart, the Philadelphia Semiconductor Index (SOX.X) exhibits stronger relative strength than the Nasdaq. Just as the Nasdaq leads the S&Ps, the Semis are leading the Nasdaq Composite. The sector is clearly attracting institutional money flow and is clearly a trend worth following at this juncture. Ask a bank robber why he robs banks and his likely reply is—it's where the money is! Traders trade trends for the same reason! To complete the sector analysis, take a look at how the Semiconductor Index compares to other sectors. For instance, the Semiconductor Index is compared to the Biotechnology Index, as shown in Figure 14-6.

Figure 14-6 shows that the Biotechnology Index is weaker than the Semiconductor Index. Other sectors within the Nasdaq should also be compared. By demonstrating relative strength, the Semiconductors should continue to show strength leading most sectors within the index, when the trend begins to turn higher.

The task at hand follows the logical top-down sequence of next looking for individual stock candidates to trade. Although you could look through thousands of stocks each day, we can limit our search to just Semiconductor stocks, which makes the task quite simple, given that this particular sector has only 15 to 20 component stocks within it.

From an investor point of view, the daily charts will serve well for stocks that are moving from a stage 1 accumulation to a stage 2 markup. By entering stocks as they move into stage 2, you participate in the trend of the stock. Continuing with the analysis, look at the stock featured in Figure 14-7.

FIGURE 14-5 Note the relative strength of the Semiconductor Index compared to the Nasdaq Composite Index.

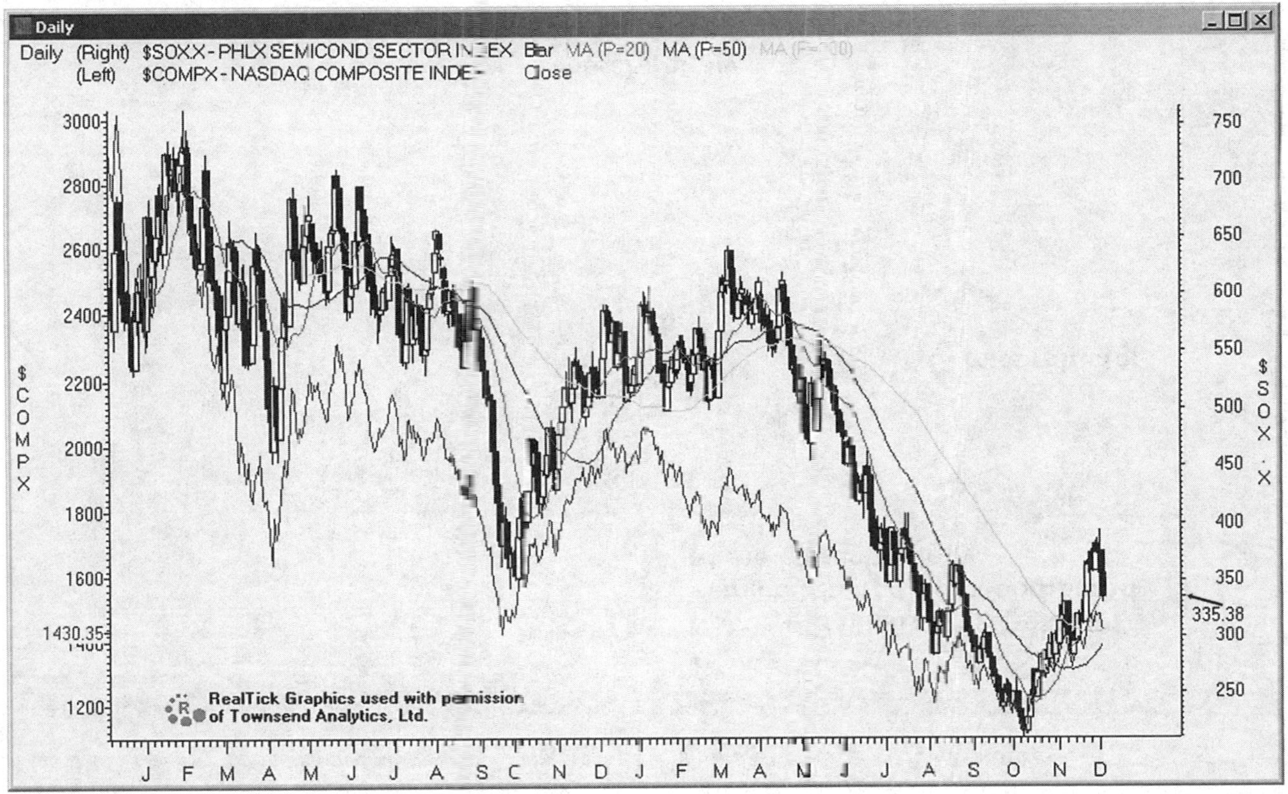

FIGURE 14-6 *Upon examining several sectors, notice the relative strength of the Semiconductor.*

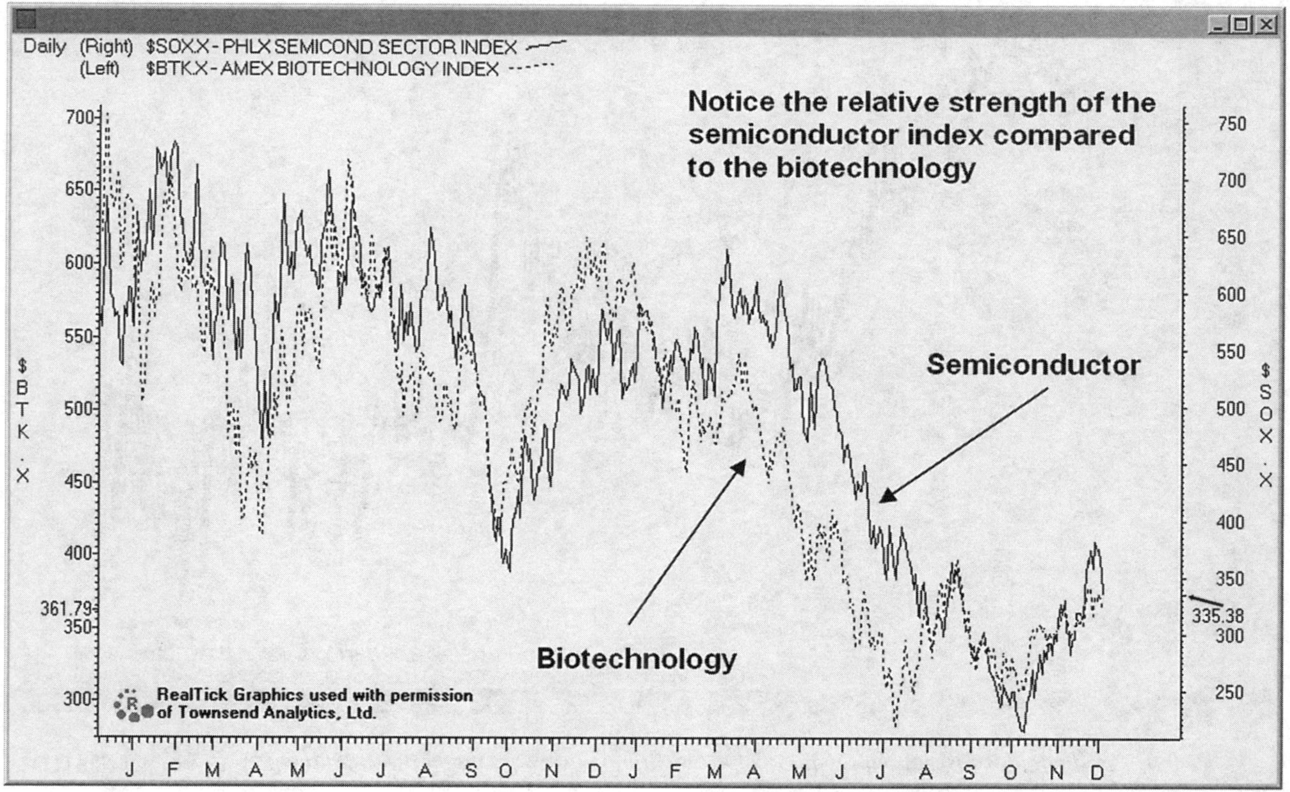

FIGURE 14-7 *A daily chart of a component stock within the sector that had been basing and broke out of the range on above average volume.*

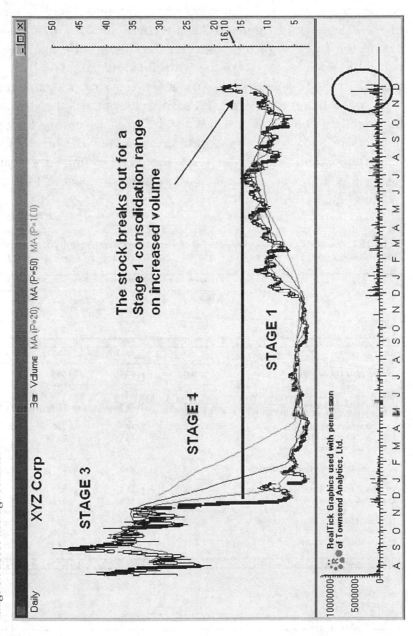

Armed with a picture of the overall market, you now want to go long a Nasdaq stock that looks to be entering a stage 2 markup phase. The stock in Figure 14-7 is a technology stock that has been basing for a period of time. Several days before the analysis took place, the stock broke out of the consolidations range on heavy volume. The catalysts for the breakout were a strong sector, money flow, and a better than expected earnings report. As the stock pulls back on light volume, it provides an ideal place to enter a long position, but prior to doing so it is prudent to review the fundamentals.

The fundamentals for the stock should be examined so that you know how it appears to the institutional investor. Figure 14-8 shows the 10-Q quarterly report for the XYZ Corp.

FIGURE 14-8   *The 10-Q report for the stock featured in the present example. This information was found on the SEC Web site. (Courtesy of www.sec.gov.)*

	Three Months Ended		Six Months Ended	
	October 31, 2002	October 31, 2001	October 31, 2002	October 31, 2001
Revenues......................	$ 21,743	$ 12,265	$ 38,533	$ 23,426
Cost of revenues*..............	13,063	7,591	23,337	13,724
Gross profit...................	8,680	4,674	15,196	9,702
Operating expenses:				
Research and development*....	2,489	1,798	5,119	3,486
Selling, general and				
administrative*............	2,710	3,384	4,790	6,623
Stock compensation charge*...	150	167	264	325
Litigation settlement........	--	3,500	--	3,500
Total operating expenses...	5,349	8,849	10,173	13,934
Income (loss) from operations..	3,331	(4,175)	5,023	(4,232)
Interest income, net..........	216	454	432	1,021
Income (loss) before income				
Taxes.......................	3,547	(3,721)	5,455	(3,211)
Provision for income taxes.....	532	--	818	--
Net income (loss).............	$ 3,015	$ (3,721)	$ 4,637	$ (3,211)
Net income (loss) per share:				
Basic.......................	$ 0.13	$ (0.17)	$ 0.21	$ (0.15)
Diluted.....................	$ 0.12	$ (0.17)	$ 0.19	$ (0.15)

Figure 14-8 shows that over the past three months and the past six months the fundamentals have improved remarkably. Over the past three months, the revenues have nearly doubled and the income and earnings went from positive to negative. The same is true for the past six months—the revenues nearly doubled and the income and the earnings per share went from negative to positive. While the fundamentals don't look great, they are showing improvement. By completing this simple fundamental check, you now know that the fundamentals look to be turning around, and combined with the top-down approach, the stars appear aligned. The stock meets several levels of criteria and has a strong likelihood to capture and hold the institutional interest we look for. As an investor, you should structure the entry on light volume pullbacks immediately following breaking out of the consolidation range. The following year of stock movement is shown in Figure 14-9.

Figure 14-10 shows that the stock pulled back to prior resistance on light volume after breaking out of the stage 1 accumulation. The rising 100-day MA was also at this level, which made it an ideal place to get long offering a low risk entry point. As the stock pulls back it makes a bullish flag pattern that implies further upside movement. This is an example of a low risk entry on a structurally sound basis of analysis. While every trade will obviously not be a winner, the statistical likelihood of having more winners than losers is undeniable. Having predetermined stops where losses are taken quickly and profits left to run, along with the statistical edge of more winners than losers, clearly beats blindly following the advice of others.

Applying the methods of analysis is vital, but acting on the analysis completes the trader and investor. It shows that the participant can use objective analysis to gain the edge for not just proper setups, but perhaps even more importantly, proper exits. As stated in the introduction, "like it or not, when you commit your capital you also commit your emotion to the market." The analysis is a hedge to temper emotions, but not a complete mitigation. This broaches the subject of when to sell. The emotional factors regarding when to sell (or buy in the case of covering short positions) are

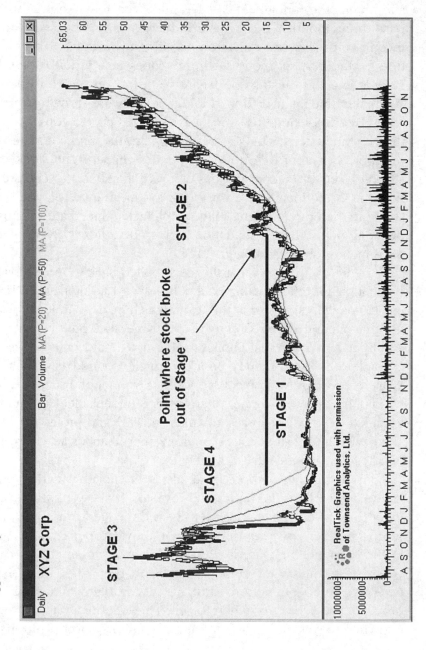

FIGURE 14-9 *After the stock broke out of its trading range, it made a strong move bigher, with little reason to be stopped out of the trade.*

FIGURE 14-10 *The stock gave you an ideal entry point as price pulled into an area of prior resistance and the 100-day MA as well as making a bullish flag formation.*

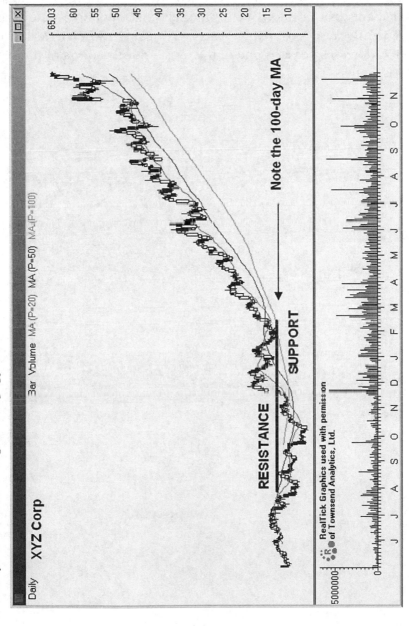

important to consider, for no trader or investor enters a trade when feeling bad about it—otherwise why make it? Conversely, most participants exit positions with precisely this emotional state of mind. Why? Because most participants lack a plan of when to sell. Chapter 15 addresses perhaps one of the most critical aspects of trading and investing.

CHAPTER 15

WHEN TO SELL

Perhaps 90 percent of all market discussions and analysis you can read and find on the Web relate to why and when to buy a stock. Too little attention is given to what to do when it is time to say goodbye to a position. Personally, I can say that exiting a trade is now intuitive to me since the same research that leads me in, also leads me out. But a more concise understanding of when to leave a trade deserves discussion. This important observation was reminded to me from a very respected friend and fellow trader, Brian Shannon. Much of what you are about to discover in this important chapter are his thoughts. Choosing the exit is somewhat of a personal decision, and brings to mind a cliché I've heard many times, "The winners take care of themselves." While I believe this is true, in order to maximize consistency and profitability, you must have a predetermined action plan.

As with any decision in the market, it is easy to let emotions dictate when to sell. If a trader allows feelings to dictate when to say goodbye to a position he or she will find the emotional battle from within paralyzing. When faced with a decision to close out a trade, some of the questions that will creep into our minds include, "Do I sell now and take a small loss, or do I buy more to average my price lower?" and "Should I sell for a small profit, or should I hold out for bigger gains?" Clearly these emotions are going to get in the way of making objective decisions, so we must have a disciplined and consistent plan of action that cuts losses at an early stage and allows our profits to run—the most basic trading goal. This plan of action you create should be based on the single most important factor, price action. In reality, knowing when to exit a position can be an agonizing experience to the undisciplined trader, especially when trading larger share size. Having exit strategies thought out in advance removes the chances of making sloppy emotional decisions.

Always remember, the market does not care what any of us think. Although the charts are a reflection of the psychology of all participants, our personal opinion simply does not count. In other words, "trade what you observe, not what you believe."

Knowing when to cover a trade is best accomplished by letting the stock tell us when to get out. Before we get to specific strategies, it is important to consider the futile nature of trying to find the single best way of exiting a position. We need to recognize that there is no single best way to do anything in the market because we all have different objectives in terms of time in a trade, levels of risk tolerance, and of capital in our accounts.

With that in mind, we will now examine seven good reasons and strategies to exit a position. By having a solid understanding of these seven incidents of market action, we will be in a better position to sell based on an objective interpretation of the message the market relays to us in the form of a price chart. For simplicity we will refer to the long side of the market in all of the examples; however, it is important to recognize that these events are also valid on the short side by simply reversing the rules.

There are seven events that should motivate you to sell. These events can be best described as:

1. Initial protective stop
2. Gaps against the prevailing trend
3. Price targets
4. Hard-trailing stops
5. Electronic trailing stops
6. Moving average crossovers
7. Time stops

Initial protective stops (IPS) give us our first decision to sell because they are based on the interest of preservation of capital. Before we can even think about taking profits, we have to first consider risk—or how much can I lose? Long before we are in a profitable position, our stock has to pass an initial test of strength, which is to hold above our initial protective stop, or our threshold for pain. Said another way—the point in which we are wrong about the position. The nature of short-term trading and investing is to be in a position only while the stock is showing positive momentum. Positive momentum means that the stock is moving in the direction we anticipated (we can have positive momentum in a stock that is dropping if we are shorting the stock). Once a stock shows signs of reversing its momentum, traders and investors should be out of that position and in cash, or better yet, in another stock where their money is working for them.

The final judge as to the success or failure of a trade is price, and it is therefore the most important consideration when exiting a position. Price action is the building block upon which support and resistance are formed, becoming the bedrock of trends. The goal of a trader is to capture as much of a trend as the market allows for, and this is why price is our most important source of information. By having a protective stop, we will not succumb to holding a position because we "think it is a good idea." The stop helps to remove emotions and opinions from the decision-making process, and this contributes to objectivity.

When initially entering the trade, the first technical consideration is price levels of support and resistance. For the same reasons we enter the position near support, we also recognize anything below it is likely to be substantial risk. Therefore, in order to protect against catastrophic loss, stops should be placed just below the most recent level of support. For shorts stops should be placed just above a recent level of resistance. In both cases (long or short), this is best determined on an hourly chart. Reviewing the chart in Figure 15-1, there are two circled areas that represented a breakout past short-term resistance that would support a good decision to buy. The arrows point out the low prior to the breakouts. If the breakout was to fail and the stock made a lower low, there would be no reason to be long a stock making lower lows. This would represent negative price momentum, a dangerous event that can lead to large losses. Another consideration is the location of the two short-term MAs. Both of the MAs are located just below the low that is pointed out, and as we know, moving averages will often act as support levels. Whenever we have more than one technical reason for being involved in a trade, it adds significance. In this case we had what appeared to be the beginnings of a new uptrend with the prior low and the rising 8- and 17-period MAs in the same location. Just below the prior higher low is often the ideal point to place our initial stop because breaking below that level would nullify the trend. See Figure 15-1.

Gaps against the prevailing trend occur when a stock in an uptrend suddenly gaps lower while you have a long position in the stock (or a stock you are shorting gaps higher). Keep in mind, gaps against the trend are not common, but when we do find ourselves in this unfortunate situation, it is best to sell the entire position. To define the significance of the gap, we do not consider 1 to 2 percent as qualification to be stopped out. Gaps of 5 percent or more are another matter. A gap of this magnitude will not typically occur unless there is a serious fundamental development. It is the market's first message to you that something has occurred that may not yet be explained in the media. Price is most important, and price just told you to get out. As a general rule of thumb for gaps, liquidate the position if the protective stop or hard stop (sell event number 4) has been violated. If the stock gaps down 5 percent but does not violate a hard stop, we need to monitor the stock closely for further signs of weakness. If it looks like liquidity may be an issue for exiting a larger position, it is a good idea to consider selling half of the position. This way if the weakness continues you will not feel trapped in the stock and reluctant to sell as it declines, waiting for a bounce that may never arrive.

FIGURE 15-1 *The protective stop is the second trade you make following the entry. Once the trade is on, the protective stop must be set and entered into an electronic environment that will trade you out if prices meet the stop. Trying to commit the stop to memory or paper is the earliest sign of poor discipline. If you're not committed to placing the stop electronically, you're not committed to being disciplined.*

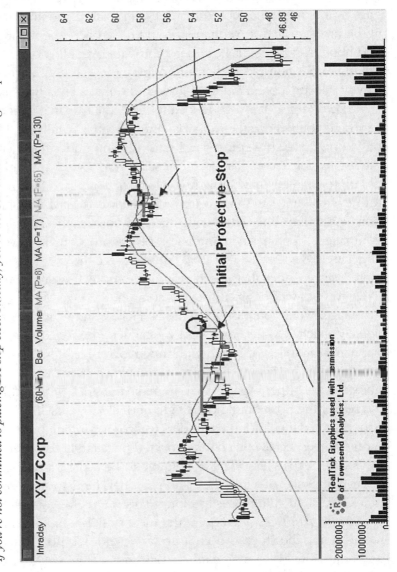

We can see in Figure 15-2, the stock gapped lower from a close near 17.00 down to just above 15.00 and did not bounce. Although it would have been a tough decision to liquidate the position on such a gap, by looking at the subsequent action, it is clearly better to have sold at the first sign of trouble than it would have been to continue to hold and hope. As a rule, it is best to get the pain over all at once by selling the entire position rather than prolonging the agony of a loser, just as slowly peeling a band aid from a wound only extends the discomfort.

Price targets. It is a good idea to have a reasonable expectation as to where you believe the stock has the potential to rally to. This is the basis of a theoretical risk/reward ratio. Exiting under these conditions means mission accomplished. If our stock is in a solid uptrend that may be approaching a prior broken level of support, there is the potential for new resistance (support once broken tends to act as resistance support). Assuming you started with a good theoretical risk/reward ratio in your original purchase, taking some of the profits makes sense at the target area. Also realize that total liquidation of the position is not warranted, since a stock that continues to have strong upward momentum is likely to follow through. By selling some of the position into potential resistance, we accomplish two things. First, it shows we are not emotionally attached to the stock, and we can let go. Second, it allows us to participate in follow-through with much lower risk if resistance is broken (breakout). This practice gives us a little cushion in case something unexpected happens (gap down) to make the stock drop suddenly. For the rest of the position, hold on tight and allow yourself to have a big winner. It is difficult for most traders to hold a winning position and let profits run, especially when the expected price target has been met. But as George Soros says, "It takes courage to be a pig." Most participants do the opposite of what they should. They tend to take profits too quickly while holding loses too long. This is a recipe for failure.

Hard-trailing stops require the most skill, but by the time we get to this point, the stock is doing the work. Our job now is to monitor and adjust our risk levels as the stock moves higher. A hard-trailing stop is based on the very definition of the trends we are trying to take money from. As we know, the definition of an uptrend is "a series of higher highs and higher lows." This implies that breaking

FIGURE 15-2 *The gap suddenly looks acceptable.*

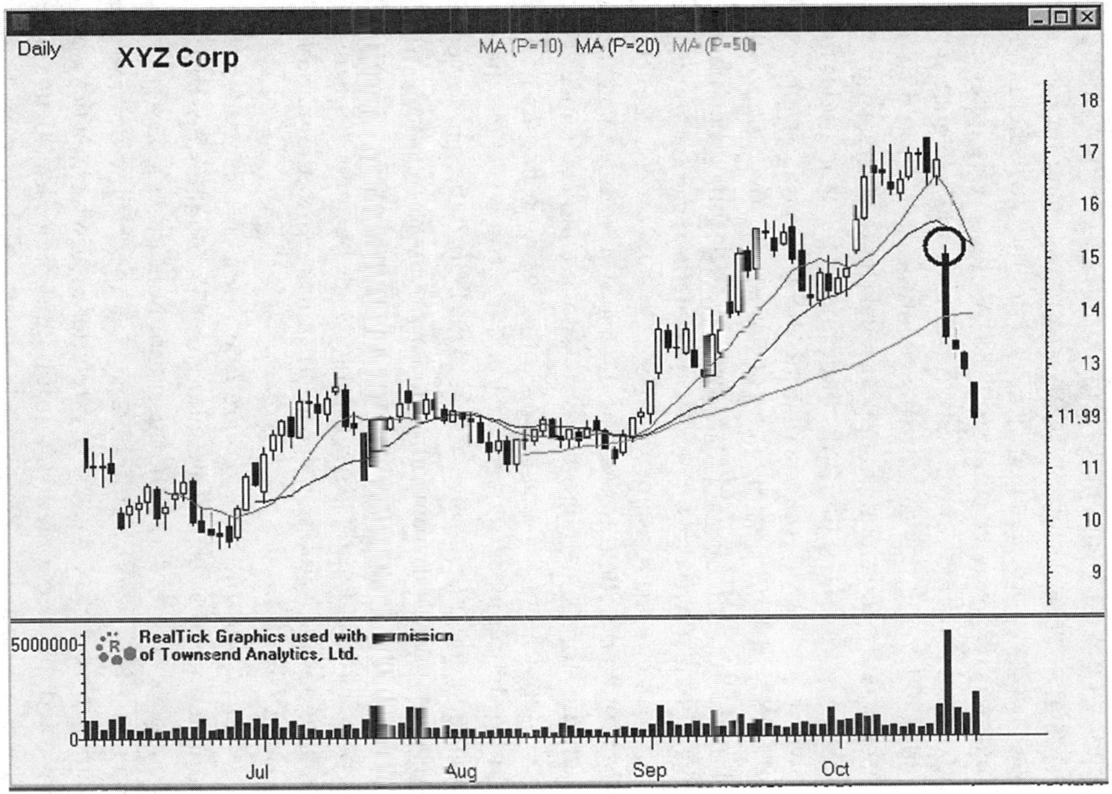
Daily
XYZ Corp
MA (P=10) MA (P=20) MA (P=50)
18
17
16
15
14
13
11.99
11
10
9
5000000
0
RealTick Graphics used with permission
of Townsend Analytics, Ltd.
Jul
Aug
Sep
Oct

the series of higher lows is a violation of the trend and that is a reason to sell. When looking at Figure 15-3, we can see how a trader would have used stop placement under the higher lows of the hourly time-frame to not only capture two nice trades to the upside, but to also sidestep disaster as the stock caved in. Assuming the first purchase was made at approximately $53 a share, the stock held the IPS and there was reason to continue to hold. As the stock gapped higher the next day, it traded above $54 and then made a higher high about midway through the day. At this point the stop should be raised to just under the lows of that support level (hard-trailing stop). Over the next couple of days, this process of raising the stop under the higher lows should have continued until the trade was stopped out just under $59 a share, locking in a gain of nearly $6. Exiting at this point allowed the trader to be in cash as the stock pulled back toward $56 over the next two days. The second purchase came two days later as the stock cleared resistance near $57.50. As you can see from Figure 15-3, the stock held above the IPS, and it should have been held with the stop being adjusted as the stock climbed higher. The stock was stopped out two days later with a gain of about $1.50. As you can see from the subsequent action, for those who held the stock on opinion and ignored price action experienced the gap lower and the subsequent sell-off, losing almost 20 percent over the next two trading sessions! This stop takes some work because you have to cancel and replace orders, but this is enjoyable work because it means you are locking in profits along the way. In this regard, the market is really working for you.

Electronic trailing stops are one of our favorite stops to use on short-term trades, especially intraday. This unique stop actually gives control of your order to the algorithm built into the system you trade with, assuming your firm offers such a tool. Many do not, and perhaps the best place to start is a free demo at www.realtick.com. They invented the electronic trailing stop, and none do it better. The ideal situation to use a trailing stop is when you buy a stock that finds rapid upside velocity, pushing the stock quickly away from your hard stop. In the situation where the stock may run $1 or more in just a few minutes, we are faced with deciding whether to sell the

FIGURE 15-3 *Hard stops work the same as IPS, the only difference is profitability. The truly unemotional trader acts accordingly either way. While profits are better than losses, enduring methods will reward both scenarios over time.*

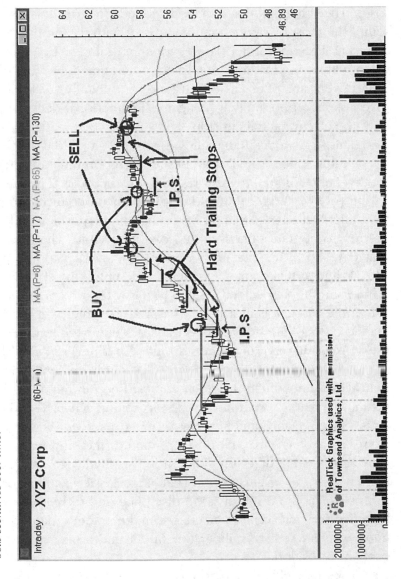

position and lock in the gains or to allow it to run further. We've all seen the stocks that can run $2 to $3 in the course of an hour or less, and we certainly don't want to allow a nice winner to turn into a loser. The emotions that can be dredged up from this experience tempt the most disciplined traders to exit with the profit rather than allowing it to run further. These stops are going to be utilized most often within the first hour of trading, when emotions from the amateur buyers are often at an extreme. Fortunately, technology has given us the opportunity to mitigate the emotional decision process with the electronic trailing stop.

This stop works in the following way. Figure 15-4 demonstrates a stock that started to rally late in the afternoon the day before. The stock continued to progress higher, and because it was showing strong positive momentum and displayed a strong technical pattern, the trader locked in partial profits on half of the position and allowed the rest to be transitioned into an overnight hold. The stock closed that day at $18.58. The next morning the stock gapped higher at $19.11, and at this point the trader was tempted to sell the stock for a quick profit, but decided instead to allow the profits to run a little. When the stock was at a price of $19.28 he entered a trailing stop market order of $.15 ($19.13). As the stock exhibited further strength, the stop is automatically adjusted higher, but never lower. The trailing stop sets an actual stop $.15 (or whatever increment you choose) below every new high the stock makes. Keep in mind that this will turn into a market order upon the stop getting activated and this can cause slippage in illiquid or fast-moving markets. As you can see from Figure 15-4, over the next 23 minutes the stop was automatically adjusted 157 times until the trade was finally stopped out $1.79 higher than the original stop. That is a classic example of letting profits run as the result of good discipline and technology working together (no intervention needed on the trader's part). Ideally a trader wants to use a trailing stop on all trades because it means a profitable position.

The most difficult decision for a trailing stop is how much room to allow the stock to have. We call this discretion. It's like going fishing. If you hook a big fish and you tighten the line too much, the fish is sure

FIGURE15-4 *The trailing stop in action. This is a ride that everyone wants to take.*

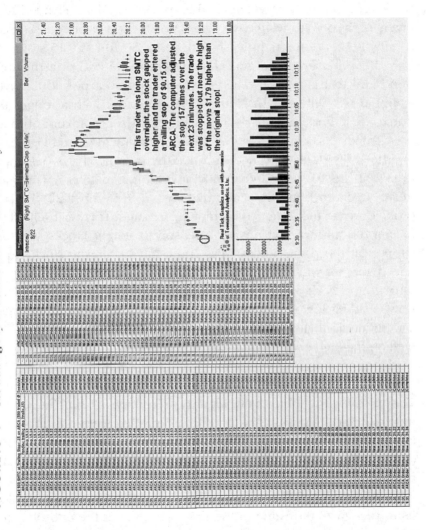

This trader was long SMTC overnight, the stock gapped higher and the trader entered a trailing stop of $0.15 on ARCA. The computer adjusted the stop 157 times over the next 23 minutes. The trade was stopped out near the high of the move $1.79 higher than the original stop!

to break off and you never taste your reward. In trading, if you set the stop too tight, you might get shaken out of the position before the stock runs its course. How much discretion you decide to give a trailing stop depends a lot on historical volatility and the price of the stock. The more volatile and higher priced stocks will need to be given extra room to wiggle while less volatile lower priced issues can usually be kept on a tight leash with just a $0.10 to $0.15 stop.

Moving average crossovers often signal the end of a prevailing trend and that is a good time to take profits on a position. For this example we will refer to Figure 15-5. Investors with a longer time horizon will find particular value using the MA crossover approach.

Trending stocks tend to stay above the rising MAs, and Figure 15-5 indicates this stock remained in a healthy uptrend that would pause briefly at the 10- and 20-day moving averages where it would find fresh buyers to bring the stock higher. On September 22, the stock broke down to the rising 50-day moving average. This swift sell-off was reason for concern, but not yet a reason to sell, as stocks often find support at the rising 50-day MA. Three days later, the stock experienced another wave of selling and that brought the 10-day MA down through the 20-day MA. This action tells us that the short-term trend is now heading lower while the intermediate term is trending higher. This indecision tells us it is time to book profits. The stock is at $28.50, well off the high near $36, but still 62 percent higher than the purchase made four months before.

MAs are simple, but often misunderstood, technical indicators. They allow us to objectively identify trends on all timeframes with incredible accuracy. One of the common misconceptions about MAs is that MA crossovers are a reason to enter a position. We have found that moving average crossovers occur in a sideways consolidating market, and it is difficult to determine when these consolidation periods will end. Understanding that MA crossovers represent indecision allows us to recognize the value of the first crossover at the end of a trend as a reason to sell. Usually an MA crossover occurs after a trend has exhausted itself, and as trend followers there should be no clearer sign that it is time to exit gracefully with our profits before the market relieves us of them.

FIGURE 15-5 *This indicates a timeless technical event that signifies the market is talking to you. The question is, are you listening? When an MA makes a cross, it indicates the trader has most likely given the stock plenty of price volatility since the MA will always lag the price. If it takes an MA to initiate a stop, the losses are likely to be bigger.*

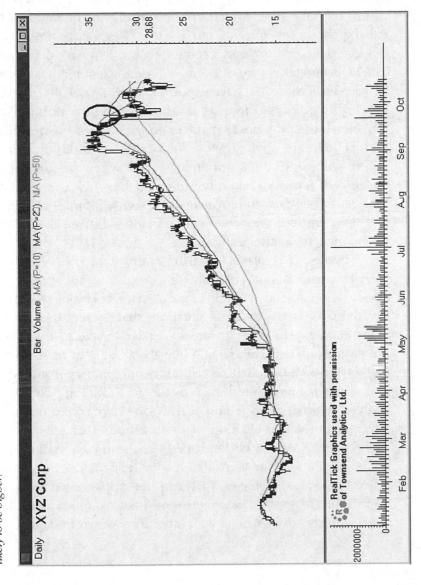

Time stops are a way of exiting a position that is stagnant. As traders, we encounter two forms of risk, and the previous six reasons to sell addressed the risk of price. This stop addresses our other form of market risk—time, which can be our biggest enemy in a trade. It can be the quiet killer of our equity. How many times have you neglected a stock in your account because it wasn't doing anything? The time stop takes care of getting out of a position if it is not working as quickly as we would have expected. We will typically give the stock two to three hours before we consider selling the position out near our cost basis. For position trades, our patience is stretched easily and we give the stock no more than one to two days to get moving before we start to think our timing is off. When we get stopped out because of time, we will often re-enter the stock if it exhibits signs that it may be ready to move later on. You will find that many stocks that time you out are not re-entered since you see the stock objectively once again after exiting.

These seven reasons to sell are not meant to be the only reasons to exit a position, but hopefully they do give you something to think about when you look at closing out your positions. Keep in mind that there are many different situations that present themselves to us in the markets. The more strategies we have to take advantage of them, the more likely we are to attain our goals being in the elite group of Market Wise Traders, who consistently take money from the market.

Keep in mind, the basics of the methodology covered in the analysis of what to trade and when (top-down) were not any single strategy, but a combination of the methods that all must confirm each other. A bias was developed on the broad market, then followed with a series of steps that lead to a specific action. Chapter 16 reflects specific strategies that can be applied to the top-down approach. These strategies represent timeless approaches that have yielded tremendous profits with little draw down in capital.

16

FAVORITE STRATEGIES

Not all trading fits neatly into a form of analysis, not even technical analysis. The following strategies represent several of our favorite. In short, they work, but like anything, they are best used in the proper situations. Apply the rules of risk management you have learned and enjoy the benefit of these timeless techniques.

THE "SHORT SQUEEZE"

Throughout the book we addressed the factors that move markets, and in general these factors include fundamentals, technicals, and psychology. We stated that fundamentals answer the question "why" prices move, but this analysis is late. Technical analysis answers the question "when," and is the chosen approach. The final, and probably hardest factor to measure, is psychology. Understanding the psychology of stock movements is often measured through technical indicators and attempts to answer the question "who?" *Who* would be a buyer and *who* would be a seller under certain circumstances? Big money can be made in a stock's movement when there is a favorable combination of the three factors listed above to uncover profitable upside opportunities.

The focus of this section will be the study of a specific technical indicator, short interest, in an attempt to uncover situations where a "short squeeze" may develop in a stock. Before we get started with analyzing the idea, we need to remember that short selling is a strategy that attempts to capitalize on a decline in share value by selling stock at a high level and later purchasing the security at a lower price. The short seller therefore represents future demand because they must buy the stock back at some future date in order to close the trade. Of course, each participant will buy back their shares at different times, but as we will see, we can make certain assumptions based on the share price where fear begins to "squeeze" the short seller. This is the opportunity.

The biggest risk to a short seller is that instead of share prices dropping, the stock's price rises. We will see later that a rising share price in a stock that is heavily shorted can lead to dramatic upward movement as short sellers add demand while covering losses. The motivation to buy back the stock by the short seller is often the fear of unlimited losses. When you buy a stock at $20 a share, the most you can lose is your entire investment, $20 a share. When you sell a stock short at $20, the potential for losses, in theory, is unlimited. The stock may rise to $40, $50, $60, or even more, as theoretically there is an unlimited upside risk! It is the fear of such an advance that can make for an explosive upside in a heavily shorted stock. The phenomenon of a rapidly rising stock with a large short interest is known as a *short squeeze*, and we will now explore the dynamics of how a short squeeze develops.

Before we continue, let us first cover some terminology. *Short interest* is defined as the total number of shares of a stock that have been sold short and not yet covered. When a person sells a stock short, exchange rules mandate that the order must be identified as a short sale. Because each short sale has to be identified as such, it is easy for the Exchanges to compile statistics on the total short interest in the market. This information is released to the public once per month by the different Exchanges. Short interest for Nasdaq stocks is tallied up on the fifteenth of each month, and that information is disseminated to the public eight business days later. For example, if the short interest is 1,500,000 shares as of August 15, that information is released to the public on August 27. Any changes to this number are released one month later. Obviously this practice can change with Exchange policy. It is the method of this strategy that matters most.

The *short interest ratio (SIR)* is the number of shares sold short (short interest) divided by the average daily volume for the previous month for the particular stock. This number is interpreted as the number of days it would take to cover (buy back) the shares sold short based on the average daily volume. The higher the ratio, the longer it would be to buy back borrowed shares. This often leads to dramatic upward momentum for the stock when the sellers become motivated to buy back their short positions. If the stock had a short position of 1,500,000 shares and an average daily volume of 500,000, then the SIR would be 3.0, meaning it would take three full days of average daily volume for the short sellers to cover their bearish bet. If the stock had an average daily volume of just 250,000 shares, then the SIR would be 6.0, meaning it would take six days of buying to cover their position. As a contrarian indicator, a higher SIR is desirable because it means it is more difficult to cover the position and the resulting buys have the potential to create significant short-term trading profits, i.e. the "short squeeze."

A *short squeeze* develops when those who sold short the stock experience losses and groups of bearish traders attempt to cover their positions quickly. Short squeezes often occur because of a news event that changes investors' perception as to the worth of a particular company. Another way a short squeeze can develop is when long holders of the stock push the price higher with aggressive buy orders in an attempt to tap into the emotional buying that a trapped short seller can provide. This can create fear on the part of the short seller. Obviously, if you are short a stock that is advancing, there is a point where it becomes fearful to continue holding the position. With that said, in order to eliminate the mounting losses and the emotional trauma of holding a big loser, the once pessimistic seller will often become a panicky buyer. It is this buying along with long-side momentum buyers that makes the stock advance at a rapid pace.

The first step in finding a good short squeeze candidate is to study the charts to see if there is any technical indication that it might be the proper time for a low risk entry into the stock. Any stock in a downtrend can be immediately eliminated because short sellers are more confident in a position that is moving in their favor. Eliminating situations that are not high probability candidates frees our time to focus on the strong stocks where the short sellers may be in trouble. At MarketWise we have proprietary databases of stocks that meet our technical criteria for an uptrending stock, but a great place to begin is to find stocks that are trading above a rising 50-day MA. If the stock is below the declining 50-day MA, you can eliminate it from the list and then focus on the stocks that are trading above the rising 50-day MA. A stock that is above a rising 50-day MA is in an uptrend and should be studied further on different timeframes to find where there may be the potential for resistance to halt the upward progress of the stock. If a stock is at a new high, it indicates that the only source of potential supply will come from profit takers, rather than people selling to get even on a position they may have been holding in their portfolios at a loss. A stock trading at a new high also indicates that it is unlikely that the short sellers are in a profitable position, and that may make them more motivated to cover their short position. See Figure 16-1.

After finding a stock in an uptrend, a quick look at the short interest table at the Nasdaq site is the next step in finding a good candidate for a short squeeze. Figure 16-2 shows that when the stock broke out in early May, the short position was near an all-time high, standing at 10,193,909 shares that had been sold short and not yet covered. Clearly the shorts appeared to be in trouble at this time. It is also important to note the high short-interest ratio at the time. The average daily volume in April was 457,574 shares, and at that rate it would take the shorts more than 22 days of buying to cover their position. This high ratio put the shorts in a precarious position, and for each share they repurchased it was like throwing gasoline into a raging fire. It was not going to be easy to cover this position.

The next step is to overlay the short position onto the price chart to come up with an approximate level that the bulk of the short

FIGURE 16-1 *The first step is to find a stock in an uptrend. This stock had broken out to an all-time high and pulled back to prior support on light volume. Anyone who had sold short in the past came into a losing position when the stock broke out and that added the potential for further demand.*

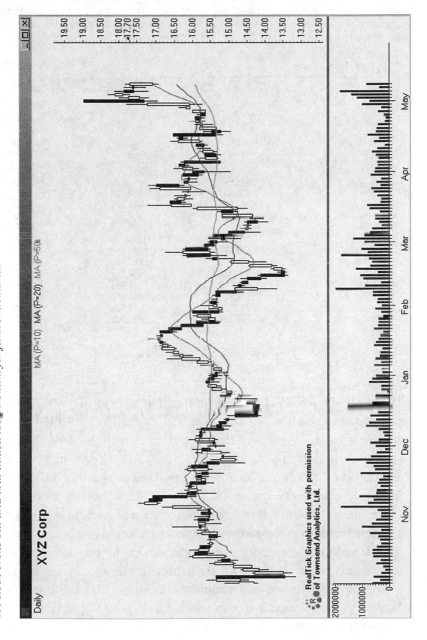

Daily   **XYZ Corp**

MA (P=10)   MA (P=20)   MA (P=50)

RealTick Graphics used with permission
of Townsend Analytics, Ltd.

FIGURE 16-2 *There are numerous sources for finding the number of shares that are short for any individual stock and the corresponding ratio to average daily volume. The site we look at most frequently is www.nasdaq.com since this site offers information on the short position of all equities markets, not just the Nasdaq.*

Short Interest

| - Short Interest | ▼ | | ▼ | | ADD | EDIT SYMBOL LIST ● |

Settlement Date	Short Interest	Avg Daily Share Volume	Days to Cover
Nov. 14,	3,839,699	448,196	8.57
Oct. 15,	3,701,933	614,939	6.02
Sep. 15,	4,020,392	401,197	10.02
Aug. 15,	4,516,845	487,105	9.27
Jul. 15,	7,723,266	1,000,670	7.72
Jun. 13,	8,978,477	344,186	26.09
May 15,	9,857,112	683,483	14.42
Apr. 15,	10,193,909	457,574	22.28
Mar. 14,	9,049,010	741,608	12.20
Feb. 14,	7,101,755	820,413	8.66
Jan. 15,	5,213,030	467,522	11.15
Dec. 13,	4,156,358	587,069	7.08

Data source: The Nasdaq Stock Market, Inc.

position was initiated at. Figure 16-3 shows that the short sellers in this stock were all in a losing position as the stock broke out to new highs. We can also figure that between November and April, while the stock traded in a range of $13.50 to $17, the short position was increased by nearly 7.5 million shares. That means that $17 should act as good support for the stock, assuming short sellers would look to cover their positions. If the stock were to pull back to $17. This pent-up demand lowers the risk with potential support just below the highs. This is a critical concept in understanding why resistance, once broken, tends to act as support. By understanding how much the short sellers are losing we can monitor the stock for anticipated urgent buying. This information answers a fundamental question as to *who* would buy the stock. By recognizing the large short position, we can understand the potential urgency buyers may have in the issue,

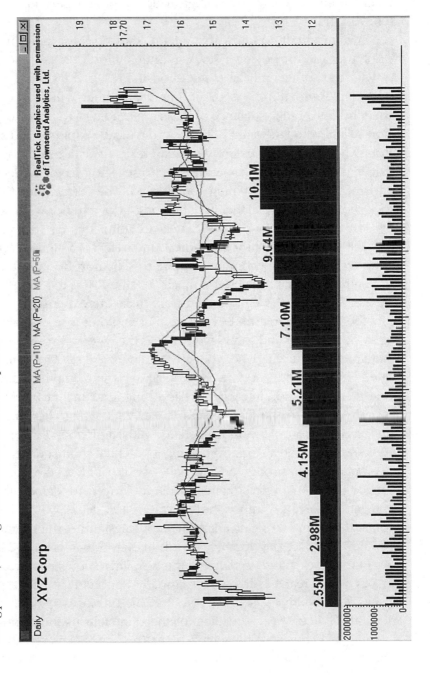

FIGURE 16-3 *From November 15 to April 15, 7.5 million shares of stock were sold short. By looking at this information on a chart, we can see that when the stock broke out to new all-time highs, all of those shares sold short were in a losing position, leaving them vulnerable to a short squeeze.*

which could be a key psychological development behind a buying frenzy in the stock.

It is important to know that a large short-interest ratio, by itself, is not a reason for buying a stock in anticipation of a short squeeze. As with any other indicator, the short-interest ratio should not be used on a stand-alone basis. The informed trader will find an edge when there is a preponderance of indicators leading to a price advance. Short sellers who take large positions are typically sophisticated speculators who have done extensive research on their targeted company and are often right. Many times those who sell short have the right idea fundamentally, but their timing could be off. The correct time to sell a stock short is when it is either in or entering a downtrend. When a short position is initiated in a stock that is trending higher, there is real potential for big trouble for the shorts. As the stock continues higher in an uptrend, it often becomes tempting to sell short because the perception may be that "it is up too much" or "the P/E is too high." However, as discussed throughout the book, these are expensive opinions to harbor. Professional traders realize that shorting a stock only once the stock rolls over and shows weakness is the higher percentage trade. Therefore, be careful who you are trading against. The true short squeeze stock candidate is when a security is in an uptrend that has attracted a large short interest and has strong fundamentals.

This leads to the final criteria to consider when choosing short squeeze candidates, the fundamentals. Although poor fundamentals would not preclude a stock from being a potential short squeeze target, a company with strong fundamentals would add to the source of demand and move prices higher. When looking at fundamentals on a momentum play, it is important not to look too deep. We will usually look at the company's news headlines for sales and earnings information, new product developments, and analyst ratings changes. In the case of the stock above, a glance at the headlines shows news reported on May 5 that reads as follows: "Company Reports First Quarter 2003 Results; Revenue Increases 50% , Net Income Increases 79%, Company Increases Guidance." Just reading this headline tells us the company is growing their business by selling more (revenue increase), they are more profitable than they were last year (net income up 79 percent), and business remains strong (increases guidance). On the day this fundamental news was reported, the stock advanced $1.05 on heavy volume; clearly the reaction from Wall Street was a positive one. The market believed the news.

When reviewing fundamentals, traders should be more interested in why others would buy or sell. It is important not to make a decision about the company, but only what others may think about the stock. There are many people who buy and sell stocks based on what the prospects for the company are, and we cannot ignore them in making our decisions because of the large impact they can have on price.

We should be able to quickly analyze the fundamental, technical, and psychological influences before making any trading decisions. When we have all three of these factors telling us the same conclusion (buy), we should act. Couple that with a high short-interest ratio and we have the ingredients for future demand. As you can see from Figure 16-4, the stock progressed nicely in its uptrend and doubled in price over the next five months.

In summary, short sellers are usually very savvy speculators; however, like any group of market participants, they aren't always right. When shorts are wrong about the direction of a stock, the move higher can be dramatic, leading to some excellent short-term profits for traders who see a short squeeze situation developing. Like any indicator, short interest should not be used on a stand-alone basis, but it should become part of a trader's arsenal. Since technical analysis is largely about measuring supply and demand, short sellers can become an excellent source of demand for a stock in an uptrend.

THE STOCHASTIC PLAY

As touched upon in Chapter 10, the stochastic indicator is an oscillator. An *oscillator* is a technical indicator that measures rate of change and momentum within a defined range of 0 and 100. The indicator measures the mathematical relationship of a securities momentum and its signs of becoming overbought and oversold. It is important to understand

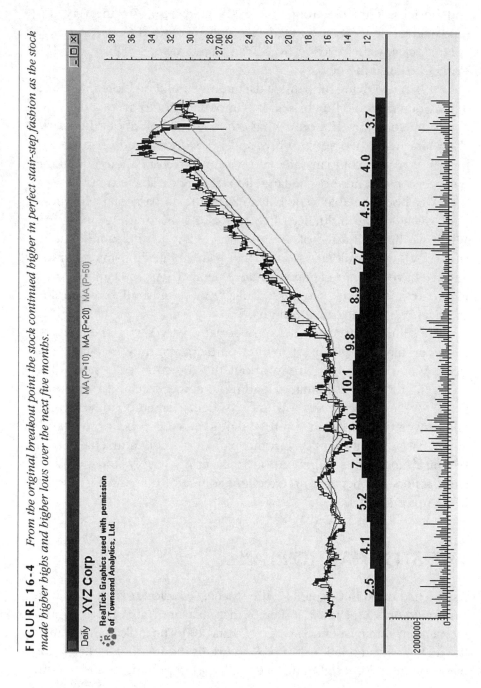

FIGURE 16-4 *From the original breakout point the stock continued higher in perfect stair-step fashion as the stock made higher highs and higher lows over the next five months.*

"overbought" and "oversold" are terms that have no fundamental representation. They are technical terms that relate to standard deviation from a historical mean price. The true value of a stochastic oscillator mathematically measures when a security is prone to reversal.

Trending stocks tend to remain in trend as long as closing prices continue to close near their highs in uptrend as lower trending securities close near their lows. See Figure 16-5. The stochastic indicator comes alive when this pattern is broken, acting as an early signal of impending reversal. In this case, the opposite is true whereby higher trending stocks close near their lows of the period and lower trending stocks close near their highs.

THE MATH

In mathematical terms the close in relation to the overall range is measured by comparing the close of the period to the low, divided by the high minus the low. See Figure 16-6.

The actual formula for stochastics is given by:

$$\%K = \frac{100 \times [C - L(period)]}{H(Period) - (L(Period)}$$

where
$$C - \text{current close}$$
L(Period) = Low of the period
H(Period) = High of the period

Again refer to Figure 16-6. As distance A gets closer to the high, %K gets larger until A = B then %K = 100. If the close trades lower, A moves toward the low and K% gets smaller until A = L then %K = 0. This is a simple example using only one period for the stochastic indicator.

If this concept seems familiar, look back to elasticity and the expansion of range we discussed in Chapter 5. The stochastic indicator measures the elasticity of price within the period selected. If the price is near or breaks the high of the range the stochastic indicator is pushed higher. As a new range is set the stochastic indicator will trade within the new range. When price reverses direction and

FIGURE 16-5 *Notice that while uptrending most every candle closes near the high of its range. When in a downtrend the candles close near the lows for most every candle. As long as prices tend to close in the direction of the trend, reversal is still unlikely.*

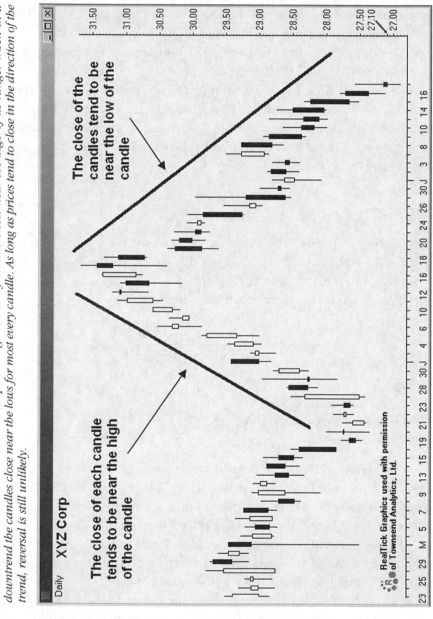

FIGURE 16-6   *In this simple, one-period example, the stochastic indicator measures the closing price to both the low (A) and the high (B) of the period.*

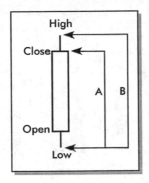

trades off the highs of the period, it will "bend over" the stochastic and begin to reflect the reversal potential of the prevailing trend. When you apply the stochastic indicator to more than one period, the indicator compares the current close to the highest high and the lowest low of the period. See Figure 16-7. Note that the stochastic indicator is comparing the current close to the elastic range of the past 14 periods. The stochastic indicator that was used in the previous examples is plotted as a line that oscillates from 0 to 100 and is designated %K. The %K line can be very sensitive and prone to giving too many buy and sell signals, so there are derivatives of %K to desensitize the indicator or slow it down. The %D line is one such derivative and is typically plotted with %K and is the MA of the %K. Just as MAs can be used to smooth out the volatility in stock prices, the %D line takes some of the volatility out of the %K line. Also realize that the period of the %D line can be customized but is typically the three-period MA of %K.

STOCHASTIC BUY AND SELL SIGNALS

The stochastic indicator is typically plotted beneath the security on a scale from 0 to 100. Traditionally the indicator is said to be in overbought territory if it gets above the 80 line. It is considered oversold if the indicator falls beneath the 20 line. See Figure 16-8.

FIGURE 16-7   *Stochastic indicator applied to 14 periods.*

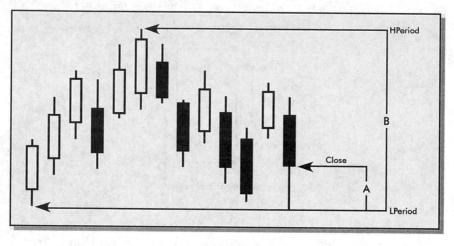

FIGURE 16-8   *The traditional stochastic indications of %K and %D.*

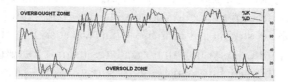

As the indicator oscillates between 0 and 100, it gains actionable levels at 80 and 20. It doesn't tell you that it will happen for sure. It just tells you that the underlying trend is getting a bit extended and a correction is probable. The 80 and 20 lines are traditionally used but if using stochastics on strongly trending stocks, the lines might have to be adjusted based on the individual stock's historical patterns. Some issues have a stochastic range at 90 and 10 for example. Therefore, it is best to relate each individual issue to its own historical relationship. For example if a stock is uptrending strongly, on the pullbacks the stochastic may not penetrate the 20 level, and it might only come down to 30. In cases like this you should adjust your oversold zone accordingly. The reverse is true for a downtrending stock.

When a stock is uptrending as the closes of the periods are near their highs, the stochastic indicator is pushed higher. As the close begins to occur away from the high of the range, the stochastic indicator is pushed over and signals the potential overbought condition. Note the movement of the stochastic indicator upon each successive candle entering the equation in Figure 16-9. Also take note that the candle that pushes the stochastic over is the classic shooting star candle which signals a reversal and halts uptrends. The rationale of the shooting star signifies the bulls' last momentous rally. The fact that the bulls cannot maintain the rally and close near the highs of the period helps confirm the bulls are tired and the bears are gaining control.

FIGURE 16-9 *The stochastic indicator begins to flatten out and gets pushed over as the closes occur off the high of the period.*

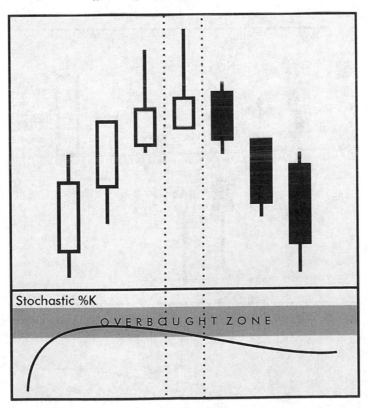

When a security is downtrending, the stochastic is pushed lower as the closes are near the low of the period being measured. Once the closes begin to move higher in the range, the stochastic begins to flatten out and moves higher. Notice how the stochastic indicator moves with each successive candle. The classic hammer candle that indicates a reversal also pushes the stochastic indicator higher. See Figure 16-10.

Referring to Figure 16-11, the stochastic indicator's %K line crosses the %D line in oversold territory, then both lines exit the oversold zone and a buy signal is given. As the stock trades higher the stochastic indicator is pushed higher until it gets into the overbought zone. Once in the overbought zone the %K crosses the %D line and both lines exit the overbought zone and the sell signal is

---

FIGURE 16-10   *The stochastic indicator is pushed lower by closes near the lows, flattens out, and then begins to rise as the closes move off the low of the range.*

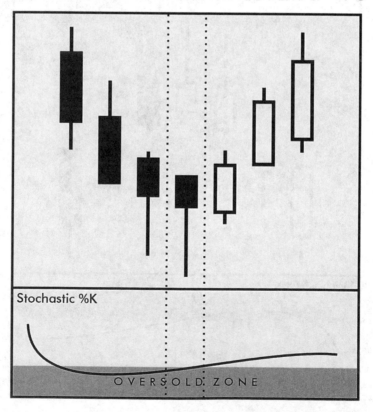

Stochastic %K

OVERSOLD ZONE

FIGURE 16-11 *The traditional buy and sell signals, the cross of %K over %D in the overbought or oversold zone, and an exit of both %K and %D from the extreme zone. %K is represented by the solid line and %D the dashed line.*

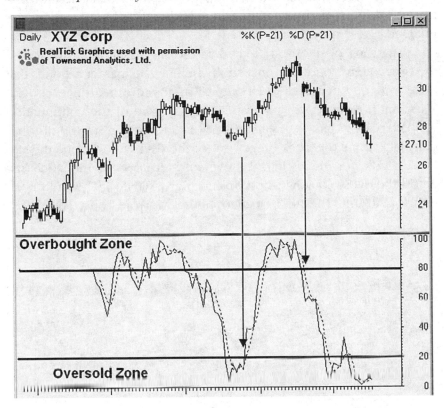

given. The subsequent action of the stock is lower. The important signal to recognize in overbought territory is the %K crossing the %D, with %K exiting the overbought zone with %D, but beneath it. Conversely, in oversold territory, %K will cross %D and both will exit oversold with %K above %D.

NONTRADITIONAL STOCHASTIC INDICATIONS

There are some patterns that the stochastic indicator gives that defy the traditional stochastic theory. Under certain circumstances, these create tradable signals that, when used in conjunction with traditional technical analysis, can lead to profitable moves. The continuation up pattern is one such situation. This pattern works best when a security has been basing in a stage 1 accumulation. Upon moving from an accumulation phase to a markup phase, the stochastic indicator moves into the overbought zone. It is at this time long positions are initiated. See Figure 16-12.

The long positions are exited as the stochastic indicator leaves the overbought zone. The philosophy behind the market action is that once a market becomes overbought it tends to remain overbought. The continuation down pattern is the opposite of the continuation up pattern. It works best when a stock is trading in a stage 3 distribution pattern. As the stock breaks out of the distribution range the stochastic indicator moves into the oversold territory. As the stochastic enters the oversold zone, short positions are initiated. The short position is held until the stochastic leaves the oversold zone. The theory

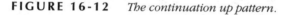

FIGURE 16-12   *The continuation up pattern.*

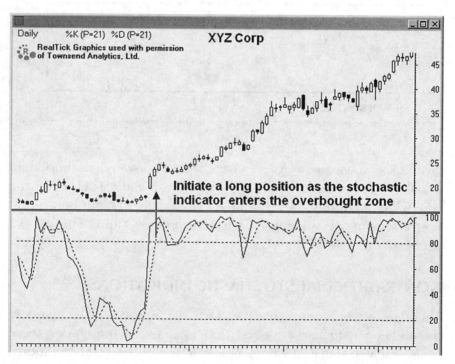

behind trading this pattern is that once a stock becomes oversold it tends to remain oversold. See Figure 16-13. In simple terms, once a trend is intact, it tends to stay intact until strong signs of reversal begin to appear. The stochastic is confirmation of the reversal.

STOCHASTIC DIVERGENCES

The divergence of price and stochastics is another nontraditional way to use stochastics. The divergence can be an early warning sign

FIGURE 16-13   *The continuation down pattern.*

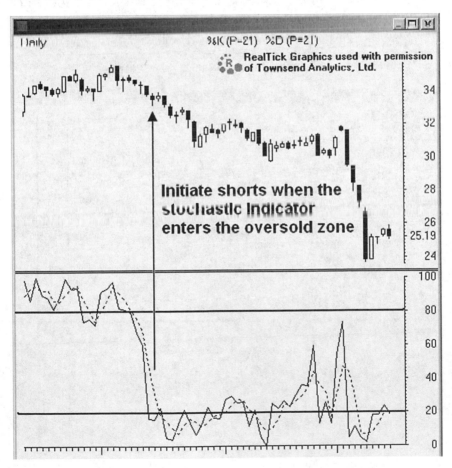

of a change in trend. The bullish divergence between price and stochastic typically occurs in a stock that is in a downtrend that is about to reverse direction. As the price makes a lower low the stochastics make a higher low. This is the divergence. After the divergence takes place wait for the downtrend to be broken by price making a higher high. It is at this point that longs are initiated. When used correctly divergences can lead to many profitable trades. See Figure 16-14.

The reverse of the bullish divergence is the bearish divergence. The bearish setup occurs while a stock is in an uptrend but is ready to turn lower. As the stock price is able to make another push higher, the stochastic indicator makes a lower high. This is the point when the divergence occurs. Short positions are initiated as the stock breaks its uptrend. See Figure16-15.

FIGURE 16-14   *A bullish divergence between price and stochastics.*

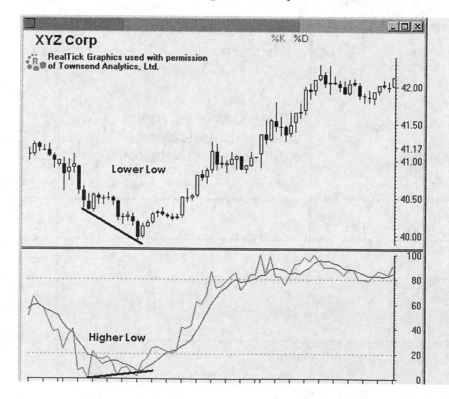

FIGURE 16-15 *A bearish divergence.*

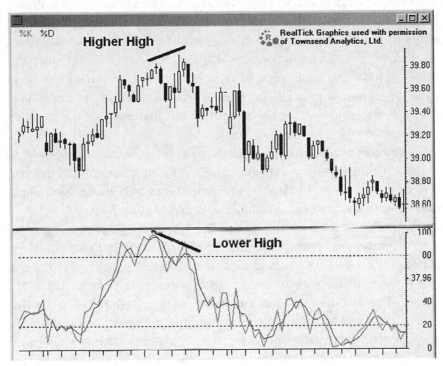

The stochastic indicator can point you in the direction of profitable trades, but remember that the indicator is a tool and like any other indicator or pattern it must be used in the context of the larger picture.

THE EARNINGS PLAY

Earnings releases are one of Wall Street's biggest news events. Trade volume increases dramatically during earnings season as dumb money rushes into the market on the heels of media hype. We have studied the potential manipulations from companies reporting earnings, Wall Street firms, and the analysts that work for them. Accounting principles used during this season seem to be stretched to the limits if not exceeding industry standards. To make matters worse, companies love to use jargon that even Generally Accepted Accounting Principles (GAAP) can't seem to understand. Earnings seem to have more ways of being reported than Baskin Robbins has ice cream flavors. Terms like "one-time charge," "beat the street," and "consensus earnings estimate" are examples of how companies can make earnings look better than they are. This leaves investors looking to analysts to make sense of the jargon, who only make matters worse with their own terminology.

Perhaps the company reporting earnings wants Wall Street to focus on their future more than their present due to current challenges they may be having. Then they like to talk about "guidance" and "pro forma," which are simply ways of looking forward or guessing what the next quarter or year will look like. This is nothing more than a distraction. Technology companies love to say things like, "on a pro forma basis we earned 15 cents a share," when in reality this has nothing to do with current earnings that may only be 2 cents a share. They also like to "pre-announce" to help soften bad news that may come forward on the day earnings are to be released. This helps cushion the impact the actual news may have on the stock's price. This kind of activity contributes to another term, "the whisper number." Now that sounds really important and I guess we are expected to believe that only important insiders could know what that number is. Perhaps we should wait to respond to the "earnings surprise," which sounds like a party! This little emotional term really gets the market frothy, when in reality all it really means is a better than expected earnings report than the "guidance" or "consensus estimate" thought.

The reaction of a stock's price to earnings announcements is an area that offers you substantial trading opportunities, but not for the ridiculous reasons and terminology stated above. Wall Street's jargon and reporting process makes earnings the most misunderstood and mistraded stock play there is. I could go on, but you get the point. I suggest you not even worry about it! Even if you understand the language of Wall Street, you can't trust it enough to trade on the news. Wall Street wants you to feel confused, that way you will use their translators, the analysts and brokers. Earnings are one of their very favorite ways to confuse the public. Our focus once again will be to look to the charts with this market cliché in mind.

BUY RUMOR, SELL FACT (NEWS)

This is one market term I don't want you to forget. Trading on earnings reports offers at least three distinct trading opportunities based on market perceptions of the amateur. How people perceive earnings reports and the jargon associated with them determines how they trade. The public will react to things that professional traders won't. This reaction from the public produces much of the opportunity for the professionals because earnings announcements are foreseeable events and the trading that takes place is based on the perception and hype surrounding them. The astute trader searches for price patterns to determine what the professionals are doing in anticipation of earnings, and fades what the amateur is expected to do once earnings are released. The price action on the charts weeks prior to earnings is the *rumor* part of the equation. The expected price action based on late amateur participation is the *fact* part of the equation. Keep in mind, this approach only applies to stocks that represent positive price action in anticipation of earnings. Shares that are depressed weeks prior to earnings are best ignored, since this would imply that once the poor news was released, professionals would buy the weakness. Not a good idea! Poor earnings, missing the consensus estimates, lower guidance, etc., can substantially punish a stock for long periods of time. Conversely, based on fact that the market discounts fundamentals in its price, this play works best when good earnings are expected, as seen through the price patterns weeks earlier. In other words, this is only a bullish play.

Professionals do not wait for the news. Instead, they trade ahead of it. Professionals look for money to flow into the stock prior to the earnings reports. Then they join that trend long before the report comes out. Traders who can read the directional bias created by the smart money taking an early position will reduce market risk greatly while increasing profit potential. Traders will look for volume to build over the normal range of the stock, and then determine on which side of the market the volume is flowing. Results come from taking risks early and not waiting for the news to be actually reported. Investors who wait to buy stock based on news reports typically lose. If a positive earnings result is expected, it will likely show on the charts. The money flow of the buying professionals generally drives the stock higher weeks before the actual figures are released. The amateurs wait for "certainty" or the actual earnings news to be released before taking action, which creates the perfect opportunity for the professional traders to sell their long positions into the buying public. This is the reason why stocks often reverse their positive direction after the release of seemingly good news. The explanation is that the stock had already discounted the news by trading up several points on the expectation of good earnings. When the earnings are finally released, professionals drive prices lower by taking profits and selling the now overvalued stock to the amateurs rushing in to buy on the good news!

To recognize where the pros are putting the money, you need to pay close attention to the price patterns of the stock several weeks before the company will report. If the trend proves positive and is confirmed with good technicals, join it as soon as possible. Do not wait for too much certainty or you will miss the low risk entry. Keep in mind, as the reporting day approaches, the likely results will be price stability (consolidation) or even weakness as professionals are taking profits in spite of the fact that amateurs may be starting to buy. The early amateur buying generally occurs because the media is more actively reporting the earnings event, with plenty of analysts willing to put in face time on television to spread their jargon and arouse emotions. The amateur loves to "bet" on outcomes, and the more aggressive dumb money starts to show up early. They will be joined soon by their less aggressive peers in the morning following the release of earnings. This is a very risky stage of the trade and the time to sell into the public buying regardless of outcome. Remember the time stop. If the trade has not worked by the day earnings are to be released, it is likely it will not. Staying in the trade beyond this time horizon puts you in a category you do not want to be in—dumb money. A word of caution, the first time you use this technique you may have a tendency to try and make the trade work no matter what, but choose stocks that only have a good earnings history and strong technical merits as we have discussed throughout the text. See Figure 16-16.

The following is an example that demonstrates the earnings play concept. XYZ Corp is a company that has good fundamentals and is technically moving higher. The chart is shown in Figure 16-17.

The 10-Q report for XYZ Corp is shown in Figure 16-18. Note the strong fundamentals.

FIGURE 16-16 *One tradable scenario for earnings releases. Notice how the security is bid up going into earnings, then sells off after the earnings are released.*

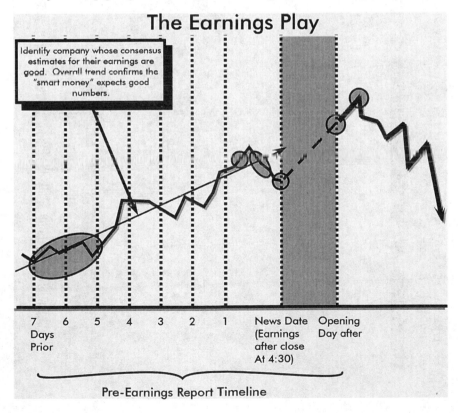

FIGURE 16-17 *The chart of XYZ Corp. The company has good fundamentals and has traded higher going into the earnings release date.*

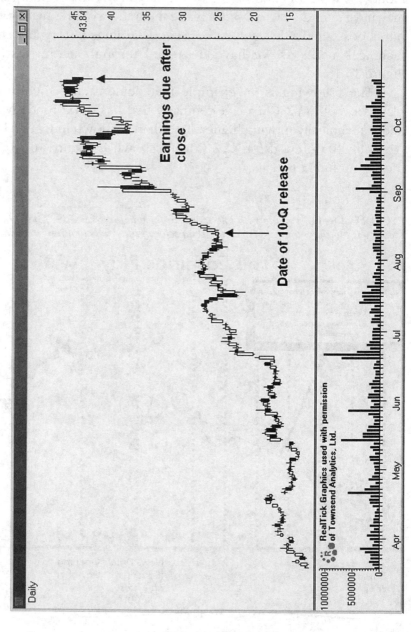

FIGURE 16-18   *The 10-Q report released by XYZ Corp in mid-August. Notice that the net revenues and the earnings have increased over the past three months and the past six months.*

XYZ Corp	THREE MONTHS ENDED JUNE 30,		SIX MONTHS ENDED JUNE 30,	
	2003	2002	2003	2002
Revenues:				
Subscriber	$ 16,307	$ 10,427	$ 30,761	$ 19,797
Advertising	609	705	1,221	1,532
Licensed services	121	174	263	357
	17,037	11,306	32,245	21,686
Cost of revenues	3,247	2,701	6,257	6,142
Gross profit	13,790	8,605	25,988	15,544
Operating expenses:				
Sales and marketing	2,866	1,434	5,376	2,731
Research and development	1,023	744	2,049	1,532
General and administrative	3,743	3,341	7,211	6,772
Total operating expenses	7,632	5,519	14,636	11,035
Operating earnings	6,158	3,086	11,352	4,509
Interest and other income, net	69	232	143	325
Earnings before income taxes and cumulative effect of change in accounting principle	6,227	3,318	11,495	4,834
Income tax expense	280	--	515	--
Earnings before cumulative effect of change in accounting principle	5,947	3,318	10,980	4,834
Cumulative effect of change in accounting principle	--	--	--	225
Net earnings	$ 5,947	$ 3,318	$ 10,980	$ 5,059
Net earnings per common share:				
Basic	$ 0.53	$ 0.31	$ 0.98	$ 0.47
Diluted	$ 0.47	$ 0.28	$ 0.88	$ 0.44

After studying the technicals and the fundamentals, the dumb money might be inclined to buy the stock going into earnings. The fundamentals are likely to remain good and the trend of the stock is to go higher, but herein lies the trap.

The analyst's consensus for the earnings of XYZ Corporation would have was $0.26. After the close on the earnings release date, XYZ Corporation releases earnings that are better than expected at $0.28 per share. See Figure 16-19.

Examining Figure 16-19, notice that the fundamentals are solid; the revenues are increasing and the earnings are increasing. The

FIGURE 16-19   *The report filed to the SEC that announced its earnings after the close in October. Notice that XYZ Corp beat the consensus estimate by $0.02.*

XYZ Corp	Quarter Ended Q3 2003	Quarter Ended Q3 2002
Revenues	$18.9 million	$12.5 million
Earnings Before Taxes	$7.5 million	$3.9 million
Net Earnings	$7.2 million	$3.9 million
Net Earnings per fully diluted share	$0.28	$0.16
Free Cash Flow [1][2]	$7.7 million	$4.1 million
Free Cash Flow per fully diluted share[1][2]	$0.30	$0.17

The analyst's consensus estimate for Q3 earnings was $0.26

company also beat the analysts' projected estimate for earnings.

The following price action of the stock is shown in Figure 16-20.

After better than expected earnings were released, the stock sold off. The amateurs bought the stock going into earnings on anticipation of good fundamentals, and they were right about the fundamental information that was released, but they were severely punished by the following price action of the stock.

The price action of XYZ Corp is an ideal example of the "buy the rumor and sell the news" concept. With solid fundamentals and technicals, the professionals buy the stock prior to the next earnings release. As earnings are announced professionals sell the stock, creating downward movement even after better-than-expected earnings reports.

Many patterns exist in the market that provide the trader and investor with a statistical edge. The most important aspect of market engagement is to understand the timeframe for which you are engaged. The methods discussed in this chapter offer timeless strategies that are based on a psychological and mathematical basis. The majority of participants do not seek to measure the human condition.

FIGURE 16-20 *XYZ Corp moves higher prior to the earnings release date, then subsequently sells off.*

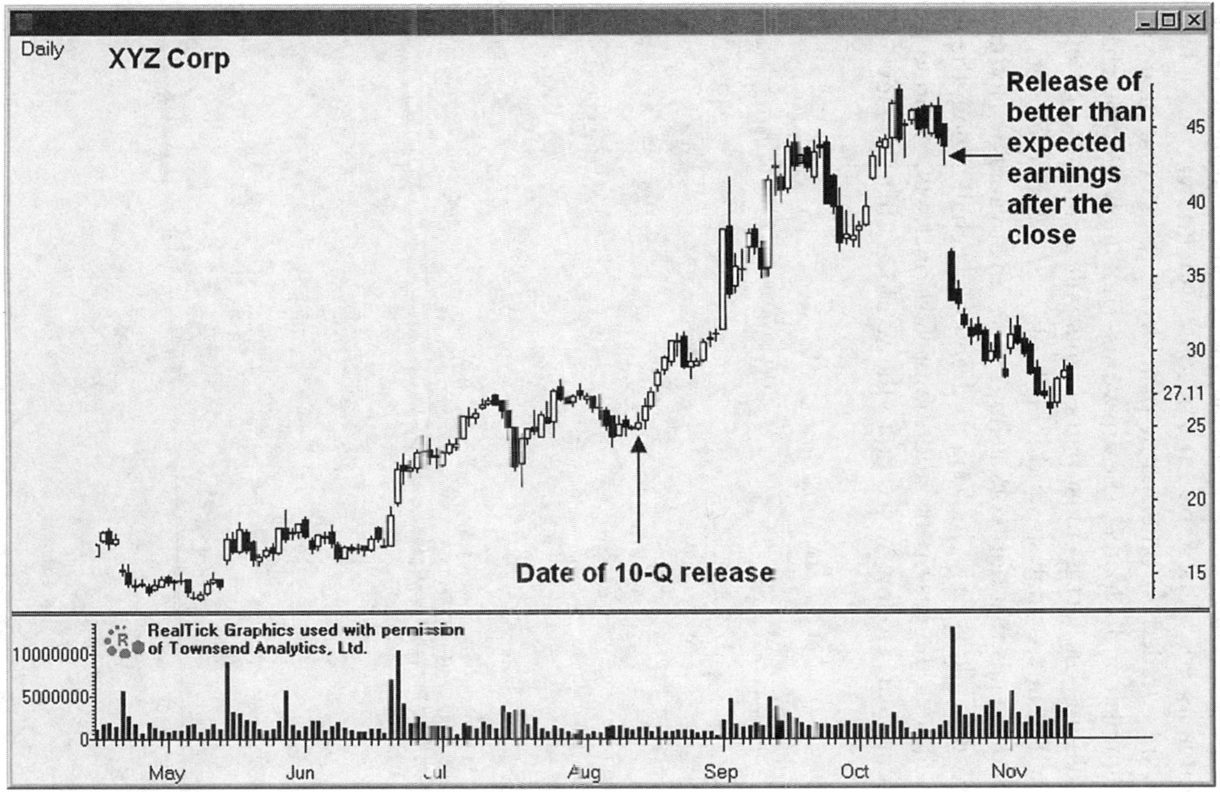

The ability to measure this behavior and illustrate patterns that continually repeat is the professional participant's advantage. It has been often asked, "if these patterns become well known, isn't it likely they will be traded by other participants to the point that their value will diminish or dissipate?" The answer is—not likely. People change, but seldom. The fact is, most participants will continue to be influenced by the news, analysts, and their brokers. Most participants are lazy, and the fact that our work is not easy is an advantage. Nothing in life worthwhile is easy. As long as the work is challenging, the amateur will seek the easy path, and the professional will continue to represent smart money. Welcome to the world of smart money!

CONCLUSION

Let us not forget the responsibility we accept as traders and investors. Like taking care of ourselves, the decisions to get in physical shape cannot come as a whim or seasonal motivation. Trading is no different; it should become a routine in your daily life. It is a state of mind and a state of understanding. It is the confluence of attitude and aptitude. I believe this is where the ultimate edge is.

Many investors never see themselves as market participants. Instead, they detach from the decision making process by relegating the responsibility to money managers. Others are mentally detached even though engaged. They cling to some newly acquired knowledge or literal interpretation of the market at the expense of acquiring the right attitude. The real essence of trading and investing is becoming part of it rather than seeing the market as some playing field that you step on and off at different times. I never see myself as in the game or out of the game, on the field or off the field. Even the institutions say, "we are on the sidelines." This doesn't make sense to me. Perhaps what they mean to say is that their money is on the sidelines. Are these institutions mentally on the sidelines as well? I think most people are. If this is true, then how would one know when to get back in the game? Your mind needs to be in the market everyday, not intrinsically, but through awareness.

I take vacations, but I am always thinking about market sentiment. It's not work; it's a way of seeing the environment around you.

Trading and investing is more about being a student of people and your surroundings than it is about being a literal student of fundamentals or chart patterns. This does not mean that because you enjoyed the food at Olive Garden that you are going to immediately buy Darden Restaurants (DRI) stock, but it does mean you should pay attention to the environment. This is where real fundamentals exist.

When getting started in trading and investing, you need a method to apply to the market. This book is one good step, but don't let yourself fall into a trap I see everyday. Don't let your sights become so targeted to literal market ideas, such as stochastics, chart patterns, or the advise of others, that you ignore intuitive signs as well. Keep your mind open. New information will fall in, and it compliments what you read on the charts. Without the psychological perspective of what drives charts and patterns, they are simply squiggly lines on an LCD monitor and this misses the point.

What I am explaining does not always translate well into books since it is intangible, but you know what I am describing. It is the feeling of Zen, or insight that only comes with experience and mastery over time. You most likely have found it in other aspects of your life, perhaps by playing an instrument or a sport. Some who pursue them with passion find that their mind clicks over into another dimension where competence is no longer conscious. This is where I believe you need to be and where most money is made in the markets. When endeavors of any kind, especially complex endeavors with many variables, become the occupation of needing a manual, the outcome will likely be ill done. The market is like that. The variables are many and the complexity great. As you process information, such as Fed rate cuts, all those cogs and sprockets must be able to turn and process the information in almost automatic fashion, leading to immediate understanding. While it does not mean this understanding will bring actionable ideas, it does improve the likelihood. This only comes after thinking through and experiencing information many times over. In order for this to happen in the market, you must first survive. This will come if you make trading a part of your life. Perhaps the best step you can take is to read often. Read books, read research reports, and study things that interest you such as technology, pharmaceuticals, etc. Through this process, you will form opinions, but these opinions will be filtered through the technical approach you have now acquired. While the approach cannot be literally interpreted, time and experience will see to it that you find your own style. I have met few people who consistently make money in the market following some literal manual or system they have little or no part in developing. I have also met few people who make money trying to literally master someone else's system. While you can start here to gain insights and understanding while learning from others, true understanding only occurs once you have found your own recipe for success. This is perhaps the hardest lesson of trading to learn.

The act of giving your money to others for management is akin to following fate and the reliance on hope and luck. This book should confirm what you already know—that the motivation of mutual funds, brokers, and traditional firms is not directly aligned with your interest. This does not mean they do not want to do well, since they do. But their methods and system of competing with other funds automatically force them into a poor mindset and method of trading. In reality, trading and investing has nothing to do with competing with the market (S&P 500). Trading and investing only relates to you. Funds charge fees and they get fees from capital. The more capital, the more fees. Therefore they compete for your money by measuring themselves against other funds. The truth is, if I manage $100,000 of my own money and make 25 percent per year on it, the fact that the market made or lost 35 percent that year has nothing to do with me. The only interest I am aligned with is making money, period. Once you give your money to someone else, you open the door to many variables that you cannot control, hence you are at the hands of fate.

The truth is, sound money management principals rely on mathematical and logical equations that give every willing participant an edge. Ignoring this responsibility is being untruthful to yourself. Luck is a lie. It persuades to believe that you have no hand in the equation or outcome. Luck is apathy and never wins over time. The truth of markets is revealed when responsibility for everything that happens to your money is at your hands, good or bad. The road to truth is in understanding the principles of risk management and the belief that one can influence outcomes, and fate does not. Once the skills are acquired to influence outcomes, the probabilities begin to work in your favor, and this takes time. Be patient and run the long race. Get rich slow.

If your life dictates that you cannot have a hand in trading and investing decisions due to time constraints, your next best approach is to become an expert, filtering the decisions of others before they commit your assets. Learn to manage the risk along the way. Regardless of whether one desires to individually manage their assets by becoming their own analyst or by overseeing the process of those who do it for you, every participant must understand the analysis and define the risk they expose their capital to. This responsibility and acquisition of knowledge will dramatically contribute to results while reducing risk.

In its most simple state, risk management means we maximize and influence the variables we can control while minimizing exposure to the variables we cannot. Time is the greatest nemesis to traders and investors. Market statisticians clearly use time as a shield to hide behind, calculating average annual returns that seem acceptable when smoothed with time. What they seem to ignore is the great volatility incurred by investors and the emotional impact it has on them. The emotional influences are what initiate fearful selling and greedy buying, both detrimental to results on any timeframe. If fund managers had it right, they would be paid strictly for performance and making money. They would forgo annual maintenance fees and be governed by "high water marks" each year as most hedge funds are. Performance would not be defined as beating the S&P 500 or some other benchmark. Performance would be defined as profitability. Most funds forget their customers may not have 20 years, and even if they do, their needs for their capital do not always mystically coincide with market cycles. Investors who need capital to send their children to college, or to enter retirement during the "tech wreck" starting in March 2000, can't pay tuition with market statistics. Individuals who understands their unique needs and timing for money, along with a foundation of knowledge, can beat the historical averages. I believe historical averages and returns are market myths that have nothing to do with me. The information we really need is the information that is not readily available. If it were, the information would have no value. Information with value is processed by each participant because information means different things to different people. It has varying degrees of risk and is not readily transferable. If it were, it would either be extremely rare or illegal to have. Information is at a premium, yet the information we get isn't what we need. A quote taken from one of my favorite books, *Against The Gods* by Peter L. Bernstein, states:

The information you have is not the information you want.
The information you want is not the information you need.
The information you need is not the information you can obtain.
The information you can obtain costs more than you want to pay.

Therefore, we must stop seeking information that will not appear. Instead, the information we need lives inside each of us in the form of our ability to relate and interpret human nature as represented on the charts. For more help and education beyond this reading, please visit us at www.marketwise.com.

INDEX

ABOUT THE AUTHOR

David S. Nassar is Founder and CEO of MarketWise University, L.L.C., and a pioneer in electronic trading, having started one of the first electronic trading firms in the nation. Seen on CNBC, NBC Nightly News, CNN, and interviewed in numerous national publications including *The Wall Street Journal, BusinessWeek, Forbes*, and many others, Nassar is a highly sought after speaker domestically and abroad. He is a New York Times bestselling author who continues to write and teach from his daily trading experiences in the market.